Insights: Readings in
Strategic Management

3rd Edition

Michael A. Hitt
Texas A&M University

R. Duane Ireland
Baylor University

Robert E. Hoskisson
Texas A&M University

Edited by
Timothy B. Palmer
Louisiana State University

South-Western College Publishing
an International Thomson Publishing company I(T)P®

Cincinnati • Albany • Boston • Detroit • Johannesburg • London • Madrid • Melbourne • Mexico City
New York • Pacific Grove • San Francisco • Scottsdale • Singapore • Tokyo • Toronto

Publishing Team Director:	Dave Shaut
Acquisitions Editor:	John R. Szilagyi
Project Manger:	Katherine Pruitt-Schenck
Production Editor:	Mardell Toomey
Production House:	Shepherd, Inc.
Cover Design:	Tin Box Studio
Marketing Manager:	Rob Bloom
Manufacturing Coordinator:	Dana Schwartz

1 2 3 4 5 6 7 8 9   PN   6 5 4 3 2 1 0 9

Printed in the United States of America

International Thomson Publishing
South-Western College Publishing is an ITP Company. The ITP trademark is used under license.

Contents

Preface

To manage effectively in the new competitive landscape of the 21st century, students must develop skills in critical thinking, problem solving, teamwork, and communication. They must be able to understand and translate valuable management concepts into practice. For these reasons, we have developed this new collection of readings to accompany *Strategic Management: Competitiveness and Globalization, 3e.*

This book has been developed to supplement *Strategic Management* in order to highlight the application of important strategic management concepts. These readings from the contemporary business press provide useful insights on how top level managers apply the critical concepts described in *Strategic Management* in the normal conduct of their jobs. They make the concepts come alive and help promote learning. Furthermore, they provide an excellent basis for classroom discussion and will contribute to the skills noted above that are critical for current students to experience successful careers.

The readings are organized by chapter topics, although many of them also provide insights on other important strategic management topics. Each chapter contains three to four articles. We commend this book to you.

We would like to thank Dr. Timothy Palmer for his invaluable assistance in selecting these readings. We are also indebted to John Szilagyi, Katherine Pruitt-Schenck, Shelley Brewer, and Rob Bloom at South-Western College Publishing for their excellent support and help on this project.

Michael A. Hitt

R. Duane Ireland

Robert E. Hoskisson

Navigating in the New Competitive Landscape:

Building Strategic Flexibility and Competitive Advantage in the 21st Century

by Michael A. Hitt
Texas A&M University

Barbara W. Keats
Arizona State University

Samuel M. DeMarie
University of Nevada at Las Vegas

A new competitive landscape is taking shape. Managers and government policy makers are encountering major strategic discontinuities that are changing the nature of competition. The technological revolution and increasing globalization present major challenges to firms' ability to maintain their competitiveness. Some of the recent important strategic discontinuities encountered include the elimination of industry boundaries, fewer distinctions between industrial and service businesses, major advances in logistics, computer aided design and communication, and opening of global markets. Firms encounter these changes at the same time they are experiencing intense foreign competition in domestic markets. These changes rival those experienced with the industrial revolution and their impact is likely to rival that of the major advances of the light bulb, telephone, printing press, and the personal computer.[1]

The development of standard management thinking was based in a time when most firms operated on a landscape that was relatively smooth with only mildly hilly terrain. Boundaries were more easily identified and firms faced a more level "playing field" with their competitors. There was reasonable availability of common information, fewer variations in international operations or involvements, similar industry-wide accounting practices, etc. However, with the changed dynamics in the new competitive landscape, firms face multiple discontinuities that often occur simultaneously and are not easily predicted. The terrain in this new landscape changes unexpectedly and has many hills, mountains and valleys. Faced with unrelenting complexity, firms must develop new strategies and new ways of organizing to deal with this exceedingly complicated landscape. It requires that they use the latest technology, continue to develop new technology, actively participate in global markets, structure themselves to gain advantage in these markets, develop and maintain strategic flexibility, and build a long-term vision that allows managers to balance short-term performance with long-term needs. In short, firms must develop the ability to effectively navigate in the new competitive landscape. Our purpose is to describe the new competitive landscape and the forces that affect it, and explore ways that firms can survive and, indeed, gain competitive advantages within this environment. To do so, requires significant revision of standard management thinking and strategic process.

The New Competitive Landscape

The new competitive landscape, driven by the technological revolution and significant globalization, is moving towards hypercompetition (rapidly escalating competition and strategic maneuvering), extreme emphasis on price, quality and satisfaction of customer needs, and an increasing focus on innovation (both in technology and new products/services). Furthermore, the time frames of all strategic actions are being reduced. In this new competitive landscape, firms exist in highly turbulent and chaotic environments that produce disorder, disequilibrium and substantive uncertainty.[2]

Technological Revolution

The new information highway (i.e., Internet) supplies information in a manipulable form and makes it available almost instantaneously.[3] It has become a symbolic and substantive engine driving the technological revolution. Significant technological trends and characteristics of this revolution include (1) the increasing rate of technological change and diffusion; (2) the information age; (3) increasing knowledge intensity (escalating importance of and emphasis on knowledge for competitive advantage); and (4) the emergence of positive feedback industries (where returns continue to increase often by building knowledge). The processing and communication of information, of course, have facilitated the rapid diffusion of technology as well as produced an information rich, computational rich and communications rich organizational environment. These changes have shortened product life cycles, made patents less effective in protecting new technology and thus less useful, and reduced the time required to develop and bring new products to the market. Furthermore, new technology is allowing firms to customize products to each customer more quickly and economically.[4]

The widespread diffusion of technology is expected to continue. Within the next 15 years, the number of computers and communication satellites is projected to double while the number of wireless communication networks will rise from 34 million to 1.3 billion. The number of Internet users will grow from 70 million in 1997 to 700 million by 2000. These developments will increase the knowledge intensity within firms and create extreme cases of information overload for many managers. These conditions call for firms to develop radically enhanced techniques for processing and integrating information and also provide a catalyst for further technological development. They also place critical importance on organizational learning for the firm to gain and/or maintain a competitive advantage.[5] All of these technological developments are occurring within a new global marketplace.

Increasing Globalization

Globalization and the development of cross-border relationships transcend the existence of multinational (or transnational) firms, and affect local businesses in domestic markets, as well. Operation in international markets is no longer reserved solely for large multibusiness corporations. New technology has allowed small organizations to become players in global markets through the creation of web pages for marketing and teleconferencing, for example.

Globalization has largely been due to worldwide economic development and the opening of domestic markets to foreign firms. In fact, economic change often leads political change. Economic development that creates needs and desires for business products forces politicians to agree on new rules to encourage further economic development and growth. One example of these new rules is the development of free-trade agreements (e.g., GATT and NAFTA). Currently, economic concerns are driving major political changes in Eastern Europe, Russia and China. The end of the cold war has opened Eastern Europe and Russia to new economies and developing market places. Additionally, China has been targeted for new investment capital by businesses in other Asian countries, North America and Europe. These changes are having immense effects. For example, China's gross domestic product recently surpassed that of Germany and is rapidly approaching that of Japan, leading some to predict that it will become a global economic superpower.[6]

New economic development and changes in political rules (e.g., free-trade agreements), make it easier for firms to enter international markets, oftentimes through strategic alliances with or acquisitions of firms currently operating in these domestic markets. Moving into new markets provides many opportunities but also multiple challenges. For example, moving into global markets increases incentives for innovation and improved opportunities to earn returns on innovation because of the expanded marketplace.[7] However, international expansion also greatly complicates operating environments. To take advantage of the opportunities for economies of geographic scope, firms must learn effective ways of coordinating operations across country borders, oftentimes in many different countries. This often requires complex structural arrangements. Furthermore, globalization creates a greater number of stakeholders and contingencies with which managers must deal and it also complicates incentive systems for managers and evaluation of the performance of a firm's various subunits. In short, increasing globalization is reshaping the competitive landscape and will continue to do so for the foreseeable future.

The new competitive landscape resulting from the technological revolution and increasing globalization is described below and depicted in Figure 1.

The New Competitive Landscape

The development of information and communication technologies and the globalization of industries have produced a blurring of industry boundaries that amounts to a massive reordering of business. As such; it becomes even more difficult to identify competitors, much less fully analyze them. For example, new communication technologies are forcing television, telecommunications and utility companies to compete and may eventually blend these formally distinct businesses into one mega-industry. Further evidence of this trend can be seen in that software manufacturers now provide financial services, airlines sell mutual funds, automakers sell insurance and provide financing, and telecommunication companies compete with broadcasters.

As a result, in the new competitive landscape, firms face significant uncertainty, ambiguity and an increasing number of strategic discontinuities. This highly volatile environment produces almost perpetual disequilibrium in the firm. In fact, the new competitive landscape may be closer to purely competitive markets (or at least

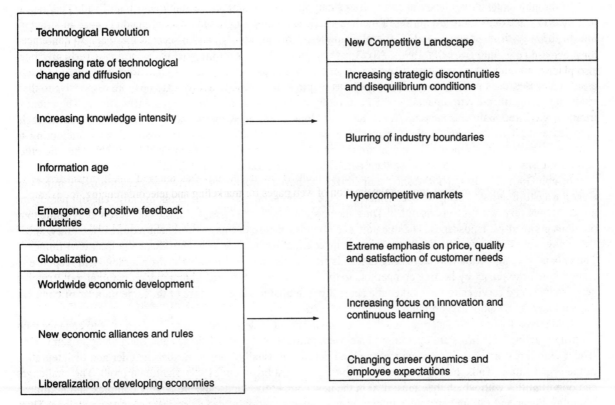

Figure 1   The New Competitive Landscape

hypercompetitive markets) than those experienced in the past. Firms have to create innovative products and services of high quality and at low prices to satisfy increasingly informed customers with distinct needs. Thus, managers are motivated to reduce the uncertainty by identifying new sources of competitive advantage.

Managers now face the task of creating a balance between the stability necessary to allow development of strategic planning and decision processes and instability that allows continuous change and adaptation to a dynamic environment. Additionally, managers must recognize and cope with multiple states of coexisting stability and instability and the fact that most of these states are only temporary. Some argue that instability is largely generated by random events, but there may be underlying order to those events and the changes they cause.[8] Thus, while random events cannot be forecasted and the depth of disequilibrium caused can only be managed at the time it occurs, top managers may use vision and foresight (proaction) during periods of destabilization to transform the organization into a new state of equilibrium (albeit temporary). These conditions require flexibility that allows firms to reduce periods of instability by making rapid and effective changes.

An example of a strategic discontinuity is the significant change in Japan's economy and financial landscape. In the 1980s, Japan's economy was red hot and its firms and financial system were considered some of the best in the world. However, more recently, a number of Japanese firms have experienced significant performance problems and Japanese commercial banks have suffered as well. For example, none of the Japanese commercial banks currently retain their Triple-A status that was evident prior to the downturn in the economy. An additional shock was sent through the Japanese economy by the collapse of the major Japanese real estate company, Sanwa Tatemono, in the Spring of 1994. This event provided a final blow for the Nippon Trust Bank that was already experiencing significant problems from excessive property loans which had gone bad. At least some of the problems experienced by Japanese banks such as Nippon Trust can be traced to globalization, particularly loans on real estate deals in North America. One-third of the estimated $600 billion in bad loans from Japanese banks are secured by U.S. properties.[9]

In the new competitive landscape, businesses can no longer expect to be stable and long lived. This fact is reflected in the extensive restructuring in the late 1980s and early 1990s and the continued changes in structure and in the way firms are managed. A useful example of this instability can be seen in the recently announced changes at AT&T. Into the early 1990s, AT&T was acquiring firms with the goal of becoming a vertically integrated telecommunications business. However, it later reversed this goal, announcing a restructuring into three separate businesses, each more focused. This move was required to allow the businesses to be more responsive to their changing competitive environments. AT&T is currently in the process of completing the trivestiture. The intent is to allow the three major businesses, AT&T Services (long distance, wireless and universal card), Lucent Technologies and NCR, to focus on their primary businesses and markets without the distraction of attempting to achieve synergies among them. There is a strong question regarding the long-term viability of NCR but the other two businesses are expected to improve their performance by operating independently.[10]

Joseph Gorman, CEO of TRW, Inc., summarizes the new environment: "There's no question in my mind that a great transformational change is occurring . . . there's a breaking of the mold economically. The old paradigms are no longer very helpful, very useful."[11] Thus, the new competitive landscape is more complex and dynamic than previous competitive landscapes. The dynamic and complex nature of this environment requires flexibility, speed and innovation. Firms must be flexible to manage discontinuities and unpredictable change in their environments. The enhanced competition and increasing demands from consumers require that firms act rapidly in response to competitors or to proact by beating competitors to the market (or even by redefining market parameters). Bringing new products and services to the market is a necessity in global markets because of the large number of competitors and increasing emphasis on innovation in these markets.

Under conditions of an uncertain and dynamic environment as described, managers often seek to enhance their control by acting as if firms are operating in a closed, rational, and predictable system. Such an approach is consistent with linear traditional management thinking because it usually leads to further disorder and disintegration of the organization. Thus, herein we argue that managers must break out of this traditional mold. The challenges and opportunities with which they must deal in the new competitive landscape are largely complex and nonlinear. Imputing linear and rational attributes to nonlinear problems will only lead to erroneous strategic actions. Thus, managers must make a paradigm shift to guide their organization's journey within this landscape.[12] In the following discussions, we explain how managers can prepare their firms to successfully navigate in the new competitive landscape.

Navigating in the New Competitive Landscape

The dynamism, uncertainty and unpredictability in the new competitive landscape requires substantive changes in many firms to be competitive. Perhaps the most important attribute that firms must achieve to operate effectively in the new competitive landscape is that of strategic flexibility.

Strategic Flexibility

The nature of the forces in the new competitive landscape requires a continuous rethinking of current strategic actions, organization structure, communication systems, corporate culture, asset deployment, investment strategies, in short every aspect of a firm's operation and long-term health. This requires flexibility and the ability to balance stable and fluid states of the organization. We argue that this requires a firm to achieve strategic flexibility. Strategic flexibility, then, is the capability of the firm to proact or respond quickly to changing competitive conditions and thereby develop and/or maintain competitive advantage.[13] The rest of this work explains the actions that individually or in combination help firms to achieve strategic flexibility and competitive advantage.

There are a number of actions that help firms navigate in the new competitive landscape. In specific, these actions directly or indirectly contribute to the achievement of strategic flexibility and competitive advantage. Among those is exercising strategic leadership which has direct effects on a firm's strategic flexibility and competitive advantage. Strategic leadership also affects these outcomes indirectly through the other major actions of (1) developing dynamic core competences, (2) focusing and building human capital, (3) effectively using new technology, (4) engaging in valuable strategies and (5) building new organization structures and culture. The actions required to navigate in the new competitive landscape and their interrelationships are shown in Figure 2 and explained in the following sections.

Because of its pervasive effect, we begin the discussions with strategic leadership.

Strategic Leadership

The strategic leaders of the firm most often are identified as members of the top management team. Thus, strategic leaders are the key decision makers in the organization. These leaders face a significant challenge in attempting to navigate the firm in the new competitive landscape; many of those challenges have been identified herein. They must be visionary leaders in addition to transformational leaders. In other words, they must develop a vision for the organization and obtain the members' commitment to achieving that vision. At the same time, they must be a catalyst for change.[14] According to Watts Wacker of SRI Consulting, "The concept of reengineering without renewing your vision only means you get more efficient at doing the wrong stuff. It's time for a complete reconnecting, reinventing and redefining of the fundamental role of business."[15]

The most important member of the top management team is the chief executive officer (CEO). CEOs, in particular, have to maintain a balance between designing and implementing dramatic transformations, while simultaneously implementing short-term projects that show achievable results. Thus, these leaders must combine a long-term vision with short-term results and ensure that both are compatible. George Hatsopoulos, CEO of ThermoElectron Corporation, suggests that in the future, successful CEOs must invent ways to manage the existing businesses while developing new ones and to maximize the company's short-term profits without sacrificing its long-term opportunities. Charles Knight, CEO of Emerson Electric Company, suggests that one of the primary challenges for a CEO in the future will be to increase output while curtailing the growth of resources (thereby increasing productivity-doing more with less). Furthermore, he believes that a majority of the future value creation will be realized in markets outside the U.S. Of course, this supports the theme of globalization and the importance of effectively exploiting global opportunities. Knight also believes that the competition for domestic markets will

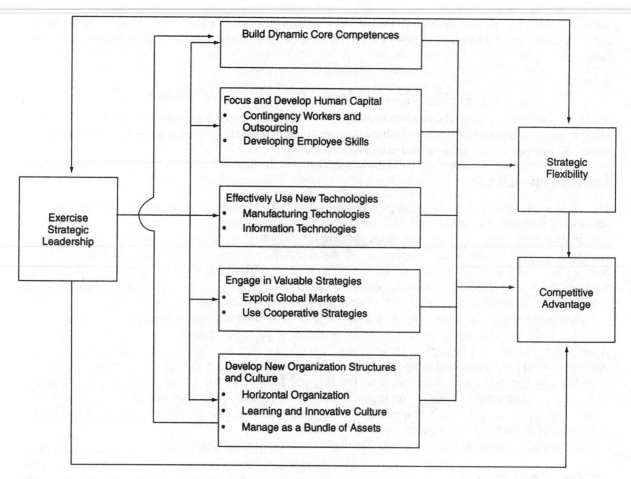

Figure 2   Building Strategic Flexibility and Competitive Advantage

be intense, but the stakes for the winner will be quite high. In other words, global market leadership will hang in the balance.[16]

Two executives who exemplify strategic leaders are Arthur Martinez, CEO of Sears, Roebuck & Co. and George Fisher, CEO of Eastman Kodak. Both executives have effected dramatic performance turnarounds in their firms while building the foundation for future viability and success. Both downscoped their firms but with the goal of growth. Transformational skills have been prominent in their success. One general manager for Sears commented, "The only aspect of Sears that remains sacred is our commitment to change." At Eastman Kodak, Fisher has emphasized systemic change and, in so doing, has dramatically shortened the development cycle of new products and has aggressively moved into international markets.[17] In both cases, these CEOs have created a new managerial mindset and culture in their firms.

The CEO's role includes development of human capital beginning with the top management team. In the dynamic and complex new competitive landscape, a heterogeneous/diverse top management team is necessary to develop the appropriate strategies. A heterogeneous top management team has varied expertise and knowledge and therefore the capacity to provide more effective strategic leadership in such an environment. However, to assure that this diverse set of skills and knowledge provides the greatest input to strategic decisions, the CEO must achieve a collaborative effort among the top management team. A top management team with more varied sets of expertise and knowledge is more likely to identify environmental changes more quickly and/or changes within the firm that require a new strategic direction.[18]

Top executives represent an important resource for firms' attempts to develop a sustained competitive advantage. Firms attempt to build top management teams that have superior managerial skills. The new competitive landscape requires knowledge of the business, ability to develop and communicate a vision for the firm and to build effective relationships with key stakeholders (e.g., international partners, customers, suppliers, etc.), leadership skills, transformational skills, a transnational perspective, capability to build a learning environment, an understanding of technology and its use in the organization, along with general management skills and other special expertise. These represent significant requirements. Yet, because members of the top management team make critical strategic decisions, the manner in which managers exercise the discretion accorded them determines the direction of the business and its ultimate long-term performance.[19]

Strategic leaders must foster and build the human capital of the firm. Effective strategic leaders should maximize employees skills rather than minimizing employee costs. This means that top managers must not only invest appropriately to recruit and select top quality employees, they must also invest in training and development to continuously build their skills and develop a corporate culture that promotes loyalty, commitment and cohesion among the employees.[20]

Perhaps the most critical skill executives must develop among their managers is that of nonlinear thinking and learning. Nonlinear thinking/learning implies an ability to conceptualize (and re-conceptualize) different and possibly contradictory information and scenarios. Integrating these capabilities among managers and other members of the organization provides for substantial strategic flexibility and hence another source of competitive advantage.[21] One of the best examples of such thinking occurs at Chapparal Steel. Interestingly, the CEO of Chapparal, Gordon Forward, refers to large corporate research centers as research cemeteries. That is because many good ideas die in them. At Chapparal, Forward suggests that every employee is in R&D. Employees are allowed and encouraged to experiment to improve operations. They have done so employing numerous unorthodox approaches that worked, including building scale models of the production system on the production floor to devise and compare alternative methods with current operations. They have improved the processes so much over time that they can produce a rolled ton of steel in 1.5 worker hours whereas the Japanese average is 5.6 worker hours and Germany's average is 5.7 hours. Dorothy Leonard-Barton refers to Chapparal Steel as "a spectacular example of a learning-laboratory corporation."[22]

The task of the strategic leader may seem daunting. Clearly, it involves taking risk. The task is aptly described by Percy Barnevik, CEO of ABB, "I'd rather be roughly right and fast than exactly right and slow. The cost of delay is greater than the cost of an occasional mistake."[23] Undoubtedly, the new competitive landscape presents a number of significant challenges to the CEO and the top management team. However, the CEO and the top management team can exercise effective strategic leadership and thus navigate the firm through the landscape maze to achieve its goals. In addition to strategic flexibility, the exercise of strategic leadership affects all of the other five components of competitive advantage as shown in Figure 2.

While much recent work has emphasized the importance of core competences in gaining a competitive advantage, there has been little focus on how to maintain the value of these competences over time. Requiring strategic leaders' vision and transformational skills, these core competences must be dynamic. That is, they must be continuously updated and/or changing to maintain their value in the marketplace (for competitive advantage). Dynamic core competences are examined next.

Developing Dynamic Core Competences

In turbulent and often chaotic environments, firms need to develop and nurture a unique set of resources to build a competitive advantage. These unique sets of resources are built into skills and capabilities, often referred to as core competences. The turbulent and changing nature of the environment suggests that these core competences cannot remain static. They must be continually evolving and developing. Therefore, firms must continue to invest in and upgrade their competences to create new strategic growth alternatives. Development of dynamic core competences requires technological and skill accumulation over time (i.e., organizational learning that is discussed in a later section). In turn, these invisible assets can be exploited and leveraged to develop new products and new markets and to out-compete competitors.[24]

Dynamic core competences help firms remain flexible and able to respond quickly to unpredicted and thereby unexpected changes in the environment. Additionally, dynamic core competences help firms partially enact their environment. In other words, firms with dynamic core competences are able to partially shape the environments in which they operate and compete. In so doing, they are better able to achieve desired outcomes.

One of the ways that firms partially shape their environments through dynamic core competences is to create new opportunities. For example, these competences can help develop new products and/or identify new markets in which the firm can effectively compete. Furthermore, the ability to leverage core competences across geographic and product business units helps firms to achieve economies of scale and scope, important for successful international diversification. Exploiting global markets is an important growth alternative in the new competitive landscape.[25] Thus, while turbulent environments present significant uncertainty for firms, the ability to create new opportunities and take advantage of them can help reduce this uncertainty. Additionally, the use of competences to build linkages and share resources across geographic and product units can heighten the uncertainty for competitors (by creating a casual ambiguity making it difficult for competitors to imitate).[26]

If firms do not continue to invest in and develop their core competences over time, thereby making them dynamic, the competences may become outdated, and limit future strategic alternatives for the firm. For example, if the competences become internally institutionalized, it may narrow the potential strategic opportunities identified and considered by the firm. In these cases, core competences become core rigidities.[27] This is exemplified by IBM's problems in recent years. In 1986, IBM was ranked as the number one corporation in America using *Fortune*'s reputation ranking. However, in 1995, the same rankings showed IBM to be 281 among America's top corporations.[28] Exemplifying this severe drop in the rankings, IBM suffered billions of dollars in net losses and had to layoff tens of thousands of employees. IBM's core competences revolved around what had been its core business, mainframe computers. IBM's competences were focused on the manufacture, marketing and servicing of large mainframe computers. As the market for this product deteriorated over time, the competences also became largely outdated. If IBM had built its competitive advantage on dynamic core competences, it probably would have pursued and emphasized new products and new markets much sooner. Once competences become core rigidities as in the IBM case, the firm may have to develop a totally new core competence to once again become competitive, perhaps in a new market. For example, recently IBM has developed a new vision and is pursuing network-centric computing.[29]

When firms are sensitive to their customers and their competitors, building dynamic core competences can better help them serve their customers and gain advantages over their competitors. Thus, dynamic core competences help firms develop strategic flexibility. In addition to the other characteristics necessary to create strategic flexibility, firms must develop human capital. Human capital plays a role in building dynamic core competences and is explained next.

Focusing and Developing Human Capital

Some firms attempt to develop strategic flexibility by focusing human capital in areas most important to the firm (e.g., in core competences). In so doing, they outsource activities in other areas and/or employ contingency workers for non-core tasks. Such actions require that firms invest significant amounts to continuously develop their human capital as well. These actions are explored below.

Contingency Workers and Outsourcing.   Approximately 25 percent of the more than 100 million employed workers in the U.S. are contingency workers. Contingency workers include those who are part-time, temporary and on contract. Some have referred to these employees, particularly contract workers, as "virtual" employees. Analysts estimate that the number of contingency workers will continue to grow and may be as much as 50 percent of the U.S. workforce by the year 2000. However, the U.S. is not the only country in which this has become a trend. The contingent workforce has been growing in Western Europe, Japan, Latin America and Canada in recent years.[30]

The use of contingency workers and outsourcing is to provide firm flexibility in reconfiguring resource deployments (and reduce costs) and reduce response times to major environmental changes. According to Michael

Malone, author of *The Virtual Corporation,* "We appear to be racing toward a protean, freelance economy in which a typical company will consist of a small core of long-term employees (to maintain the enduring relationships with suppliers, distribution channels, and customers) surrounded by an ever-changing cloud of contractors, semi-permanent employees, and company-to-company relationships."[31] However, firms must take care not to overuse contingency workers or to outsource too many or critical functions, because the potential costs of such actions include lower employee morale, motivation, commitment and productivity and loss of critical capabilities and control. Furthermore, contingency workers, particularly in conjunction with more permanent employees, must be managed in a delicate and sensitive manner. Thus, while this strategic approach can provide significant flexibility to firms, there are a number of potential subtle and hidden costs that must be weighed carefully in the decision to use contingency workers.

Technical and professional workers represent one of the fastest growing segments of contingency workers. Some firms, in fact, are hiring temporary chief financial officers and managers. As many as 20,000 interim managers are working in the United Kingdom. These high caliber professionals possess strong managerial skills, such as the ability to see the big picture, and can readily interact with other internal and external professionals (e.g., bankers, lawyers, etc.). As a result, they can offer short-term solutions to corporate crises and managerial resource deficiencies.[32]

Contingency workers, in some cases, receive less pay, but in nearly all cases, receive few or no benefits. Given that benefits represent approximately 60 percent of total compensation costs, the use of contingency employees can represent a significant reduction in labor costs. An additional benefit to a smaller permanent workforce is the ability to make strategic moves more quickly. With fewer encumbrances and employees to gain commitment to changes, firms are able to implement major strategic changes rapidly and more efficiently.

Similar to the use of contingency workers is the outsourcing of some firm operations. In recent years, many firms have outsourced functions that are not core to their businesses and on which they are unable to build a competitive advantage. For example, approximately 20 percent of the largest U.S. firms have outsourced the information technology function and U.S. corporations and spent about $38 billion on such outsourcing in 1995 (its growth is predicted to be 22 percent annually through 1999). Firms can reduce costs, often significantly, through outsourcing. For example, Boeing Co. estimates that it saves approximately $600 million annually by outsourcing a number of aircraft components and parts.[33]

While the use of contingency workers and outsourcing activities can produce benefits for a firm, it also may create static rather than dynamic flexibility. With fewer employees and activities, the firm may be able to act/react faster but may not possess the capabilities to change in the ways needed. Firms can lose control over outsourced functions and be at the mercy of their suppliers. Furthermore, firms using significant numbers of contingent employees may actually reduce rather than build their skill set and knowledge base, necessities to survive in the new competitive landscape.[34]

Because of the critical importance of human capital, the costs of contingency workers can be high. For example, not only can firms lose important employee skills by using more contingency workers, they also lose employee loyalty and commitment. Employees who lack commitment may be unwilling to expend extra effort on behalf of the organization when needed. Furthermore, these employees may be less motivated and thereby less productive than permanent employees in similar positions. Finally, contingency work arrangements often preclude the organization from capturing the benefits of firm specific knowledge or capabilities that are often developed by permanent employees.[35]

The management of contingency workers is also an important issue. Contingency workers sometimes are treated in less personal ways and often feel much more insecure about their longer-term employment opportunities. Substantive use of contingency workers can also create potential friction between this group of employees and those of a more permanent nature. Therefore, it may be difficult to integrate the two groups of employees to work cooperatively on major projects and programs.[36] Finally, employment of contingency workers in critical positions where safety (or confidentiality) is a concern may be a mistake. For example, safety problems have occurred in units employing contingency workers in the petrochemical industry.[37]

Thus, we may conclude that contingency workers and outsourcing must be used with great care. Their use may create static rather than dynamic flexibility. That is, firms using such approaches may have the flexibility to change but not the skills necessary to change in the ways necessary to navigate effectively in the new competitive landscape.

Developing Employee Skills.   Firms need to develop dynamic strategic flexibility. That is, they must have the knowledge and skills (capabilities) to make the types of changes needed to gain an advantage in the new competitive landscape. To do so, they need to invest significantly in the development of human capital. Such investment is necessary to have dynamic core competences and contributes to organizational learning (discussed later). Research suggests that U.S. firms may not be developing their human capital appropriately to achieve dynamic flexibility relative to their international competitors. For example, firms from England, France and Germany invest about .25% of their countries' GNP in employee training and development programs while U.S. firms invest about .05% of the GNP on skill development. On a per employee basis, U.S. companies spend about $1800 on training and development programs while British and German companies spend about $5000 and $8000 respectively.[38]

Intel is a firm that invests heavily in human capital. As an example, it offers free voluntary employee development programs (e.g., language training, technical skill training). Many Intel employees take advantage of these opportunities. Recently, when one of Intel's businesses experienced a downturn in demand, it was able to deploy 90 percent of employees to other (often new) business areas largely because of the new skills the employees acquired from the voluntary development program.

In short, our arguments suggest that developing human capital helps create dynamic strategic flexibility while use of contingency workers and outsourcing, now popular in industry, largely creates static flexibility. Therefore, we argue that increasing emphasis be placed on continuously developing human capital. Such emphasis is particularly important in the deployment of new technologies.

Effective Use of New Technology

New technology is being developed in many areas but perhaps the most significant developments have occurred in manufacturing and information technologies. Thus, we focus on those two.

Manufacturing Technology.   New and emerging technologies have altered the economies of manufacturing and increased the ability to produce more product variety and flexibility by taking advantage of economies of scope. Among the advanced manufacturing technologies that facilitate the development of strategic flexibility are computer integrated manufacturing (CIM), flexible manufacturing systems (FMS), and computer-aided design and computer-aided manufacturing (CAD/CAM). These manufacturing technologies, when properly implemented, help firms customize their strategies such that they can simultaneously manufacture products of high variety at low cost, and design and commercialize new products in much shorter time cycles.

These sophisticated manufacturing technologies help firms exploit economies of scope and improve their responsiveness to environmental changes. Increased speed arises from the ability of the system to incorporate new product design variance as well as the more effective integration of design and manufacturing activities. Technology provides the ability to implement flexible, modular production set ups and rapid changeover of tools used in the production process that is software driven and expandable to include a broad range of design families. Economies of scope arise from the ability to manufacture a broader range of product components and families as well as from the internal synergies resulting from integration of the firm's subunits, particularly between design and manufacturing.[39]

Investment in advanced manufacturing technology (AMT) expands the firm's strategic flexibility because it provides opportunities for future technological growth (e.g., through new product designs). As a result, implementation of AMT and CAD/CAM systems, in addition to facilitating the integration of design and manufacturing units, can also help build linkages with suppliers and customers. In fact, software is becoming an important part of most manufacturing processes. For example, often, new manufacturing facilities are equipped with software that accounts for approximately 20 percent of the total costs.[40]

Some argue that modular product designs are perhaps the most significant source of strategic flexibility. A modular product design creates standardized interfaces in a product architecture that permits a range of variations in components without requiring changes in the overall product design or other components in the product. Also, the new technologies described above provide resource flexibilities that improve the ability of the firm to cope with internal and external contingencies. Thus, in addition to other benefits, new AMT can increase the strategic flexibility of firms.[41]

Application of sophisticated new technologies has led to the development of mass customization. Mass customization is a process by which firms apply technology and management methods to produce flexibility and rapid responsiveness and thereby customize products to customers' special needs. Mass customization is likely to become the norm approach to manufacturing products by the year 2000.[42] George Fisher, CEO of Eastman Kodak Co., suggests that ". . . the need for new technologies, improved quality, and faster development-to-market cycle times will increase as we move literally from mass marketing to markets of one."[43]

In 1991, Andersen Windows offered its customers 86,000 different products. This complexity resulted in calculations for price quotes requiring several hours and up to 15 pages of information. In addition, 20 percent of the truckloads of Andersen Windows contained an error, which was very costly. Because of these problems, Andersen implemented new technology to provide mass customization of windows for customers. Using an interactive computerized catalog for retailers, Andersen now offers 188,000 different products with most customized. Now fewer than one in 200 truckloads contain an inaccurate order. Andersen is continuously working to improve its technology to produce purer forms of mass customization.[44]

Information Technology.   The other critical domain for new technology application is information (and communication) technology. In fact, some firms may use innovations in information systems to gain a competitive advantage. The computerized reservation systems developed by U.S. airlines exemplify this approach. One of the best examples is the SABRE system developed and implemented by American Airlines. The development of the initial system required four and one-half years, over 400 person years of effort, and cost a total of $30 million (in 1960 dollars). This computer reservation system represented a revolutionary innovation and made other carriers captive to the American Airlines system. American Airlines charged rent for the use of its system and acquired significant first mover advantages with this innovation. American Airlines has recently introduced a new system with open architecture called EAAsy Saber. Expectations are for EAAsy Saber to again represent a revolutionary innovation by American Airlines.[45]

While much emphasis has been placed on vertical information systems, firms must also develop and utilize horizontal information systems to help coordinate activities across units. Such coordination is particularly important in firms that have adopted horizontal structures (discussed in a later section) and firms operating in global markets that desire to achieve economies of scope across separate international locations. Such information systems in combination with the vertical information system can aid firms in making faster and higher quality strategic decisions and in developing and moving new products to the market more quickly. Essentially, such an information system helps coordinate and share the firm's collective knowledge across major operations.[46]

Horizontal information systems are being used to coordinate across global operations by such firms as Sun Microsystems, Gillette and Goodyear Tire & Rubber Co. Sun Microsystems offers 24-hour technical services through a single phone number by drawing on employee teams in California, England and Australia. The teams coordinate their efforts electronically through a horizontal information system. Goodyear, on the other hand, can redirect output from its Turkish plant, when demand for its tires in Turkey is low, to other locations in Europe where demand remains strong. Thus, horizontal information systems also help coordinate manufacturing and moving products to locations where demand is strongest.[47] In effect, both vertical and horizontal information systems provide support for the utilization of organizational capabilities and competences. The increasing knowledge intensity present in the new competitive landscape requires the effective use of information technology to support managerial operations and required innovation as well.

MBNA, a credit card company, uses the most up-to-date information technology to ensure accuracy and speed in its transactions. MBNA focuses on the high end of the credit card market where customers demand speedy service and accuracy. As a result, MBNA has standards that include processing customer address changes in one day, answering all telephone calls within two rings and transferring customer calls to the correct party within 21 seconds. Credit line increase requests are processed within 15 minutes for platinum card holders and 30 minutes for standard cardholders. These times require sophisticated technology and current information databases.[48]

Bill Gates, founder and CEO of Microsoft, predicts that the information highway will become the world's department store. He suggests that products will be available for examination, comparison and customization globally through the information highway.[49] Thus, use of new technology can contribute to strategic flexibility and increase speed of action. It also can facilitate coordination across international operations including, strategic alliances. These strategies are discussed next.

Engaging in Valuable Strategies

While there are many firm strategies, our focus is on two that have the greatest opportunity to contribute to strategic flexibility and competitive advantage over time, exploiting global markets and using cooperative strategies.

Exploiting Global Markets.   In general, firms that diversify into international markets tend to outperform their domestic competitors. Furthermore, these firms tend to be more innovative than others because of the larger markets in which to obtain the returns as well as providing the resources necessary to develop major new innovations. International markets also create opportunities to expand product life cycles and to earn greater returns on innovations. In addition to these incentives to move into international markets, increasing globalization places strong pressures on firms to do so. For example, increasing globalization creates greater competition in most firms' domestic markets. Thus, they may seek to enlarge their markets rather than competing solely for a domestic market with more contestants. As a result, an increasing number of firms, large and small, are attempting to exploit global markets. Interestingly, a recent survey showed that approximately 50 percent of small businesses in the U.S. were operating in international markets, up from 20 percent in the early 1990s.

Effective implementation of international diversification requires coordination of subsidiary/business activities across country locations. In the new competitive landscape, multinational corporations can no longer compete as a collection of independent subsidiaries. Rather, they must integrate their activities across geographic locations in order to share resources and gain economies of scope. Multinational firms must develop into transnational organizations that provide for global coordination (to share resources and gain economies of scope) and at the same time allow local autonomy (to take advantage of the opportunities in local country markets).[50]

The challenge of transnational firms is to identify and exploit cross-border synergies, and balance local demands with the global vision for the organization. This requires a networking flexibility. Networking flexibility refers to the ability of firms' subunits to develop networks of relationships with external parties to improve the firms' acceptance by these parties and improve the satisfaction of customer needs. These relationships may be developed at the local, national, regional and even global levels. For example, a firm may establish a strong relationship with a local supplier in one region and product area but with a global supplier in another product area.[51]

Building an effective transnational organization requires a corporate culture that values global similarities in both cultures and markets. Research has shown that firms with such values operating in global markets outperform firms with other types of values. An appropriate corporate culture is also necessary to promote an internationally integrated organization.[52] For example, Asea Brown Boveri uses a corporate culture to foster an internal cooperative attitude and clearly is an organization that emphasizes geocentrism. Use of sophisticated computer mediated networks (e.g., intranet) facilitates coordination across country boundaries and helps diffuse the corporate culture.

Research has found powerful forces within international organizations that restrain the sharing of assets and authority across divisions/subsidiaries operating in different countries. One of the most critical forces restraining the sharing of assets is the continued domination of the home market in the decision processes of the firm. Thus, there was resistance to including other country perspectives and political pressures both within and outside the firm that sustained current decision making authorities and processes.[53]

Yet, interdependence among international businesses within a multinational firm demands high levels of coordination and collaboration. To do so, requires increased sharing of information across country borders, socialization of managers through in-house training, and establishment of horizontal structures to integrate the various organizational units in making key decisions. The implementation of sophisticated information system networks is often necessary to facilitate the sharing of information and knowledge. Texas Instruments changed its manufacturing and sales organizations to encourage and facilitate the sharing of resources at its various locations throughout the world. For example, it now uses a ten-person team to plan and oversee the building of manufacturing facilities. Use of this cross-functional, cross-geographic team has helped the firm complete plants eight months faster than competitors. The traditional country sales groups were replaced by a team of product specialists that routinely moves across countries and continents. These innovations help TI operate its 17 plants world-wide as a single, virtual manufacturing facility.[54]

Michael Porter predicted that over the next 25 years there will be enormous growth and opportunities in international markets, but it will also be a time of unfettered competition. To take advantage of these opportunities, Porter suggests, will require integrating company activities into distinctive competitive systems. Such integration will demand a high level of coordination across functional and geographic boundaries.[55]

Beyond transnational organizations is the notion of a stateless corporation. A stateless corporation is one that does not claim a home country and thus does not allow any country to dominate its decisions. Such organizations should be more flexible to compete in global markets and better able to be open to new product ideas throughout the world. As such, these organizations are likely to be more innovative.

Thus, while it is critical that firms be willing to enter new international markets, they must find means of coordinating the activities to gain the benefits of these markets. Larger markets have many potential benefits but to realize those benefits, firms must coordinate across those markets and share resources. One popular means of entering international markets is by using cooperative strategies.

Using Cooperative Strategies.   Strategic alliances (a form of cooperative strategy) are becoming more common in both domestic and international markets. Alliances may be used to develop new technology and/or to enter new markets, particularly international markets, because a partner helps share the risks and the costs. Attempts to commercialize particularly complex technologies have a high potential of failure because of the significant resources and capabilities required, but the probability of success in these ventures can be increased by a strategic alliance. Partners share the costs and contribute different competences. In face, one of the primary benefits of strategic alliances is that firms can integrate complementary competences and effect knowledge transfers to increase the possibility of new venture success.[56] Furthermore, strategic alliances may enable firms to push the limits of technology by combining their technological and creative resources and by providing more access to capital as well as greater managerial capabilities.

Texas Instruments formed a strategic alliance with local partners to build manufacturing facilities in Europe and Asia. In Italy, it built a plant in cooperation with the Italian government, each paying 50 percent of the $1.2 billion cost. This alliance and others in Asia have helped save Texas Instruments more than $1 billion in manufacturing facilities. Furthermore, the firm gained strategic geographic positioning in emerging markets and partners with knowledge of those markets and of the local culture.[57]

While strategic alliances have advantages, they also have some disadvantages. For example, firms participating in such alliances must be concerned about their partners' strategic intent in cooperating on the venture. In past years, some firms have formed joint ventures with the intent of gaining access to and knowledge of new technology that when inculcated into their own organization helps them become an effective competitor with their former partner after the venture is dissolved. In addition, a joint venture can be largely shaped by powerful partners who then guide the trajectory of the venture outside of originally established goals of the other partners. Therefore, firms must be careful in choosing partners to ensure that their goals will be met by establishing the alliance.[58]

Another form of cooperative strategy is the R&D consortium. Such consortia generally are formed by a group of potential competitors to combine resources and knowledge to develop and transfer technology across organizational boundaries. In particular, such consortia have been developed by domestic competitors in response to significant competition from foreign firms in domestic and global markets. To date, such collaborations have been moderately successful in the U.S. and more successful in other countries such as Japan.[59]

One of the newest forms of cooperative strategy is the interorganizational network. Both informal and more formal (contractual) networks of firms are developing to gain their competitive advantages. Networks are particularly popular among small entrepreneurial firms. Forming such networks allows smaller firms to compete against larger ones. Those networks reduce the resource and market power advantages of large firms. For example, the Kentucky Wood Manufacturers Network of small firms obtained a $2.5 million contract with Disney World that was divided among the network firms according to their capabilities. Similarly, eleven British chemical manufacturers formed a network called UK Fine Chemicals which they market as a virtual company that allows the customer to deal with a single organization (the network). Networks are becoming increasingly common among service firms as well, such as advertising agencies.[60]

Despite the potential problems, using cooperative strategies such as strategic alliances and networks, can improve a firm's market power, strategic flexibility and its core competences in order to gain and maintain competitive advantages. Many of the actions discussed previously, and particularly the strategies, require specific organizational structures and cultures for their implementation.

Develop New Organizational Structures and Culture

Implementation of an international strategy as well as cooperative strategies requires a structure that facilitates coordination and collaboration across country borders. Horizontal structure facilitates implementation of these strategies and increases strategic flexibility as well. Additionally, developing dynamic core competences and building human capital requires a culture that emphasizes organizational learning. A culture that values innovation, in addition to organizational learning, will increase the use of new technology and improve a firm's strategic flexibility. Finally, managing firms as bundles of assets provides greater strategic flexibility. Thus, we explore these types of structure and culture.

Horizontal Structures.   Traditionally, the most common organization structure was vertical and often rigidly hierarchial with sequential operations and coordination among the various functional units. However, the new competitive landscape requirements for innovation and speed of action have lessened the value of vertical structures. Vertical structures tend to be slow in developing and implementing decisions and less facilitative of innovation. As such, organizations are beginning to develop flatter and more horizontal structures to enhance innovation and speed of strategic actions. For example, creating groups of people with different perspectives can enhance creativity. Furthermore, such groups are believed to develop and commercialize new products faster than the older sequential process used by organizations.[61]

John Marcotti, President of The Enterprise Group, suggests that "We're hollowing out corporations. And that is challenging us to invent a new theory of the firm to replace the internal specialization or division of labor which we've had with us since Adam Smith . . ." Further, Pasquale Pistorio, CEO, SJS-Thompson Microelectronics, stated that "I believe the challenge (of the next 25 years) is to convert today's cumbersome verticalized companies into decentralized but cohesive, flexible and horizontal organizations."[62]

In the more traditional hierarchical structures, coordination was usually achieved through establishing standards, developing plans and schedules, and encouraging mutual adjustment by the functional units. However, firms wishing to take advantage of the innovative and speed properties of a horizontal structure will use more formal integrating mechanisms. Among these are boundary spanners, task forces, teams, integrating committees/departments and sophisticated information networks. These formal horizontal integrating mechanisms have the purpose of increasing the breadth, frequency and quality of information shared across functional specialties and business units.[63]

For horizontal structures to be effective, certain potential barriers must be overcome or managed. Most common among these organizational barriers are the independent frames of reference of the different unit or team members (if cross-functional teams) and organizational politics. Individuals who work within a distinct specialization (e.g., functional area) often have common educational backgrounds and work experiences. They face similar types of problems and often use similar criteria to evaluate and solve those problems. Therefore, individuals with common specializations frequently develop cognitive models that closely resemble one another. These individuals have similar cognitive biases, use similar heuristics and likely have common tacit knowledge. If individuals from different functional areas are then selected to form a cross-functional team (a common mechanism used to exploit the potential advantages offered by coworkers' diversity of experiences), their cognitive models often differ which creates the potential for conflict as teams focus on critical decisions. For example, cross-functional teams developed to design and commercialize new products may find it difficult to agree on the criteria for an effective product design. Similarly, functional units' goals may differ creating organizational political problems and goal conflicts for teams composed of members from different units. Also, problems can arise from unequal resource allocations to different units within the organization, thereby creating real or perceived power differences among team members representing different units. These power differences can lead to dysfunctional processes within the team.[64]

To avoid many of these problems, some organizations have largely eliminated functional unit boundaries and created many autonomous work teams. In these cases, the structure is largely horizontal rather than vertical. In fact, many of the more recently popular reengineering processes have been designed to create horizontal structures. If these horizontal structures are able to integrate the different knowledge and expertise of team members from across the organization, innovation should be enhanced and with effective communication, productivity and speed of decision making should also improve.

GE Medical Systems, American Express Financial Advisors and Ford Motor Company's Customer Service Division all have implemented a process-based horizontal organization. These organizations are structured around core business processes such as customer service, account management, etc. The tasks are driven by process objectives as opposed to functional roles. Key managers are referred to as process managers rather than department heads. For example, GE Medical Systems has a vice president of global sourcing. The hierarchy is flattened by eliminating unwanted tasks and combining other related tasks, thereby reducing the number of employees needed. Ford's Customer Service teams are now staffed by three people compared to 25 in the former functional structure. The result is a more flexible and faster acting organization. Teams in GE Medical Systems' x-ray facility now install machines at customer sites in one-third the time required with the old structural arrangement.[65]

Advancing technology has facilitated the use of teams and thus horizontal organizations. With the development and implementation of internal computer supported networks, firms can now create virtual teams. These virtual teams may be composed of individuals at disparate locations, even across country boundaries, yet communicate instantaneously with team members. Recent advances in collaborative software, internet/intranet technologies and personal desktop video conferencing have facilitated the use of virtual teams.[66]

Thus, horizontal structures can aid a firm's strategic flexibility by making it more innovative and by facilitating the development and implementation of strategic actions rapidly. Speed and innovation should help the organization be more responsive to environmental changes and demands. Innovation and learning can also be facilitated by the organization's culture.

Building a Learning and Innovative Organization Culture.
David de Pury, co-chairman of the board for Asea Brown Boveri, stated that "Innovate or die is the first rule of international industrial competition." He suggests that over time, companies that rely solely on improving productivity are not likely to survive. Only those firms that develop and market new, unique goods and services gain an advantage over their competitors. Research supports de Pury's observations by showing that firms introducing more innovative products in global industries where they compete earn greater returns than their competitors.[67] Organizational learning is a critical component of competitiveness in a dynamic environment characterized by the rapid development and diffusion of new technology, the growing requirements for innovation and the need to respond to changing competitive conditions. Firms can extend their learning capacity by finding partners with complementary knowledge bases and skills or through a process of continuously updating their own competences (e.g., by developing dynamic core competences). In particular, organizational learning is important for the development and implementation of innovation.

The primary purpose of a learning organization is knowledge creation. The one sure source of lasting competitive advantage is knowledge. When markets shift, new technologies are introduced, the number of competitors continues to increase, and new products become rapidly obsolete, firms must consistently create new knowledge (innovate), diffuse it throughout the organization and find ways to capitalize on it. Jack Callahan, recently retired president and CEO of the Allstate Business Insurance Group, agrees. He stated, "You will only win in the 21st century by building knowledge, growing knowledge workers and putting knowledge workers at the center of organization."[68]

To build the capacity for continuous organizational learning, firms must construct appropriate strategic architecture. Strategic architecture is an overarching set of corporate values and priorities upon which specific strategies are built. For example, firms that have strong values for innovation and thus encourage, expect and reward innovation from all employees are the most successful innovators in their industries. Furthermore, firms must be willing to set aside existing successful products for new innovations in order to continuously maintain their competitive advantage. For example, Intel, Sony and Mitsubishi use a concept of systematic abandonment whereby when they introduce a new product, they simultaneously establish the date at which they will deliberately abandon that same product. Afterwards, they immediately begin developing the next generation of that new product with the intended commercialization date to correspond with the sunset date established for the current product.[69]

Organizational learning helps firms to continuously develop and change their core competences. However, organizational learning alone does not translate into a core competence. Rather, the firm must utilize and convert the learning into firm specific resources and skills. Furthermore, organizational learning cannot be incremental and linear for firms to survive. In periods of dynamic change that produce strategic discontinuities, learning must be nonlinear and involve a configuration of skills and competences.[70]

Such learning has been referred to as self-sustaining or meta-learning learning. Meta-learning involves the simultaneous conceptualization of different and contradictory forms of knowledge. It may create additions to or substitutes for current knowledge.[71] Chevron, with $32 billion in annual revenues and operating in 100 countries, provides an example of meta-learning. In 1992 Chevron created a new position called Process Master, with the responsibility to oversee the different processes across its six refineries. Process Masters take innovations developed in one refinery and work with managers at the other refineries to adapt and implement them. Sometimes they transfer with little change (linear learning) but at other times must be revised significantly or changes made in the refinery to make them work in another location (often nonlinear learning). Chevron also publishes a "Best Practices Resource Map" that is distributed to all employees. This map contains brief descriptions of the innovations and official as well as grassroots groups responsible for them (and directions for contacting them). The publication of the resource map has led to the formation of new groups, such as one focused on competitive intelligence.[72]

Organizations with strong competences can take advantage of positive strategic opportunities to develop market power while weaker organizations will be forced to adapt by developing effective abilities to learn and translate that learning into new competences. As a result, even those organizations with strong market power must continually develop their competences or, over time, will lose their market power as they become vulnerable to environmental changes and competitors' new competences and strategic actions.[73]

Firms have to build knowledge to innovate. Innovations are necessary in many areas including new products and services and new processes to manufacture the products or provide the services. Linear learning may contribute to incremental innovations but nonlinear learning is necessary for the radical innovations often required in the new competitive landscape.[74]

Finally, firms may reconfigure their assets to create greater strategic flexibility. Managing firms as bundles of assets often reduces or eliminates the linkages between businesses.

Managing Firms as Bundles of Assets.

A turbulent environment with discontinuous changes makes it difficult to predict attractive industries to enter. Yet, firms must attempt to do so and invest appropriately in the businesses operating in such industries to maintain competitive advantage.

In the context of unpredictable changes, once attractive industries may become unattractive in relatively short periods of time. New technological developments and entry of new competitors can create discontinuities in a market and make it less attractive for existing competitors. For example, CCH, once named Commerce Clearinghouse, was a highly successful firm as a major provider of critical information to law and accounting firms. However, the emergence of electronic databases largely eliminated the demand for its services, almost over night.

As a result, firms must be prepared to exit some businesses and enter others rapidly. The significant restructuring in the late 1980s and early to middle 1990s was partially designed to help build more flexibility in large overdiversified firms. Firms must accumulate and build competences that enable them to develop new strategic assets more quickly and efficiently than their competitors. Only then can firms develop and sustain competitive advantages.[75] In this context, firms are less concerned about managing a portfolio of assets where stability of such factors as risk are assumed. Rather, the intent is to manage a bundle of assets that can be aggregated, disaggregated or reconfigured quickly to respond to competitive conditions.

Attempts to build flexibility in the management of a firm's assets may be exemplified in the wave of mergers that began in the middle 1990s. Some have referred to the latest rush of mergers and acquisitions as the fifth merger wave of this century.[76]

Managing firms as bundles of assets is difficult to do effectively. Managing firms as portfolios of assets is a practice that began in the late 1970s and early 1980s and was promoted by some leading scholars and consulting firms (e.g., the Boston Consulting Group). While it was attractive and popular among many executives, it relies on now obsolete assumptions. Subsequent experience with this approach has shown that many firms managing assets as a portfolio also were short-term oriented and thereby not investing for the long term. These firms often overly emphasized financial controls and produced less innovation in their markets over time than their competitors.[77]

To manage firms as bundles of assets requires a different form of structure than has been used by most firms in the past. In general, firms must be managed as loosely coupled bundles of assets.[78] For example, some firms have attempted to allow significant local autonomy to their widely geographically dispersed units but maintain some centralized control, oftentimes attempting to use organizational culture as the primary linkage. One prime example of such a structure can be found in Asea Brown Boveri (ABB). Percy Barnevik, CEO of ABB, suggests that ABB is a company of many cultures (meaning multicultural management teams), but one with a common corporate culture. He noted that the glue that holds the organization together involves the overall information reporting system (reporting real-time performance to the top executives from each of the businesses and profit centers). There's another soft kind of glue described in ABB's policy bible; it includes the firm's mission, values and expectations, along with guidelines for overall behavior. In other words, it is used as a guide to the corporate culture.[79]

In order to increase economy and effectively implement a loose coupling between major business units, firms are increasingly using a subsidiary structure. In such cases, the autonomous units are easier to sell or spin-off (i.e., there are lower costs associated with these changes). Oftentimes the potential spin-offs are poor performers and the parent firm is creating looser linkages to reduce its risk. However, by decentralizing the decision making, the heads of those units may also become more long-term oriented and improve performance over time. George Hatsopoulos, CEO of ThermoElectron Corporation, has a goal of spinning off new ventures. He refers to them as spin outs (to differentiate them from poor performers) and gives the managers of these ventures an equity position to provide incentives for long-term investments. Over a period of 1984–1995, ThermoElectron completed 12 spinouts, many of which have been quite successful. The Corporation maintains a majority equity position in each business and provides the infrastructure, such as financial and legal services, employee benefits administration, risk management and investor relations, that produced loosely coupled linkages.[80]

An example of managing a firm as a bundle of assets is the recent major change announced by AT&T dividing itself into three new independent businesses. Some have referred to AT&T's actions as trivestiture. This is an extreme form of managing as a bundle of assets because the three new businesses have no linkages among them (except for common shareholders). In so doing, executives in each of the independent businesses can focus on that firm's markets and operations without concern for the need to coordinate with the other two businesses. The intent is that each of the independent businesses will operate in a competitively unimpeded and cost efficient manner. The stock market reacted positively to AT&T's announcement. Of course, there are critics of this move, specifically suggesting that the split up is because of past mistakes. Regardless of the prior reasoning, the increasing subsidiaries, spin-offs (spinouts) and breakups (e.g., AT&T) suggests a wave of the future, managing firms as bundles of assets.[81]

Thus, executives desiring to manage firms as bundles of assets in order to build strategic flexibility must also manage the paradox . . . be prepared to move swiftly to eliminate underperforming assets in deteriorating markets and/or acquire assets in rapidly developing attractive industries, while at the same time making long-term investments in their core businesses and core competences. This requires strategic leadership (discussed earlier) as well as an organizational culture that emphasizes learning and innovation.

Conclusions

The world is changing; nation-states and political systems are dissolving (e.g., old Soviet Union, Eastern Europe) and in some cases, creating strife and chaos (e.g., Bosnia). The development of new technology and opening of global markets are changing the nature of competition and consumer demands are stronger. The recent pervasive restructuring that characterized most industries suggests that managers are attempting to respond to the challenges presented by the evolving new competitive landscape. Undoubtedly, firms that are overdiversified should down-scope and firms that are over or undersized should rightsize.[82] However, that is only the first step toward being strategically competitive over the long term, particularly in the new competitive landscape.

In a competitive environment in which difficult to predict strategic discontinuities occur frequently, the top management of firms must search for ways of achieving temporary equilibrium (balance forces of stability and instability). However, concomitantly they must be prepared to disrupt equilibrium (destabilize units) within the firm if necessary to prepare for future contingencies. A number of managers (public and private) may experience difficulty in creating the needed changes. First, they may find it difficult personally to give up power as is usually required to create a horizontal organization. This type of change often requires that managers delegate responsibility and authority for gathering, translating and disseminating information and for making critical decisions across multiple levels and units in the organization. Second, even if they can accept the loss of power, they often must overcome significant resistance to change and organizational politics (whereby people try to buffer their fiefdoms from change to maintain their power bases).

Herein, we have discussed a number of actions that top executives must take in order to navigate their firms successfully in the new competitive landscape. Most important among those is developing strategic flexibility. To build strategic flexibility and competitive advantage requires exercising strategic leadership, developing dynamic core competences, focusing and building human capital, effectively using new technologies, employing valuable strategies and implementing new organization structures and culture. In general, strategic leaders must be prepared to radically transform their organizations. Additionally, several of the strategic actions recommended will contribute further to the technological revolution, globalization and general environmental turbulence. For example, development and use of new technology feeds the technological revolution. Exploiting global markets further enhances globalization. Development of and introduction of innovations, particularly when done with speed and regularity, further contribute to environmental dynamism.

While the strategic action mechanisms described are important, they can only create competitive advantage if implemented effectively. Below we provide some action steps for managers to build strategic flexibility and competitive advantage:

1. Exercising Strategic Leadership
   * Develop and Communicate a Long-Term Vision
   * Encourage and Gain Commitment to Continuous Change
   * Build Nonlinear Thinking Among the Management Teams and, Indeed, All Employees
2. Build Dynamic Core Competences
   * Create and Support a Corporate Culture that Emphasizes Continuous Learning
   * Provide Effective Skill Development Programs with Regular Updating to Include the Latest Technology
   * Produce Incentives for Continuous Skill Development and for Acceptance of Change
3. Focus and Develop Human Capital
   * Make Limited Use of Contingency Workers and Outsourcing
     —Identify the least valuable units (those that cannot provide a competitive advantage)
     —Consider outsourcing these units but only to excellent, reliable and ethical suppliers
     —Consider using contingency employees in peripheral jobs but minimize their numbers and impact on core functions

- Develop Human Capital
  - —Recruit the best employee talent
  - —Invest substantial resources in developing new employee skills and capabilities
  - —Reward employee skill development
4. Make Effective Use of New Technology
   - Through Continuous Environmental Scanning Regularly Identify the Newest and Most Effective Technology Relevant to Your Business (e.g., Information Technology, Manufacturing Technology)
   - Make a Commitment to Have the Newest and Best Technology and Updating of Skills to Use It.
   - Allocate Necessary Resources to Acquire and Implement Up-to-Date and Best Technology Available.
5. Engage in Valuable Strategies
   - Exploit Global Markets
     - —Identify international markets where your firm can participate and add value
     - —Enter those markets using the most effective entry method (e.g., strategic alliance with partner from country where market is located)
     - —Build a transnational management team (e.g., culturally sensitive and knowledgeable top management teams) and with a loosely coupled cooperative structure (e.g., corporate culture emphasizing cooperation, compensation/incentives for cooperation)
   - Engage in Cooperative Strategies
     - —Where risks are high and/or adequate internal resources are unavailable, search for partner to develop a cooperative venture
     - —Select partners with complementary resources and appropriate strategic intents
     - —Find ways for your firm and the partner to reach both's goals (make it a win-win partnership)
6. Develop New Organizational Structures and Culture
   - Implement a Horizontal Organization
     - —Where possible develop teams (particularly cross-functional ones)
     - —Provide managerial attention and support (e.g., incentives, financial resources, training, moral support) to the teams (and individual members thereof)
     - —Integrate the horizontal with the altered vertical structure (plan it; do not allow it to "evolve")
   - Develop a Learning and Innovative Organization Culture
     - —Inculcate the building of knowledge into the values of the organization
     - —Develop a program to create nonlinear (e.g., review of major decisions and actions by group of knowledgeable managers)
     - —Build a structure that diffuses knowledge throughout the organization (e.g., jobs with the responsibility to spread best practices from one unit to others)
   - Manage Firm as a Bundle of Assets
     - —Continuously evaluate the various businesses and units for their criticality and risk
     - —Spin-off (spin-out) the riskiest businesses/units, while maintaining an equity interest
     - —Focus on and give primary managerial attention to the most valuable core businesses/units

To transform an organization and achieve even moderate levels of success, core skills that are critical to build appropriate core competences must be identified and developed. It will require managerial and organizational introspection and openness to change. To do all of this, requires that top management (strategic leaders) engage in nonlinear thinking and adopt a systemic perspective of the firm. Because most business education programs (e.g., MBA) and business experience have emphasized a linear and sometimes shorter-term perspective (much less a nonsystemic perspective), a new kind of strategic leader is needed. The significant amount of restructuring experienced in recent years signifies firms' initial attempts to deal with the new competitive landscape. However, much more is required to effectively navigate in this competitive landscape. The successful top executives of the 21st century will be considerably different from those of the 20th century.

References

1. R.A. Bettis and M.A. Hitt, "The New Competitive Landscape," *Strategic Management Journal* 16 (1995): 7–19; R.M. Kanter and P. Stonham, "Change in the Global Economy: An Interview with Rosabeth Moss Kanter," *European Management Journal,* 12 (1994): 1–9; T.A. Stewart, "A New 500 for the New Economy," *Fortune,* 15 May, 1995, pp. 165–178.

2. See for example: R. D'Aveni, *Hypercompetition: Managing the Dynamics of Strategic Maneuvering,* (New York: The Free Press, 1994); M.A. Hitt, R.E. Hoskisson, R.A. Johnson and D.D. Moesel, "The Market for Corporate Control and Firm Innovation," *Academy of Management Journal,* 39 (1996): 1084–1119; I. Prigogine and I. Stengers, *Order Out of Chaos,* (Toronto: Bantam Books, 1984); R.D. Stacey, "The Science of Complexity: An Alternative Perspective for Strategic Change Processes," *Strategic Management Journal,* 16 (1995): 477–495.

3. "Beyond the Millennium: CEOs Size Up the Future," *Chief Executive,* March 1995, pp. 38–41.

4. Bettis and Hitt (1995); S. Kotha, "Mass Customization: Implementing the Emerging Paradigm for Competitive Advantage," *Strategic Management Journal,* 16 (1995): 21–42.

5. "Snapshot of the Next Century," *Business Week: Special Issue of 21st Century Capitalism,* June 1994, p. 194; D. Lei, M.A. Hitt and R.A. Bettis, "Dynamic Core Competences Through Meta-Learning and Strategic Context," *Journal of Management,* 22 (1996): 549–569; P. Eng, "Cybergiants See the Future—and Its Jack and Jill," *Business Week,* 19 April 1997, p. 44.

6. M. Weidenbaum, "The Changing U.S. Role in Southeast Asia," *Executive Speeches,* 9, 4 (1995), pp. 17–19.

7. M.A. Hitt, R.E. Hoskisson and R.D. Ireland, "A Mid-Range Theory of the Interactive Effects of International and Product Diversification on Innovation and Performance," *Journal of Management,* 20 (1994): 297–326.

8. Prigogine and Stengers (1984); Stacey (1995).

9. H. Sender, "Shotgun Weddings," *Far Eastern Economic Review,* 157, 48 (1994), pp. 48–52; M. Rosenthal, "Distress Signals," *Institutional Investor,* December, 1995, pp. 101–103.

10. C. Arnst, L.N. Spiro and P. Burrows, "Divide and Conquer?" *Business Week,* 2 October 1995, pp. 56–57; H.R. Gold, "Brave New AT&T," *Barron's,* 11 March 1996, pp. 33–39; L. Ford, "Will AT&T Bobble its Triple Play," *Institutional Investor,* June, 1996, pp. 99–105.

11. G.P. Zachary, "Behind Stocks' Surge is an Economy in Which Big U.S. Firms Thrive," *The Wall Street Journal,* 22 November 1995, pp. A1, A5.

12. R. Chia, "From Modern to Postmodern Organizational Analysis," *Organization Studies,* 16 (1995): 579–604; R.A. Thietart and B. Forgues, "Chaos Theory and Organization," *Organization Science,* 6 (1995): 19–31.

13. M.A. Hitt, R.E. Hoskisson and J.S. Harrison, "Strategic Competitiveness in the 1990s: Challenges and Opportunities for U.S. Executives," *Academy of Management Executive,* 5, 2 (1991), pp. 7–22; R. Sanchez, "Strategic Flexibility in Product Competition," *Strategic Management Journal,* 16 (Special Issue): 135–159.

14. S. Finkelstein and D. Hambrick, *Strategic Leadership* (St. Paul: West Educational Publishing Company, 1996); M.A. Hitt and B.W. Keats, "Strategic Leadership and Restructuring: A Reciprocal Interdependence," in R.L. Phillips and J.G. Hunt, eds., *Strategic Leadership: A Multi-Organization Level Perspective* (Westport, CT: Quorum Books, 1992), pp. 45–61.

15. J. Chun, "Search for Tomorrow," *Entrepreneur,* May, 1997, p. 112.

16. "Beyond the Millennium . . . ," (1995).

17. D. Sparks, "Arthur Martinez, *Financial World*'s CEO of the Year," *Financial World,* 25 March, 1996, pp. 48–58; L. Grant, "Can Fisher Focus Kodak," *Fortune,* 13 January, 1997, pp. 77–79.

18. Finkelstein and Hambrick (1996); K. Bantel and S. Jackson, "Top Management and Innovations in Banking: Does the Composition of the Top Team Make a Difference?" *Strategic Management Journal,* 10 (1989): 107–124; M.F. Wiersema and K. Bantel, "Top Management Team Demography and Corporate Strategic Change," *Academy of Management Journal,* 35 (1992): 91–121.

19. R.P. Castanias and C.E. Hellfat, "Managerial Resources and Rents," *Journal of Management,* 17 (1991): 155–171; D.C. Hambrick and S. Finkelstein, "Managerial Discretion: A Bridge Between Polar Views of Organizational Outcomes," in B. Staw and L.L. Cummings, (Eds.), *Research in Organizational Behavior* (Greenwich, CT: JAI Press, 1987), pp. 369–406.

20. W.S. Sherman, M.A. Hitt, S.M. DeMarie and B.W. Keats, "Organizational Morphing: The Challenges of Leading Perpetually Changing Organizations in the Twenty-First Century," Working Paper, Texas A&M University, 1997.

21. R.E. Hoskisson and M.A. Hitt, *Downscoping: How to Tame the Diversified Firm* (New York: Oxford University Press, 1994); J. Kerr and E. Jackofsky, "Aligning Managers With Strategies: Management Development Versus Selection," *Strategic Management Journal* 10 (1989): 157–170.

22. J. Martin, *Cybercorp* (New York: Amocom, 1996).

23. R. Joyce, "Global Hero," *International Management,* 47, September 1992, pp. 82–85.

24. C.K. Prahalad and G. Hamel, "The Core Competence of the Corporation," *Harvard Business Review,* 68, 4 (1990), pp. 79–93; Lei, Hitt and Bettis (1996); J. Badaracco, *The Knowledge Link,* (Boston, MA: Harvard Business School Press, 1991); R. Reed and R.J. de Fillippi, "Causal Ambiguity, Barriers to Imitation and Sustainable Competitive Advantage," *Academy of Management Review,* 15 (1990): 88–102; H. Itami, *Mobilizing Invisible Assets,* (Cambridge, MA: Harvard University Press, 1987).

25. Hitt et al. (1994); M.A. Hitt, R.E. Hoskisson and H. Kim, "International Diversification: Effects on Innovation and Firm Performance in Product Diversified Firms," *Academy of Management Journal,* 1997, 40: 767–798.

26. J. Barney, "Firm Resources and the Theory of Competitive Advantage," *Journal of Management,* 17 (1991): 99–120; G. Dosi, "Sources, Procedures and Microeconomic Effects of Innovation," *Journal of Economic Literature,* 26 (1988): 1120–1170.

27. D. Leonard-Barton, *Wellsprings of Knowledge,* (Boston, MA: Harvard Business School Press, 1995).

28. Although some studies have questioned the value of *Fortune*'s reputational rankings (e.g., Fryxell & Wang, 1994), in a recent Keynote Address at the Texas Conference, Barry Staw reported that his research showed these rankings to be related to firm outcomes.

29. I. Sager, "The View From IBM," *Business Week,* 30 October, 1995, pp. 142–150.

30. E. Dravo, "How to Play the Jobs Recovery," *Financial World,* 163, 7 (1994), p. 121; S. Overman, "Temporary Services Go Global," *HR Magazine,* 38, 8 (1993), pp 72–74; L. Reynolds, "Washington Confronts Part-Time America," *Management Review,* 83, 2 (1994), pp. 27–28.

31. "The Next 25: What Today's Leading CEOs, Management Gurus, and Futurists See Coming for Your Company, Your Job and Your Life Between 1995 and 2020," *Industry Week,* 21 August, 1995, p. 48.

32. J. Chuang, "A Skill of One's Own," *Inc.,* 16, 12 (1994), pp. 27–28; J. Fierman, "The Contingency Workforce," *Fortune,* 24 January, 1994, pp. 30–36; J. Oliver, "Enter Slowly, The Board Room Temp," *Management Today,* May 1994, pp. 56–58.

33. M.A. Hitt, R.D. Ireland & R.E. Hoskisson, *Strategic Management: Competitiveness and Globalization* (St. Paul, MN: West Publishing Co., 1997).

34. D. Lei and M.A. Hitt, "Strategic Restructuring and Outsourcing: The Effect of Mergers and Acquisitions and LBOs on Building Firm Skills and Capabilities, *Journal of Management,* 21: 835–859; P. Capelli, L. Bassi, H. Katz, D. Knoke, P. Osterman and M. Useem, *Change at Work* (New York: Oxford University Press, 1997).

35. J. Pfeffer, "Competitive Advantage Through People," *California Management Review,* 36, Winter 1994, pp. 9–28.

36. D.C. Feldman, H.I. Doerpinghaus and W.H. Turnley, "Managing Temporary Workers: A Permanent HRM Challenge," *Organizational Dynamics,* 23, 2 (1994), pp. 49–63; J.L. Pearce, "Toward an Organizational Behavior of Laborers: Their Psychological Involvement and Effects on Employee Co-Workers," *Academy of Management Journal,* 36 (1993): 1082–1096.

37. T.A. Kochan, J.C. Wells and J. Smith, "Consequences of a Failed IR System: Contract Workers in the Petrochemical Industry," *Sloan Management Review,* 33, Winter (1992), pp. 79–89; T.A. Kochan, M. Smith, J.C. Wells and J.B. Rebitzer, "Human Resource Strategies and Contingent Workers: The Case of Safety and Health in the Petrochemical Industry," *Human Resource Management,* 33, 1, (1994), pp. 55–77.

38. M. Useem, "Corporate Education and Training," in C. Kaysen (Ed.), *The American Corporation Today* (New York: Oxford University Press, 1996).

39. D. Lei, M.A. Hitt and J.D. Goldhar, "Advanced Manufacturing Technology, Organization Design and Strategic Flexibility," *Organization Studies,* 17 (1996): 501–523; P. Nayyar and R.K. Kazanjian, "Organizing to Attain Potential Benefits From Information Asymmetries and Economies of Scope in Related Diversified Firms," *Academy of Management Review,* 18 (1993): 735–759.

40. D. Morley, "Dream on . . . Again," *Manufacturing Systems,* 12, 7 (1994), p. 10.

41. T.K. Das and B. Elango, "Managing Strategic Flexibility: Key to Effective Performance," *Journal of General Management,* 20 (1995): 60–75; J.E. Ettlie and J.D. Penner-Hahn, "Flexibility Ratios and Manufacturing Strategy," *Management Science,* 40 (1994): 1444–1454; S.A. Snell and J.W. Dean, "Strategic Compensation for Integrative Management: The Moderating Effects of Jobs and Organizational Inertia," *Academy of Management Journal,* 37 (1994): 1109–1140; R. Sanchez, "Strategic Flexibility in Product Competition," *Strategic Management Journal,* 16 (1995): 135–159.

42. S. Kotha, "Mass Customization: Implementing the Emerging Paradigm for Competitive Advantage," *Strategic Management Journal,* 16 (1995): 21–42; B. Pine, *Mass Customization* (Boston: Harvard Business School Press, 1993); B. Pine, B. Victor and A.C. Boynton, "Making Mass Customization Work," *Harvard Business Review,* 71 (1993), pp. 108–119.

43. "The Next 25 . . . ," p. 43.

44. J. Martin, "Are You as Good as You Think You Are?" *Fortune,* 30 September, 1996, pp. 142–152.

45. W.C. Schulz, "The Emergence of the Real-Time Computer Reservation System as a Competitive Weapon in the U.S. Airline Industry 1958–1989: A Paper on Strategic Innovation," *Technovation,* 12, 2 (1992), pp. 65–74.

46. A.C. Boynton, "Achieving Dynamic Stability Through Information Technology," *California Management Review,* 35 (1993), pp. 58–77.

47. Zachary (1995).

48. Martin (1996).

49. W. Gates, *The Road Ahead* (New York: Viking Press, 1995); N.D. Meyer, "A Sensible Approach to Outsourcing," *Information Systems Management,* 11, 4 (1994), pp. 23–27.

50. Hitt et al. (1997); K. Roth and A.J. Morrison, "Implementing Global Strategy: Characteristics of Global Subsidiary Mandates," *Journal of International Business Studies,* 23 (1992): 715–735; C.A. Bartlett and S. Ghoshal, *Managing Across Borders: The Transnational Solution* (Boston: Harvard Business School Press, 1989).

51. A.J. Campbell and A. Verbeke, "The Globalization of Service Multinationals," *Long Range Planning,* 27, 2 (1994), pp. 95–102.

52. J.L. Calof and P.W. Beamish, "The Right Attitude for International Success," *Business Quarterly,* 59 (1994): 105–110.

53. I. Turner, "Managing International Organizations: Lessons From the Field," *European Management Journal,* 12 (1994): 417–443.

54. P. Burrows, L. Berman and P. Engardio, "Texas Instruments Global Chip Payoff," *Business Week,* 7 August, 1995, pp. 64–66.

55. "The Next 25 . . . ," p. 54.

56. Hitt, Ireland and Hoskisson, (1997); K. Singh, "The Impact of Technological Complexity and Interfirm Cooperation on Business Survival," *Academy of Management Best Papers Proceedings,* (1995): 67–71.

57. Burrows, Berman and Engardio (1995), p. 65.

58. E. Garnsey and M. Wilkinson, "Global Alliance in High Technology: A Trap for the Unwary," *Long Range Planning,* 27, 6 (1994), pp. 137–146; J. Hagedoorn, "A Note on International Market Leaders and Networks of Strategic Technology Partnering," *Strategic Management Journal,* 16 (1995): 241–250; M.A. Hitt, B.B. Tyler, C. Hardee and D. Park, "Understanding Strategic Intent in the Global Market Place," *Academy of Management Executive,* 9, 2 (1995), pp. 12–19.
59. D. V. Gibson and E.M. Rogers, *R&D Collaboration on Trial: The Micro-Electronics and Computer Technology Corporation* (Boston: Harvard Business School Press, 1994).
60. M.A. Hitt and B.A. Bartkus, "International Entrepreneurship," in J.A. Katz and R.H. Brockhaus, Sr. (Eds.), *Advances in Entrepreneurship, Firm Emergence and Growth* (Greenwich, CT: JAI Press, 1997), in press; Martin (1996) *Cybercorp.*
61. D.G. Ancona and D.F. Caldwell, "Bridging the Boundary: External Activity and Performance in Organizational Teams, "Administrative Science Quarterly, 37 (1992): 634–665; D.G. Ancona and D.F. Caldwell, "Demography and Design: Predictors of New Product Team Performance," *Organization Science,* 3 (1992): 321–341; M.A. Hitt, R.E. Hoskisson and R.D. Nixon, "A Mid-Range Theory of Interfunctional Integration, Its Antecedents and Outcomes," *Journal of Engineering and Technology Management,* 10 (1993): 161–185; R.W. Woodman, J.E. Sawyer and R.W. Griffin, "Toward a Theory of Organizational Creativity," *Academy of Management Review,* 18 (1993): 293–321.
62. "The Next 25 . . . ," p. 50.
63. P.S. Adler, "Interdepartmental Interdependence and Coordination: The Case of the Design/Manufacturing Interface," *Organization Science,* 6 (1995): 147–167; R. Daft and R.H. Lengel, "Organizational Information Requirements, Media Richness and Structural Design," *Management Science,* 32 (1986): 554–571; J.R. Galbraith, *Complex Organizations* (Reading, PA: Addison-Wesley, 1973); D.A. Nadler and M.L. Tushman, *Strategic Organization Design* (Glenview, IL: Scott Forsman and Company, 1987).
64. Hitt et al. (1993); M.A. Hitt, R.D. Nixon, R.E. Hoskisson and R. Kochhar, "The Birth, Life and Death of a Cross-Functional New Product Design Team," Paper presented at the Academy of Management meetings, (1996), Cincinnati, OH.
65. R. Jacob, "The Struggle to Create an Organization for the 21st Century," *Fortune,* 3 April, 1995, pp. 90–99.
66. S.M. DeMarie, A.M. Townsend, M.A. Hitt and A.R. Hendrickson, "Virtual Teams, Computer-Mediated Communication, and Organizational Change: An Adaptive Structuration Theory Framework for the Study of Emerging Organizational Form," unpublished working paper, University of Nevada at Las Vegas, 1997.
67. L.G. Franko, "Global Corporate Competition: Who's Winning, Who's Losing and the R&D Factor as One Reason Why," *Strategic Management Journal,* 10 (1989): 449–474; D. de Pury, "Innovate or Die is the First Rule of International Competition," *Research-Technology Management,* 37, September/October, 1994, pp. 9–11.
68. I. Nonaka, "The Knowledge Creating Company," *Harvard Business Review,* 69, 6 (1991), pp. 96–104; M.A. Verespej, "To Lead or Not to Lead?" *Industry Week,* 9 January, 1995, pp. 17–18.
69. M.J. Kiernan, "The New Strategic Architecture: Learning to Compete in the Twenty-First Century," *Academy of Management Executive,* 7, 1 (1993), pp. 7–21.
70. Lei, Hitt and Bettis, (1996); A.D. Meyer, A.S. Tsui and C.R. Hinings, "Configurational Approaches to Organizational Analysis," *Academy of Management Journal,* 36 (1993): 1175–1195.
71. G. Hamel, "Competition for Competence and Interpartner Learning Within International Strategic Alliances," *Strategic Management Journal,* 12 (1991): 83–104; C.K. Prahalad and R.A. Bettis, "The Dominant Logic: A New Linkage Between Diversity and Performance," *Strategic Management Journal,* 7 (1986): 485–501.
72. J. Martin (1996).
73. B. Levitt and J.G. March, "Organizational Learning," *Annual Review of Sociology,* 14 (1988): 319–340.
74. W.S. Sherman and M.A. Hitt, "Creating Corporate Value: Integrating Quality and Innovation Programs," in D. Fedor and S. Ghosh (Eds.), *Advances in the Management of Organizational Quality,* (Greenwich, CT: JAI Press, 1996), Volume 1, pp. 221–244.

75. C.C. Markides and P.J. Williamson, "Corporate Diversification and Organizational Structure: A Resource-Based View," *Academy of Management Journal,* 39 (1996): 340–367.

76. Hitt, Hoskisson, Johnson and Moesel (1996).

77. Hitt, Hoskisson, Johnson and Moesel (1996).

78. J.D. Orton and K.E. Weick, "Loosely Coupled Systems: A Reconsideration," *Academy of Management Review,* 15 (1990): 203–223.

79. Joyce (September, 1992), p. 85; M.F.R. Kets de Vries, "Making a Giant Dance," *Across the Board,* 31, October 1994, pp. 27–32.

80. "How Can Big Companies Keep the Entrepreneurial Spirit Alive?" *Harvard Business Review,* 73, 6 (1995), pp. 183 & 188.

81. C.J. Loomis, "AT&T Has No Clothes," *Fortune,* 5 February, 1996, pp. 78–80.

82. Hoskisson and Hitt (1994); M.A. Hitt, B.W. Keats, H. Harback and R.D. Nixon, "Rightsizing, Building and Maintaining Strategic Leadership and Long-Term Competitiveness," *Organizational Dynamics,* 23, 2 (1994), pp. 18–32.

Compaq to Acquire Digital, Once an Unthinkable Deal

The PC Maker Grew Rapidly As Competitors Shunned Risk

by Evan Ramstad and Jon G. Auerbach
Staff Reporters of THE WALL STREET JOURNAL

In 1985, *Digital Equipment* Corp. was a behemoth. It sold speedy corporate computers that were seen as the future of high technology. Only IBM could outmuscle it. Sales that year: $6.69 billion.

In 1985, *Compaq Computer* Corp. was in its third year of a new business. The idea: Clone other people's best-selling computers. Sales that year: $504 million.

Monday, highflying Compaq, now the world's biggest seller of personal computers, agreed to buy struggling Digital for $8.55 billion in cash and stock, or $57.40 a share. Digital shares closed Monday at $55.44.

What happened between 1985 and Monday is, in many ways, the story of modern computing.

For Compaq, the purchase of Digital puts it in position to compete directly with giants *International Business Machines* Corp. and *Hewlett-Packard* Co. In a ruthlessly competitive market, the move gives Compaq the ability to move beyond PCs into a whole new realm: high-end computing—Digital makes powerful workstations and Internet servers—and servicing computer operations for big companies, which alone is estimated to bring in about $6 billion a year for Digital.

"We have now all the major pieces in place," says Eckhard Pfeiffer, Compaq's chief executive officer.

But while a boon for Houston-based Compaq, the folding of Digital into the younger computer marker is a sad commentary on a company that helped pioneer the computer era. More than any other, Digital, based in Maynard, Mass., symbolized the high-tech boom that came to be known as the Massachusetts miracle. Digital's success spawned numerous imitators along the Route 128 highway that arcs around Boston.

Founded in 1957 at a time when IBM owned the industry, Digital introduced its first computer, called the PDP-1, in 1960, bringing computers out of back offices and into the hands of the general public. Unlike previous machines—hulking mainframes that could cost millions—the PDP-1 fit on a desk. At $120,000, it was cheaper than anything on the market. It was an instant hit.

Digital went on to become the leader of the burgeoning minicomputer market. By the mid-1980s, Digital was the No. 2 computer maker in the world, second only to IBM. In 1988, sales topped $11.4 billion, with profits at an all-time high of $1.3 billion.

Compaq was then a mere pipsqueak. Founded in 1982 with help from venture capitalists, the company set out to make a modified version of IBM's nascent personal computer. Compaq's version was a 20-pound machine that could be carted around.

When IBM launched a portable PC of its own in 1984, Compaq went after IBM's core PC business: desktops. With cheaper prices and specialized features, Compaq and other clone makers gradually ate into IBM's PC market share, increasing the significance of chip maker *Intel* Corp. and software *Microsoft* Corp.

In the fall of 1986, Compaq upset the industry's balance of power. IBM didn't want to use Intel's latest chip just yet, enjoying sales from the current version. So Compaq beat Big Blue to it, rolling out a computer using the new 386 microprocessor. Sales in 1987 doubled to $1.2 billion.

At Digital, however, founder Kenneth Olsen was insisting that terminals attached to minicomputers were all most people needed. He also criticized Digital customers' desire to move to standard, open computer systems from machines that had proprietary operating systems.

In 1992, with the company's other businesses slumping, Digital directors forced Mr. Olsen to resign. The directors, many of whom were close friends of Mr. Olsen, chose Robert B. Palmer, his polar opposite. While Mr. Olsen drove a minivan and wore flannel shirts, Mr. Palmer, who is 57 years old, fancied Italian suits, drove a Porsche and took grueling runs to clear his mind.

A Texan who left home at 15 and put himself through college to become a sought-after chip engineer, Mr. Palmer took over a company that had reported $4 billion in losses, was saddled with a work force topping 130,000 and was hemorrhaging money. He slashed more than 60,000 jobs, which made him unpopular with employees. He became insular, infrequently seeing colleagues outside the office, say people who have worked with him.

With his semiconductor expertise, Mr. Palmer helped develop a blazingly fast microprocessor called Alpha that remains the fastest in the market. He invested heavily in it, and even sued Intel for patent violations in hopes of making it Digital's core business.

Digital was plagued by sales-force problems that Mr. Palmer proved unable to repair. In an industry of cut-throat sales competition, Digital gained a reputation as unresponsive and arrogant. Mr. Palmer himself was reluctant to make customer calls. He began traveling more, to meet prospective buyers, only after his board begged him to press the flesh more often, say directors. Business was lost to Hewlett-Packard and IBM.

Though Digital remains the nation's No. 4 computer maker, the company's numerous missteps turned the former powerhouse into a second-tier player.

Compaq, by contrast, hardly hesitated to push the personal computer into more advanced uses. In 1989, it introduced the PC server, which is at the center of computer networks. That same year, it led nine other PC makers in refusing to go along with an IBM proprietary design for moving data inside a PC. From then on, Rod Canion, Compaq's founder, said, "It's been fairly clear that what we had developing here was a steamroller."

However, it would be his top lieutenant, Mr. Pfeiffer, who paved the way for Compaq's fastest growth. With Compaq struggling to compete with a raft of cheap computers in the early 1990s, the board ousted Mr. Canion and promoted Mr. Pfeiffer, a German-born sales and marketing executive who had argued for cutting the bells and whistles and lowering PC prices.

Mr. Pfeiffer, who is 56, was promoted in October 1991, just after Compaq suffered its first quarterly loss. Noting the strides of its lower-cost competitor, *Dell Computer* Corp., Mr. Pfeiffer shocked the industry and caused a bloody price war by deciding to cut gross profit margins almost in half, to about 22%. By the end of 1994, Compaq had passed IBM to lead the world in PC sales. The next year, its total passed Digital's.

Since then, Compaq has been racing to match Dell's production efficiencies—which are achieved largely by waiting to build computers until an order comes in—while continuing to grow quickly through a multitude of sales avenues, including dealers, retailers and, most recently, the Internet. The company missed Mr. Pfeiffer's goal to be producing, by the end of 1996, all of its PCs on a build-to-order basis. Knowing by mid-1996 that the company wouldn't make it, Mr. Pfeiffer urged his top 200 managers to redouble their efforts. "This is the last thing," he implored them at a meeting. "This one is going to stick." Compaq at last began changing production last July and aims to finish this summer.

To be sure, Compaq has had its share of goofs. Its notebook business is a distant third to Toshiba and IBM. It failed in a foray into producing printers. And it has had trouble in Japan. None of those problems, however, has dented its financial performance.

Now Compaq is the world's leader in PC servers, a high-margin and fast-growing part of the business. It turned the home-computer business upside down by leading the push to offer PCs priced below $1,000. And the recent acquisition of Tandem Computer Inc. gave it a new line in specialized systems and a seasoned sales force of 6,000 to go with the 2,000 sales people it hired last year. Digital will add 7,000 more salespeople to that mix.

Digital has never been able to make major inroads in PCs, dropping out of the consumer market a couple of years ago. Accounting for just over $2 billion in sales, the PCs it makes now are used for the broader systems it installs.

To make the deal with Digital work, Compaq will need to boost efficiency and profits at Digital, which lags behind most of the computer industry. Digital's sales in fiscal 1997, ended in June, fell to just above $13 billion, the lowest this decade, and it was just barely profitable, with net income of $140.9 million.

Compaq is considering further layoffs. One person familiar with Compaq's thinking says eventual cuts could reach 10,000 of Digital's current 55,000 jobs, although the magnitude hasn't been decided. Earl Mason, Compaq's chief financial officer, declined to comment on layoffs, except to say that any plans will be disclosed when the transaction closes, which is expected in the second quarter.

People who have been following the negotiations don't expect Mr. Palmer to stick around long. That wouldn't be surprising, given Compaq's recent history. The company acquired Tandem last summer for $3 billion, and Tandem's well-regarded chief executive officer, Roel Pieper, stayed only to help with the integration; he left the company two weeks ago.

Mr. Palmer says he will remain at Digital to "make sure . . . the integration goes smoothly," but he wouldn't comment on whether he will remain beyond a transition period.

Under the terms of the deal, Compaq will pay $30 in cash and about 0.945 shares of its common stock for each of Digital's approximately 149 million shares. Although the deal was initially valued at $9.6 billion, it was worth $8.55 billion after Compaq's shares Monday fell nearly 9%, or $2.75, to $29 in composite trading on the New York Stock Exchange.

Both companies have said a combination has made sense for some time, and the two courted off and on since 1995, when Compaq first approached Digital. Then, the two generally agreed on a purchase price of between $9 billion and $10 billion—about the same as the current deal, based on Compaq's closing share price Friday. But Digital's board balked, convinced that sales of computer systems built around the Alpha chip were about to take off, insiders say.

They didn't. Worse, a sales-force reorganization left important customers uncovered, and Digital was forced to acknowledge that a glut of its personal computers were backlogged in retail channels.

The companies talked again in summer 1996, but Compaq made it clear it was interested mainly in Digital's service business and was put off by Alpha's problems, say people close the matter. But Digital agreed to sell Alpha and its manufacturing facility for $700 million to Intel in October, settling the nasty patent dispute. Though the deal still needs regulatory approval, it changed the landscape, and Compaq decided to make a move last month.

After face-to-face meetings and a slew of telephone calls, Mr. Palmer and Mr. Pfeiffer met in New York last Friday to begin final negotiations at the St. Regis Hotel. Mr. Pfeiffer was joined by chief financial officer Earl Mason, while Mr. Palmer was joined by director Frank P. Doyle, a retired GE executive who played a crucial role in negotiating the Intel settlement.

Again, the companies reached fairly quick agreement on price, which some saw as low, despite its premium of about 25% over Digital's closing price Friday. Digital has cash reserves of about $2 billion that could swell closer to $3 billion if pending asset sales and the deal with Intel get a green light from federal regulators. Plus, Digital has tax-loss carry-forwards estimated at about $3 billion that can shield some of Compaq's net income from taxes.

"It looks pretty cheap," says Tom Jackson, a portfolio manager with Prudential Investments, which owns more than six million Digital shares. Mr. Jackson, who has been pressing Digital to consider selling, was disappointed that the purchase price wasn't any better than what was discussed two years ago.

Mr. Olsen, the Digital founder who now runs a closely held company that makes high-end computers, says that he was "saddened" by the Compaq purchase, but that "it's probably a good thing" because Digital was losing market share to more nimble competitors. "They needed something to save them," he says.

Compaq Chairman Benjamin Rosen says Compaq recognized early on that the PC was becoming a commodity, meaning it needed to pay less attention to technology. "It took Digital longer to make this change," he says. Though the company has been responding recently, he notes, "It was a much more difficult job moving down than up."

Ever aggressive, Mr. Pfeiffer said late last year that he wants Compaq to reach $50 billion in sales by 2000. Now, he says he intends to raise that goal when the dust settles a little later this year and challenge IBM, which has annual sales of $78 billion. "This is a major step in that direction," Mr. Pfeiffer says.

Creating a Great E-Commerce Business

by J. William Gurley

I continue to be amazed at the large number of technology companies focused on electronic commerce. Hundreds have built software and hardware targeted specifically at enabling the future of E-business. The products include everything from Web product catalogs to encryption tools to digital certificates that verify the authenticity of documents. Meanwhile, one company after another joins this or that industry consortium, which is always announcing *the* global technical standard for online transactions that will get E-commerce rolling. If only SET or OBI or OPS or OTP (every standard has a three-letter acronym) were available, *then* we really would be surfing for dollars. Quite frankly, many of these standards are either efforts by companies to lock up key technologies, or efforts by mainstream financial institutions to make sure they are not rendered obsolete.

These acronym bearers are indulging in an interesting form of hypocrisy. On the one hand, they cite Dell and Cisco, which sell billions of dollars of products online, as evidence that serious business can be done over the Web. On the other hand, they insist that serious business can't be done without standards. Then how is it that Dell and Cisco are selling billions of dollars of products without turning to these marvelous technological tools? Perhaps the technologies help the technologists more than businesses or consumers.

While I'll grant that some of these standards may eventually help grease the skids for E-commerce, what I am trying to point out is that technology is *not* the key to creating great Internet commerce. Instead, the companies that will do well—the ones that will garner most of the transaction fees—are the ones that will take the time to understand the context of the industry in which they operate. Rather than aggregate technology, they must aggregate context.

It's not surprising that tech guys have had a hard time collecting tolls on the information highway. Let's say you build a Web-mail to help companies sell online. Let's say you charge for this service by asking for a percentage of sales. What type of companies will you attract? Confident companies would never use your service, because they anticipate large numbers of users and consider your fees egregious. On the other hand, timid companies that are unsure of their success will be attracted to your low up-front costs. Good luck with this strategy.

The home-run opportunities belong to companies with people who deeply understand how a particular industry works; who understand how the Internet as a channel can serve that industry. These companies will build Websites that aggregate buyers and sellers to help facilitate both the decision-making process and the subsequent delivery of products or services. Kevin Jones of *InteractiveWeek* calls these butterfly businesses, because if you draw a picture of a service that aggregates buyers and sellers, it involves two triangles pointing inward at the single Web source.

I prefer to call these sites vortex businesses, since their success involves aggregating not just the two butterfly wings of buyers and sellers, but also technology, content, and commerce. This is not easy to pull off. Over the past year, my partners and I at Hummer Winblad have received several business plans from companies that want to build Websites aggregating buyers and sellers in one industry; once they have mastered the technology, they say, they'll bring the same model into another industry. This proposition is doomed from the outset. It assumes, incorrectly, that the most difficult challenge is assembling good technology. The hard part isn't assembling technology; the hard part is aggregating context.

There are four keys to giving a site the context needed to create an industry-transforming vortex. First, you need industry-specific content that is competitive with the leading trade magazines. The goal is not to attract advertisers as much as to attract eyeballs, i.e., buyers, who will in turn attract suppliers. In theory, trade magazines are in a great position to become vortex businesses. But few publishers have the vision necessary to quickly exploit this opportunity.

The second key element in giving a site great context is understanding the features and specifications a customer would typically evaluate to make a purchase decision. The intricacies of such decisions vary enormously from industry to industry. Product catalogs, for example, need to be set up in a way that is intuitive to people in a given industry, and search routines need to be set up to follow the thinking of a typical industry decision-maker. This is one reason that it will be very difficult for any company to build vortex sites in multiple industries.

The third piece of necessary context is a complete understanding of the way products or services are moved in each industry. How are products ordered? How are they delivered? What can be changed? What can't? Since different industries have different models of distribution, vortex businesses need to figure out how they can fit into, and perhaps improve, the existing logistical structure. In some industries, vortex companies may simply facilitate the matching of buyers and sellers, and take a commission for arranging the sale. In others, meanwhile, vortex companies will take physical ownership of the product and distribute it. So existing distributors have a great opportunity to move into E-commerce—provided they're able to deal with the necessary cultural change.

The last piece of the puzzle is to take the information generated at the Website and make it available in various forms to the industry community. Vortex companies will be able to watch and learn as customers pick through features and specifications. They will also be able to set up chat rooms, bulletin boards, and surveys where buyers can reveal information pertinent to suppliers. These data will be more valuable than any marketing data ever collected, and it will be up to the vortex company to figure out how to use this information without alienating or angering its customers.

Which industries are ripe for a vortex business? First, you need a large market with significant fragmentation, i.e., many independent buyers and sellers. Next, industries whose products come in complex configurations will value a more uniform way to search for product and service information. Likewise, industries with complicated or expensive distribution processes will find value in a single, automated site that concentrates information. Last, acquiring the data needed to build the content on the site must not be overly difficult.

There are a few examples in the current world from which to learn. While not profitable, consumer-focused companies such as Amazon.com, CD-Now, Auto-by-tel, and CarPoint appear to be on a sustainable track. But even these businesses differ in their approaches. Amazon.com takes physical ownership of the product, for example, while most music sites do not.

While consumer opportunities are somewhat interesting, business-to-business ones are the most promising. In almost every nook and cranny, there lies a chance to become the New Age facilitator for an industry, and I believe that the vortex model will be the premier way to extract rent on the Internet. So far, success stories are few, while trials are abundant. Pick your favorite industrial product, and you may find an attempt at a vortex. I have even seen a business plan for copypaper.com. For an interesting example of a traditional company trying to put this model into effect online, check out Aspect Development (www.aspectdv.com). Aspect publishes a widely used catalog of electronic parts. Now it is making the transition to the Web, and the company's site holds great promise.

Vortex businesses are likely to have one very powerful edge over traditional distribution and manufacturing operations: They will get increasing returns, rather than diminishing marginal returns. As a site becomes successful, the chances of its becoming ever more successful increase. The more buyers are attracted, the more sellers will be drawn in, and the more products that are available, the more customers will be drawn in. That, in turn, makes content aggregation easier—vendors must bring you their content, rather than your having to go gather it. Everything gets drawn to the center of the vortex. The implication is clear: Great vortex businesses will tend toward natural monopolies, and there will be no such thing as second place.

J. William Gurley is a partner with Hummer Winblad, a venture capital firm. Neither he nor his firm has financial interests in the companies mentioned. To receive an expanded version of Above the Crowd, *visit www.news.com; to subscribe to the E-mail distribution list, send E-mail to listserv@dispatch.cnet.com with the following in the message body: subscribe atc-dispatch. If you have feedback, please send it to atc@humwin.com*

Read Your History, Janet

by John Steele Gordon

For now, Bill Gates has won peace by agreeing to make available versions of Windows 95 with the Microsoft Explorer browser disabled. But this is only the opening in what could turn into a decades-long war between Microsoft and trustbusters. Justice's ultimate goal may be to permanently dismember future Microsoft operating systems, to boost the chances of Netscape Navigator as an alternative browser. Eleven state attorneys general are subpoenaing Microsoft. The lynch mob is forming. The guy's gotten too big for his boots. Go get him.

Let's assume for the sake of argument that Gates is hell-bent on taking over the entire computer business, using his dominance of desktop software as an opening wedge. Does he have the power to succeed? Do we, that is, need the Department of Justice to protect us from this juggernaut? History says no.

Go back to 1969. The Microsoft of the day was the International Business Machines Corp.—seemingly invincible, with a 65% share of the computer market. The little guys were being squashed: Burroughs, Sperry, General Electric, Honeywell, Control Data. More, perhaps, to protect them than to protect consumers, the U.S. government sued IBM, demanding that the company be dismantled.

The battle raged for 13 years. By the time the Justice Department dropped its case in 1982, mainframes had begun a long, slow fade from glory. Before the decade was over, IBM was heading into serious trouble and was soon to lay off thousands of employees. While IBM was declining, a new giant was arising. In 1982 Intel sold $86 million worth of microprocessors. A year earlier, Microsoft had sold its first copy of MS-DOS.

The history books are filled with government assaults on powerful combines that succumbed to market forces without help from the U.S. government. The Department of Justice sued to break up J.P. Morgan's steel trust, U.S. Steel Co., which won that case in 1920. But no lawyers could protect Big Steel, as it was called, from obsolete technology. An antitrust prosecution in 1967 forced Schwinn Bicycle Co. to lessen its grip on bicycle dealers; foreign competition and complacency put Schwinn into bankruptcy in 1992.

The United Shoe Machinery Co., attacked as a monopoly by the government in 1918, won in the Supreme Court but lost in the world marketplace; remnants of this once powerful giant survive only as a part of a British company known as United Machinery Group, headquartered in Leicestershire.

General Motors never suffered a government antitrust attack, but lived for years in holy terror of one. Alfred D. Chandler, the Pulitzer-prize-winning business historian at Harvard, recalls what Alfred P. Sloan, GM's chairman from 1937 to 1956, told him about pulling punches. Sloan knew that if GM topped 45% in market share it would have an antitrust problem, but telling his managers to stop at 45% was like telling them not to work hard. And Sloan was right. American automobile technology and manufacturing largely went to sleep in the postwar years. Detroit's unanticipated blow from the Japanese in the 1980s was nearly fatal.

Chandler remembers when Radio Corp. of America dominated radio and television the way Intel and Microsoft dominate the desktop today. "There was a consent decree against RCA that said not only do you have to license everything, but in domestic markets you can't charge royalties," Chandler says. "So guess who they licensed to? Japan. The Japanese electronics industry is based on this. And when [General David] Sarnoff went to Japan in 1960 he was awarded the Order of the Rising Sun as one of the great contributors to Japan. I said they ought to give that to the antitrust [lawyers]!"

In the name of protecting competition, Washington killed the once great Pan American World Airways. The government said Pan Am was so powerful that it should not be allowed to acquire domestic routes. Lacking feeder traffic, Pan Am lost ground to foreign competitors. By the time the ban was lifted in 1978 it was too late. Pan Am died in 1990.

The trustbusters say they are only doing their duty. The 108-year-old Sherman Act forbids monopolizing a market or engaging in any "restraint of trade." In most cases these prohibited acts boil down to one of three things: having too large a market share (that is, sheer bigness); tying the sale of one product to the sale of another; and predatory pricing.

How much is too much market share? It depends on how a company got there. Merely controlling 90% of the virgin aluminum market got Alcoa in trouble in a landmark 1945 case, even though there was considerable evidence that its dominance was due more to superior foresight and engineering than to nefarious business practices. Much lower percentages can trigger an antitrust prosecution if they are the result of mergers. In a 1962 Supreme Court case that represents the giddy limits in antimonopoly prosecutions, Brown Shoe Co., with 1% of the shoe retailing market, was forbidden to acquire Kinney, with 1%. Nowadays it would probably take more than a 2% market share for the Supreme Court to stop a merger.

Tying? That's the crime Microsoft stands accused of: If you want the latest Windows, you have to take our browser, too. The economic theory here is that a company with monopoly power in one market can leverage its way into an unjustified position in another market.

History offers little support for this theory. Robert Bork, the eminent legal philosopher, made a good case in his 1978 book *The Antitrust Paradox* that the government shouldn't worry about tying contracts at all. Suppose General Motors has a hot sports car that people are lining up to buy. Suppose it demands that all the buyers, as a condition of getting the Corvette, take out a car loan from a GM finance subsidiary. It's easy to see how such an offer would damage competing lenders, but how would it injure consumers? If GM attempted to extract a price for the two products that exceeded their combined value to consumers, people would buy their cars elsewhere.

And yet the courts have again and again interpreted the Sherman Act's ban on "restraint on trade" to forbid tying contracts. IBM was forced to stop making users of its accounting machines buy IBM cards; International Salt was similarly challenged for the way it leased salt-dispensing machinery; Hollywood was enjoined from block-booking of movies. In the days of block-booking, movies were cheap entertainment. Today a movie ticket can cost you $9.

In practice, this line of cases raises prices for consumers. Fred L. Smith Jr., of the Competitive Enterprise Institute, explains: "We could sell left shoes and right shoes separately. We don't do that because we find that when a person wants a left shoe they want a right shoe, too. The reason we don't separate them is we lower the transaction cost of buying shoes."

Lastly there is the offense of predatory pricing, also part of the case against Microsoft. The company's sin, if you agree with this theory, is giving its browser away instead of charging money for it. Why is charging too little viewed as an evil? In theory because once competition is wiped out, the predator would be able to gouge consumers. It's just a theory. There is scant evidence that any would-be monopolist ever made money this way.

The populist thinking behind the theory of predatory pricing goes back to that classic of the muckraking era, Ida Tarbell's *History of the Standard Oil Company,* published in 1902. It depicted a ruthless John D. Rockefeller buying out his competitors at his own price and crushing those who refused by underpricing them until they were bankrupt. Once his monopoly was complete, of course, it was argued that Standard Oil would jack up prices, and Rockefeller would drain America's wealth into his own pockets. The government did succeed in breaking Standard Oil into pieces. But what keeps the price of oil down? That breakup—or the discovery of huge quantities of oil elsewhere, by other players?

As Bork points out, the history of the antitrust laws shows that they make little sense if the point is to defend consumers. They are better understood as efforts to defend weak competitors. He wrote two decades ago: "The general movement has been away from the ideal of competition and toward the older idea of protected status for each producer, away from concern for general welfare and toward concern for interest groups, and away from the ideal of liberty toward the ideal of enforced equality."

In a 1993 epilogue to his classic, Bork took some satisfaction in noting that courts had come a long way toward his view of how antitrust should work. But now the populists hold sway again. The anti-Microsoft suit could be a big step backwards.

Forget the courts, Janet. Trust the market.

John Steele Gordon is the author of Hamilton's Blessing *(Walker & Co., 1997), a history of the national debt. Research: Dolly Setton.*

From Steer to Eternity

by Leigh Buchanan

The sky is low, the color of skim milk, and a breeze rattles the scraggly mesquite trees that ring the entrance to Capitol Land and Livestock, a cattle dealer in Schwertner, Tex. Behind the company's stately, porticoed main building, a brown-and-white Charbray lumbers through a labyrinthine arrangement of open-air pens, gates, and alleys, stopping at last inside the squeeze chute, a narrow metal stall that restrains her movements. Wielding a tool that looks like a giant hole punch, a worker clamps a yellow plastic tag on one ear. The calf flares a nostril but appears otherwise unflustered.

Inside that thumbnail-size tag lies a tiny radio-frequency transponder. When the worker waves a metal wand over it, a unique ID number is transmitted wirelessly to a Dell laptop computer perched on an overturned trash can a few feet away. Jim Schwertner, Capitol's 46-year-old president, leans over the computer and watches as the number appears in an Excel spreadsheet. He then types in the fact that the worker is squirting TSV2, a vaccine for respiratory disease, into the calf's nose and injecting worming medicine into her flank. The computer is also cabled to a switch box with multiple serial ports resting on a chute-side table. The ports feed the computer output from an electronic scale and a digital thermometer inserted into the calf's rectum: this animal weighs a healthy 592 pounds and has a normal temperature of 101 degrees. Her vitals punctiliously recorded, the calf is released and trots off to her pen.

Capitol Land and Livestock, a $150-million company founded 51 years ago by Schwertner's father, doesn't look like the epicenter of an industry revolution. But the business—along with a handful of others, many of them in Texas—is experimenting with a technology-driven model of supply-chain integration and management that could, among other things, raise the price cattle producers get for their wares by 5% or more, reduce costs by 20%, significantly improve the quality and consistency of the meat sold in supermarkets and restaurants, and help quell public fears about beef safety. "It is the single biggest thing ever to happen to this industry," says James Herring, CEO of Friona Industries L.P., an operator of feedlots and feed-manufacturing companies and one of Schwertner's partners in the supply-chain project.

At a time when companies in many industries are consolidating suppliers and demanding new informational intimacy with business partners, the beef system is a prime example of how even the smallest organization can use relatively inexpensive technology to build a better product and secure relationships with customers. And while beef producers are among the first to embrace such a sophisticated system, the model has implications for any industry in which raw materials of variable quality is transformed into finished products of variable quality by a multiplayer manufacturing chain.

The umbrella term for what the beef companies are doing is "source verification and performance-data tracking," the creation of a kind of bovine audit trail that captures every event in an animal's life, from birth to butcher. Schwertner's company is using a primitive version of the system, but he expects to have a more sophisticated model in place in a few months. What won't change are the ear tags: each calf is outfitted with a tag containing a small antenna that's attached to an integrated circuit storing a unique ID. The tags work roughly like bar codes: when swept by an electronic reader, they transmit their ID numbers wirelessly to a computer.

At Capitol Land and Livestock, the ID number is stored locally in a spreadsheet, along with other information the company has about the animal. The spreadsheet is then sent on a disk to Schwertner's business partners—in this case, the companies he supplies. In the new model, all of Schwertner's data will be transmitted by modem to a database running at a third-party vendor or an industry association, where it will be joined over time

Where's the Beef?

What follow are the four most common links in the beef-manufacturing chain. Retailers and distributors are also involved, but since information is tracked using ear tags that are removed at the packing plant and sent back to the rancher, their ability to enter information into the system is currently limited.

What They Do	Data They Review or Collect
Ranchers: They breed cows and bulls to produce calves, both for meat and as replacements for the herd. They generally sell the calves once they are weaned, at six to eight months, and weigh 500 to 600 pounds.	Genetic history; birth data and weight; weaning date and weight; medical treatments, vaccinations, and other significant incidents
Stockers/Growers: Their objective is to add weight as fast as possible while keeping the animal healthy. They sell animals at about 750 pounds, when they are 10 to 12 months old.	Periodic weight measurements; medical treatments, vaccinations, and other significant incidents
Feed-yard operators: They feed animals a high-energy diet for 90 to 200 days, until they reach approximately 1,100 to 1,200 pounds.	Feed-ration ingredients; weight measurements; medical treatments; vaccinations, and other significant incidents; animal origin and history
Packers: They slaughter the animal; chill, age, and cut up the carcass; and pack those pieces in boxes for shipment to distributors and retailers.	Live-animal weight; carcass weight, warm and chilled; yield, grade, and quality of meat; carcass defects

by information collected by a series of owners using a variety of tools: radio-frequency identification (RFID) readers, handheld and laptop computers, electronic weigh scales, scanners that read drug-container labels—even a gadget that performs ultrasounds to determine how much fat an animal carries.

As the animal moves down the manufacturing chain, both new and past owners will be able to check that database, using the Internet, for relevant chunks of its biography. At the top, ranchers can find out how much weight an animal gained at each stage of production and how much red meat it rendered at the packing plant—information they'll use to make decisions about culling, grazing, and breeding. At the bottom, packing-plant workers can check for things like needles that may have broken off in a calf's flank or drugs that have not had time to pass through its system. Even retailers will eventually be able to contribute, noting, for example, whether a slab of meat received from the packing plant broke down into 9 steaks or 16.

Large ranchers have been collecting some of this data for years, scribbling it in notebooks as animals are weighed, checked for pregnancy, or given injections, and then keying it into herd-management programs back in their offices. But recording which heifer bred with which bull tells them nothing about the quality of the porterhouse that resulted from that union. Using data on a calf's development fed back into the system by subsequent owners, however, ranchers can decide whether to breed two specific animals again or whether to sell the bull and put the cow out to pasture. The information can also help ranchers, feedlots, and packers identify the best and worst among their suppliers—information they weigh when deciding who receives the favor of their business.

"This technology has shown us that preconceived ideas we've had about cattle are completely wrong," says Schwertner. "For example, the industry has for a long time thought that if you had a group of cattle that all came from the same rancher, that looked alike and had the same genetics, they should all perform similarly. Not true. And now that we know that, we don't have to go out and pay more for one-ranch cattle anymore. We know what we buy at the auctions is just as good."

Such performance data—whether it is used to improve product quality, locate the source of defects, or choose the best suppliers—is important to any number of industries. Food production is the most obvious: in a situation like last year's hepatitis scare, strawberry producers could have used such a system to quickly determine at what stage the fruit became contaminated. Forestry companies have an interest as well. The industry is trying to build a market for certified wood products, and in order to prove that finished goods have been grown and harvested in ecologically sound ways, they must be able to leave a trail of digital bread crumbs from landowner to retailer. Applications even extend as far afield as the high-tech industry, where PC manufacturers that buy from circuit-board assemblers and other small companies could keep glitches to a minimum by noting the conditions of each component's manufacture and determining at what stage of production problems crept in.

In fact, shared information is becoming such a crucial part of supplier-customer transactions that it is almost as important as the product being exchanged. "Buyers are forming links with sellers who are willing to invest in the technology and to agree on the management practices that will allow this [collection and dissemination of information] to happen," says Bill Helming, a member of the board of directors of the Supply Chain Council, a national trade association. That information helps players all along the chain reduce costs and improve quality. "As a result, the chain has the choice of charging a premium or competing on cost," says Helming. "There's enormous economic leverage."

Jim Schwertner, like most beef producers implementing supply-chain technology, is doing so within the context of an alliance formed for that purpose. These alliances include representatives from every stage of the manufacturing process: ranchers, stockers/growers, feedlots, packing plants or slaughterhouses, and, in some cases, retailers. (See "Where's the Beef?" on page 70.) While all the companies in Schwertner's alliance—called Beef Advantage—have revenues of more than $100 million, most of the calves that travel through its pipeline originate on small ranches, those with fewer than 500 head of cattle and annual sales of under $250,000. It is these small businesses that may ultimately benefit from the system.

Calves that are born on small ranches now enter the Beef Advantage chain through Capitol Land and Livestock, which buys them either directly or through auction barns; the scant data that accompanies the animals generally travels verbally or on paper. But Schwertner expects that those ranchers, even the smallest, will start tagging their own cattle and entering information into the system when the Internet-accessible database is up and running. Under such an arrangement, the electronic audit trail that now begins with Schwertner would start with the small ranchers, who would also be able to use end-of-the-line performance data to make better breeding and management decisions.

Schwertner's company functions like a typical brokerage business: it buys cattle in large volume, takes title to them, and immediately resells them. Every day, Capitol's 15 buyers spread out across south and central Texas, purchasing cattle and trucking them to headquarters, where they are sorted by size, sex, and quality. Then the telemarketers hit the phones, cutting verbal deals with feedlots until every last Charbray and Black Angus is gone. "My dad has this philosophy: We don't go home at night with any inventory left unsold," says Schwertner.

A calf passing through Schwertner's outfit is tagged, weighed, measured, and dosed with medicines; Schwertner then supplements data collected at the squeeze chute by typing in any printed information passed along by the animal's previous owner, such as birth date and weight at time of sale. All that information will be available to James Herring on a spreadsheet when the calf makes its next stop: Friona Industries, with headquarters in Amarillo, Tex. Herring is also a member of Beef Advantage and has agreed to buy a certain number of Schwertner's beasts as part of the alliance agreement, which also includes terms for sharing information and for adopting the technology to do so.

In the time the Charbray enjoys Friona's hospitality, she may double in weight, and all the while Herring will be adding information to his own spreadsheet, which he shares with Schwertner. Combining Schwertner's data with information he gets back from Cargill Foods' Excel Corp., a packing plant that is the next link in the chain, Herring is able to calculate what conditions—how much an animal is fed or when it segues from grass to grain—produce the highest-quality carcass for the lowest cost. And like Schwertner, Herring will use that information when he's figuring out whom to buy from, possibly cutting exclusive deals with suppliers whose product brings the most return. "Using an integrated production process like this, we can create a superior product," he says.

So far, Schwertner's and Herring's biggest investment has been the tags, which go for between $3 and $11 each, depending on the manufacturer. Prices are dropping, however, and should settle in at around $4. In addition, Schwertner has spent $25,000 on readers, computers, and the serial devices that allow him to take chute-side measurements. But the expected returns dwarf that outlay.

First, there are the savings born of efficiency, which Herring estimates at 20% or more. For example, new owners, lacking information on an animal, will usually subject it to a regimen of drugs that may duplicate doses administered earlier in the chain and increase the amount of time the animal takes to clear the medications out of its system. Knowing an animal's age and rate of weight gain makes it easier to determine when to switch it from grass to grain—the less time it spends on grain, the less cost to its owner. And since restaurants, supermarkets, and other customers buy beef according to specific grades and weights, producers can use feedback on which calves throw those numbers out of whack to winnow the offending bulls and cows from the breeding pool.

And then, of course, there are the premiums. Buyers—particularly at the later stages—desperately want consistent size and quality. Packers, for example, don't want to waste time cutting excessively fatty meat down to a quarter-inch trim. And supermarkets want beef that they can easily divide into steaks and cuts of approximately the same size. As a result, these buyers have traditionally docked their suppliers for calves that are too large, too small, or exhibit other peculiarities. Schwertner says he's spoken with several buyers who are willing to pay extra to suppliers who can deliver a predetermined size and quality. "Our customers aren't paying more yet for source-verified animals, but I know they will," he says. "Our goal is to try to get a 5% premium."

A third advantage is improved food safety: the system aims to mitigate the effects of—if not eliminate entirely—the kinds of mad-cow and E. coli incidents that make Frank Perdue a richer man. "If there is a scare, the system provides a mechanism to trace products that have been contaminated, which avoids the destruction of uncontaminated products and minimizes losses," says Lee Curkendall, vice-president of product development at AgInfoLink, the new systems integrator that is acting as sherpa through this high-tech terrain for several alliances. "Participants in the chain can also adjust their environmental and management practices to reduce possible contaminants." If, for example, a packing plant discovers a chemical residue in certain calves, it can notify the supplier, who can comb through those animals' histories looking for common strands or anomalies. Perhaps they all hail from a particular pasture where pesticides have been incorrectly applied.

At the back of everyone's mind, of course, is the hope that source verification and performance-data tracking in the beef industry will bring carnivores who have defected to paler products back to their rib eyes—meaning more money for all. "We're not just losing market share to pork and chicken; we're also losing it to people not buying meat," says Bob Nunley, the owner of Coyote Ranch, in Sabinal, Tex., and a member of Rancher's Renaissance, another alliance that is experimenting with the technology. "Someone goes to a store and spends a lot of money on a steak and it's too tough to eat— we've lost a customer."

In Nunley's vision, alliances that could track their beef and thus guarantee its quality would trumpet the fact through labeling: consumers would grow to associate a divinely marbled rump roast with Rancher's Renaissance, for instance, and gladly pay more for it. "Right now, nobody knows whose meat they're buying," says the rancher. "We need to be able to differentiate the product—to show we're a group of people producing quality stuff."

Coyote Ranch looks anything but high tech: a handful of ramshackle buildings surrounded by 9,000 acres of mesquite, agorita berries, and guajillo. But if Schwertner's outfit is the *Spirit of St. Louis*—the earliest of adopters using the most basic of technologies—then Nunley's is the *Concorde*. The ranch is serving as a test site for a sophisticated implementation of the technology that may ultimately become the prototype for a national cattle-tracking system. (See "Equal-Opportunity Beef," page 75.)

Rancher's Renaissance—a 20-company alliance with members in Hawaii, California, and Texas—chose Coyote Ranch as its beta site because of Nunley's familiarity with computers: the lean, laconic rancher does programming as a hobby and developed most of the business's inventory software. Charged with testing the data-collection aspects of the system prior to the establishment of an alliancewide database, Nunley began putting ear tags on his cattle last October. But the use of tags is where Nunley's and Schwertner's systems part company.

In the Rancher's Renaissance system, which should be fully deployed in March, there will be little keying of information into a laptop. Rather, sophisticated software will handle nearly everything. To start, Nunley will log on to the computer and select which bovine characteristics he wants the software to recognize—whether or not a cow is pregnant, for example. He will then take a "work card"—a 10-by-30-inch piece of plastic embedded with several transponders—that is dedicated to that particular characteristic and place a label indicating a possible outcome ("yes," for pregnant; "no," for not pregnant, recheck) next to each transponder. The person working the chute

EQUAL-OPPORTUNITY BEEF

Americans loved red meat and democracy. So what could be better than a nationwide system that ensures all flank steaks are created equal?

A national source-verification and performance-data-tracking system similar to those being implemented by several beef alliances was proposed in December by a task force of the National Cattlemen's Beef Association and was scheduled to be voted on at press time. Like the alliance databases, which would feed into it, the national database would be maintained by an unbiased third party. Any cattle company that put information on its animals into the system could track how they fared up and down the road—even if it didn't know who had bought them. (Performance data, searchable by ID number, would be blind, so a rancher might know how much fat a packer found on one of his calves, for instance, but not who that packer was.) The system would be supported by fees from companies using the information to improve their products. "The goal is that ranchers would never have to pay to put data in—just to get it out," says Anne Anderson, a 25-year veteran of the Texas cattle industry and a member of the task force.

If the national system gets a thumbs-up from the association, Anderson expects it will be operational by 1999. But it could be several years before a critical mass of companies participates. "There will be a pretty big gap between the time the alliances and some of the progressive thinkers come in and the time coffee-shop talk gets others to use it," she says. In addition to a pervasive fear of technology among many players ("They're just so intimidated by the Internet," Anderson says), some ranchers are worried that the system might provide the smoking gun in the case of a health scare. If a disease or infection is traced back to their beef, says Anderson, "they don't want to be put out of business, and that's a very real option."

—L.B.

can then simply scan an animal's ear tag and point his wand at the appropriate transponder on the card: the joyful tidings that #431B is with calf will travel via radio frequency to the computer, which may be 800 feet away in the cab of a pickup truck. Nunley also plans to set default results ahead of time, so that if all the calves passing through his chute come from one place or are undergoing the same treatment, that information will be automatically registered for each one. "The point is to save these guys from having to do a whole lot of data entry out in the field," says Curkendall. "They're cow punchers, not key punchers."

Once the proprietary software running on the computer has stored the data, the ranch will transfer a copy of it over the Internet to a Structured Query Language database running at a nonprofit technology provider to the industry. Using a password, members of the alliance will be able to access the database—also over the Internet—and run queries against individual ID numbers to see how their animals performed at different stages. They will also be able to pull reports comparing that performance with various averages (for example, how did the tenderness of my animals compare with all others processed by this packer?)

Members of Rancher's Renaissance are deploying the system with the guidance not only of AgInfoLink but also AgriInitiatives, a two-year-old consultancy to the agriculture and natural-resources industries, in Austin. (The companies are also working with Beef Advantage.) Anne Anderson is the CEO of both: she, Curkendall, and another partner devised the model for the source-verification and performance-data-tracking system and founded AgInfoLink when they couldn't find an existing technology company that could handle all the pieces.

What both companies aim to do, Anderson says, is to get all the players in the supply chain to focus on creating the best product for the end consumer, rather than simply passing off material to the next link. "We in the cattle industry have unfortunately had a somewhat cannibalistic relationship, with buyers and sellers making money at the expense of each other," she says. "We have to realize that we're all in the food business; we're all part of the same manufacturing process."

Anderson herself is a medium-sized producer—her family's ranch, Coyote Creek, in Rock Island, Tex., currently hosts about 800 head of cattle. Although she does not yet belong to an alliance and has no one to share data with, she has already begun outfitting her animals with ear tags in anticipation of the day when she will. "I want to get more for my calves, and I know I won't even have the opportunity if I don't do this," says Anderson, who collects information in an Excel spreadsheet on her Dell laptop. She also evangelizes among her smaller neighbors. Her most recent convert is a ranch with only 38 head; the rancher, excited by the technology but not ready to relinquish the old way of doing things, had the names, not the numbers, of his cows embossed on the outside of the tags.

Such small and medium-size players are the original source of 90% of the nation's beef. Anderson believes that once they begin sharing information among themselves and with their customers, they can—in addition to becoming part of the alliances—forge their own competitive entities with marketing power comparable to those large partnerships. "If we get bigger pools of high-quality cattle, we may get a premium because there will be more good cattle per day that are available," says Anderson. "If we're all getting information back and using that information to improve decisions, it can have economic ramifications for the entire area."

That kind of thinking is fairly new for small businesses, but it makes enormous sense for many industries, says the Supply Chain Council's Bill Helming. "In the early days we took a Darwinian approach: it's me or you. Now companies are learning to compete as a chain"—even if it's a horizontal chain encompassing players that might normally be considered rivals, he explains. Cooperation among small companies also makes them more attractive suppliers to large customers. "In the past, people have said, 'All these mom-and-pops are too hard to do business with. I have to negotiate separate terms with every one,'" he adds. "If everyone will agree to act in a standard way and use this technology for leverage, that can make for a very effective collaboration. It could totally change the playing field."

Leigh Buchanan (leigh.buchanan@inc.com) is the editor of Inc. Technology.

Competitive Advantage and Internal Organizational Assessment

W. Jack Duncan, Peter M. Ginter, and Linda E. Swayne

Executive Overview

It is generally agreed in the strategic management literature that internal organizational assessment is less developed theoretically and practically than other areas of situation analysis. This paper presents a four stage approach to analyzing a firm's internal strengths and weaknesses and illustrates how the technique can facilitate strategy formulation through the integration of value chain concepts and the incorporation of the most recent findings on internal resources and capabilities. A case example is used to illustrate how the approach can be applied by strategic decision makers as a tool for exploring the potential of their companies for sustained competitive advantage.

Jay Barney observed that "the development of tools for analyzing environmental opportunities and threats has proceeded much more rapidly than the development of tools for analyzing a firm's internal strengths and weaknesses."[1] Indeed, discussions of strategic management comfortably refer to strategic issue diagnosis, scenarios, Porter's industry attractiveness analysis, and a multitude of other techniques designed to examine potentially important strategic factors outside the organization.[2]

Discussions of internal organizational assessment, by contrast, are more often functional assessments of financial, human resource, information systems, and marketing strengths and weaknesses, rather than attempts to identify the present and potential competitive advantages of the firm. Effective strategic management requires an understanding of organizational resources and competencies as well as how each contributes to the formation of organizational strengths and ultimately to the development of a competitive advantage.

Focusing on the uncontrollable external environment highlights the importance of adapting to change, fitting organizations to the larger environment, and understanding that the rules of success are written outside individual business firms. The relatively more sophisticated status of external environmental analysis may reflect little more than threat bias, or the tendency to focus on the things that can do harm to organizations. Adaptability, fit, understanding externally imposed rules of success, and competitive forces, however, are only part of the formula for achieving competitive advantage.

Strategic decision makers need a systematic technique for scanning their internal organization. By paring down long lists of strengths and weaknesses and determining which ones are competitively relevant, they can understand precisely how each competitively relevant strength and weakness has the potential for adding or subtracting value. On the basis of this information, they can develop an array of generic strategies that will most likely lead to sustained competitive advantage. Even though the process can be easily adapted to the corporate level, our objective is to provide a business level technique for systematically assessing the relationship between internal strengths and weaknesses and sustained competitive advantage. This technique takes existing ideas and assembles and integrates them into a four-stage decision process that can be easily and efficiently used by strategic decision makers. The recommended approach uses the primary and support activities in value-chain analysis as the domain for searching out strengths and weaknesses, examines each strength and weakness in terms of its ability to create or reduce competitive advantage, and suggests specific ways firms may achieve a more competitive position in their market places.

A Closer Look at Competitive Advantage

Understanding competitive advantage is an ongoing challenge for decision makers. Historically, competitive advantage was thought of as a matter of position, where firms occupied a competitive space and built and defended market share. Competitive advantage depended on where the business was located and where it chose to provide services. Stable environments allowed this strategy to be successful, particularly for large and dominant organizations in mature industries.

The ability to develop a sustained competitive advantage today is increasingly rare. A competitive advantage laboriously achieved can be quickly lost. Organizations sustain a competitive advantage only so long as the services they deliver and the manner in which they deliver them have attributes that correspond to the key buying criteria of a substantial number of customers. Sustained competitive advantage is the result of an enduring value differential between the products or services of one organization and those of its competitors in the minds of customers. Therefore, organizations must consider more than the fit between the external environment and their present internal characteristics. They must anticipate what the rapidly changing environment will be like, and change their structures, cultures, and other relevant factors so as to reap the benefits of changing times. Sustained competitive advantage has become more of a matter of movement and ability to change than of location or position.[3]

The question of an enduring value differential raises the issue of why a firm is able to achieve a competitive advantage. To answer this, it is necessary to examine why and how organizations differ in a strategic sense. Identifying strengths and weaknesses requires introspection and self-examination. It also requires much more systematic analysis than it has received in the past.[4]

Assessing the Potential for Competitive Advantage

External environmental analysis is accomplished by scanning, monitoring, forecasting, and assessing. These successively more detailed environmental sweeps help ensure that genuinely important opportunities and threats in the external environment are not overlooked. Internal organizational analysis should take place in much the same way, through the successively detailed stages of surveying, categorizing, investigating, and evaluating. Although the terms are arbitrary, they are meant to convey the idea of successively more detailed sweeps of the internal organization. Each stage in the process achieves a critically important task that is highlighted in the discussion.

Figure 1 provides an overview of these four stages. The entire process will be illustrated by a case study of Ingram Micro, a leading worldwide wholesale distributor of microcomputer products as a case study.[5] A brief description of Ingram Micro is provided in Figure 2.

Stage One: Surveying Potential Strengths and Weaknesses

Identifying an organization's strengths and weaknesses is difficult because characteristics that appear as one or the other may, on closer examination, possess little or no significance for competitive advantage or disadvantage. The list of strengths and weaknesses generated by conventional techniques is usually little more than an initial impression of what a firm does well and where it needs improvement. The list is usually long, not very concrete, and agreed on by only a relatively few people.

However, even a superficial list of possible strengths and weaknesses is important to initiate strategic thinking and to focus thinking on areas where the firm can actually add or lose value.[6] This approach requires a survey of infrastructure, human resources, technology development, procurement, inbound and outbound logistics, operations, marketing and sales, and service activities. Accomplishing the initial survey is a matter of looking at financial statements, staffing standards, information resources, organization charts, and customer and employee surveys and interviews. The findings are then compared with industry standards and historical trends, and judgments are made as to whether the organization's performance represents strengths or weaknesses relative to others in the strategic group.[7]

In the case of Ingram Micro, as illustrated in Figure 3, potential strengths included the experience of the management team, administrative and financial support from Ingram Industries, and leading-edge information and inventory control models. Potential weaknesses included extremely high debt and financial leveraging, dependency on a relatively few and powerful suppliers, and potentially excessive family control.[8]

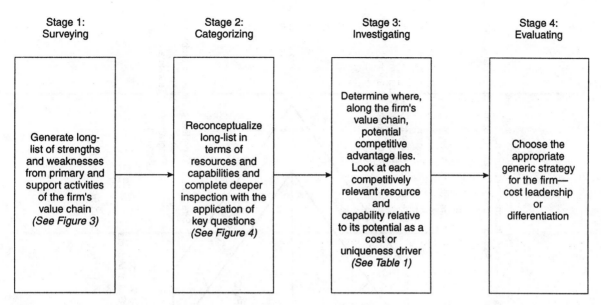

Stage 1: Surveying	Stage 2: Categorizing	Stage 3: Investigating	Stage 4: Evaluating
Generate long-list of strengths and weaknesses from primary and support activities of the firm's value chain *(See Figure 3)*	Reconceptualize long-list in terms of resources and capabilities and complete deeper inspection with the application of key questions *(See Figure 4)*	Determine where, along the firm's value chain, potential competitive advantage lies. Look at each competitively relevant resource and capability relative to its potential as a cost or uniqueness driver *(See Table 1)*	Choose the appropriate generic strategy for the firm—cost leadership or differentiation

Figure 1   Internal Environmental Analysis Process

Ingram Micro is a leading worldwide wholesale distributor of microcomputer products. Located in Santa Ana, California, Ingram markets microcomputer hardware, networking equipment, and software products to more than 100,000 reseller customers in more than 120 countries. Ingram's more than 1,100 suppliers include Apple Computer, Cisco Systems, Compaq, Hewlett-Packard, IBM, Intel, Toshiba, and U.S. Robotics. Some of its major customers include CompUSA, Micro Warehouse, Sam's Club, and GE Capital Technologies. It offers one-stop shopping through an inventory of over 36,000 products.

The company began as part of Ingram Industries and has relied throughout its history on other entities in the Ingram family of businesses for financing, cash management, tax and payroll administration, insurance, and administrative services. In 1996, Ingram Micro engaged in a public offering to raise the capital necessary to accomplish a split-off, but planned to continue to rely on the larger company for selected services.

Ingram Micro has grown rapidly since 1991 and increased net sales and net income from $2.0 billion and $30.2 million to more than $9.0 billion and $85.0 million respectively. Over 30 percent of its net sales are generated internationally. In 1994, it formed the Ingram Alliance Reseller Company, a master reseller business.

Figure 2   A Profile of Ingram Micro

Stage Two: Categorizing Organizational Differences

The second stage of internal organizational analysis involves more detailed categorization of the strengths and weaknesses highlighted by the initial survey. The critical task in this stage is to understand precisely what types of strengths and weaknesses a firm possesses in an absolute sense and relative to competitors.[9] Do the organization's strengths and weaknesses lie in tangible or intangible resources or both? Are they represented primarily by the presence or absence of the skills and experiences of employees relative to doing the actual work of the organization? Do

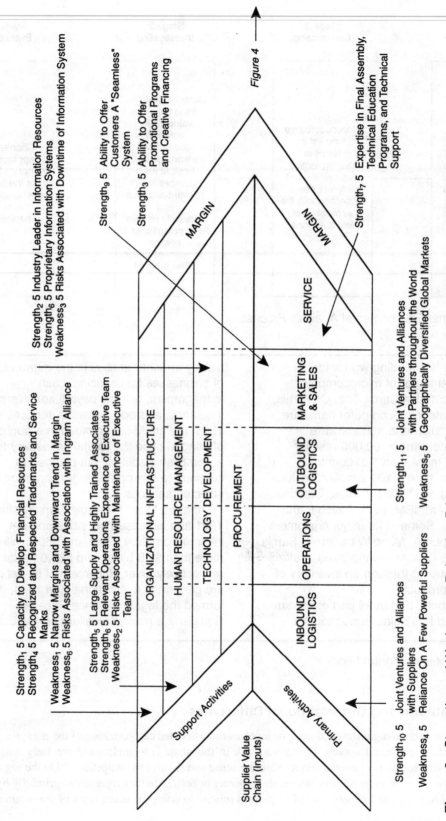

Figure 3 Strengths and Weaknesses Related to Primary and Support Value Activities in Porter's Modified Value Chain

Figure 4

Strength₁ 5 Capacity to Develop Financial Resources
Strength₄ 5 Recognized and Respected Trademarks and Service Marks
Weakness₁ 5 Narrow Margins and Downward Trend in Margin
Weakness₆ 5 Risks Associated with Association with Ingram Alliance

Strength₅ 5 Large Supply and Highly Trained Associates
Strength₆ 5 Relevant Operations Experience of Executive Team
Weakness₂ 5 Risks Associated with Maintenance of Executive Team

Strength₂ 5 Industry Leader in Information Resources
Strength₆ 5 Proprietary Information Systems
Weakness₃ 5 Risks Associated with Downtime of Information System

Strength₉ 5 Ability to Offer Customers A "Seamless" System
Strength₃ 5 Ability to Offer Promotional Programs and Creative Financing

Strength₇ 5 Expertise in Final Assembly, Technical Education Programs, and Technical Support

ORGANIZATIONAL INFRASTRUCTURE
HUMAN RESOURCE MANAGEMENT
TECHNOLOGY DEVELOPMENT
PROCUREMENT

INBOUND LOGISTICS | OPERATIONS | OUTBOUND LOGISTICS | MARKETING & SALES | SERVICE

MARGIN

Support Activities
Primary Activities

Supplier Value Chain (Inputs)

Strength₁₀ 5 Joint Ventures and Alliances with Suppliers
Weakness₄ 5 Reliance On A Few Powerful Suppliers

Strength₁₁ 5 Joint Ventures and Alliances with Partners throughout the World
Weakness₅ 5 Geographically Diversified Global Markets

they lie in managers' and employees' ability or inability to integrate and coordinate resources and skills? This reframing requires that one understand real and potential differences relative to competitors.

In stage two, potential strengths and weaknesses are categorized as strategic resources or capabilities, and more specific measures are developed for each. This is important because it is these resources and capabilities, along with a firm's purpose and aspirations, that ultimately make it different and suggest the path or paths to sustained competitive advantage.

The resource-based view argues that the key to sustained competitive advantage are those factors available for use in producing goods and services that are valuable and costly to copy.[10] Resources, as we use the term, may be tangible or intangible human assets. Human resources are often skill based and involve expertise in designing, producing, distributing, and/or servicing the products or services of the firm. They relate to skillfulness in accomplishing tasks required by one or more of the primary value activities. Tangible resources include things such as land or location, while intangible resources include such things as goodwill. The basic assumption is that resources are unevenly distributed and developed across firms, and explain, to some extent, the ability of an organization to effectively compete. Organizations with marginal resources break even, those with inferior resources disappear, and those with superior resources make profits.[11] One writer noted: "Basing strategy on the [resource] differences between firms should be automatic rather than noteworthy."[12]

Yet another potential source of sustained competitive advantage is the "purposeful coordination of resources."[13] An organization's ability to deploy and integrate to produce desired results is defined as a capability.[14] Unfortunately, "there are almost as many definitions of organizational capabilities as there are authors on the subject."[15] We will use the term to describe the ability to integrate or link skills and resources. Whereas human resources relate to expertise in actually doing the work of the organization, capabilities relate to putting things together in unique and innovative ways. Capabilities involve the integration of primary value activities, support activities, and/or primary and support value activities.

Capabilities, therefore, may be thought of as architectural abilities or bonding mechanisms whereby resources are combined in new and innovative ways. As a result, they accomplish learning, change, and ongoing renewal for individuals and organizations.[16] Capabilities, or the linking activities in the value chain, represent the collective learning in organizations, coordinating diverse operational skills and integrating multiple streams of technologies.[17] Sustained competitive advantage is based on the acquisition of resources that possess a unique relationship to the external environment and are integrated in innovative ways. An important element in judging sustained competitive advantage is understanding precisely what are our tangible and intangible resources, what skills and experiences do our employees possess, and how good are we at coordinating resources and skills. An important question is how competitively relevant are our resources, competencies, and skills?

Deeper Inspection ASSIST Analysis (an acronym for assessment of internal factors for strategic advantage) is useful for systematically determining the competitive relevancy of our resources and capabilities. This technique is an attempt to more effectively integrate into the strategy formulation equation internal factors leading to competitive advantage.

As illustrated in Figure 4, the first step in ASSIST analysis begins after the reframing of each potential strength and weakness as a resource or capability. In the second stage, each strength and weakness is then subjected to a series of questions to better understand whether or not it represents a real or potential competitive advantage or disadvantage. The questions are:[18]

1. *Question of Value.* Does the resources or capability represent something of worth to customers? Do competitors have something of worth to customers that the organization does not possess?
2. *Question of Rareness.* How many competitors possess the resource or capability? If it is rare and others do not possess it, it is a strength. If it is rare, and competitors possess it, but the organization does not, it is a weakness.
3. *Question of Imitability.* If competitors do not possess the means of obtaining the resource or capability, it is a strength. If the organization does not possess the resource or capability, and has no means of obtaining it, it is a weakness.
4. *Question of Sustainability.* How able will the organization be to maintain the value, rareness, and lack of imitability of the resource or capability? Can the competitors sustain their advantage?

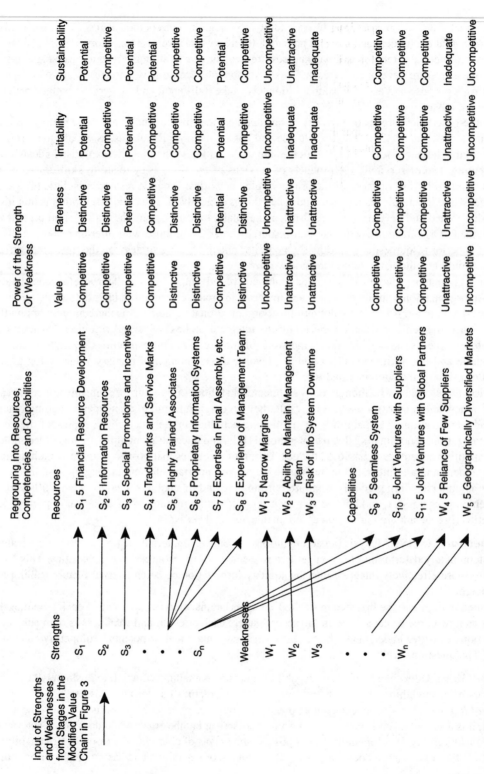

Figure 4 Assessment of Internal Factors for Strategic Advantage (ASSIST)

Assessing the Extent of Competitive Advantage The third step is to assess the extent of the competitive advantage or disadvantage possessed by each of the identified strategic resources and capabilities. Alternative values are assigned according to the following definitions:

- *Inadequate.* The resource or capability is below the minimum required to be in the business.
- *Adequate.* The resource or capability is the minimum required to be in this business or to minimally compete.
- *Attractive.* The resource or capability is better than the minimum required to compete but does not represent a particular advantage (or disadvantage in the case of a weakness). It will merely get the attention of appropriate individuals.
- *Potential.* The resource or capability is sufficient to attract attention and represents an important strategic consideration.
- *Competitive.* The resource or capability represents a clear competitive advantage/disadvantage relative to members of the strategic group.
- *Distinctive.* The resource or capability cannot be duplicated by competitors.

Figure 4 illustrates how the potential strengths and weaknesses of Ingram Micro were "categorized." This more detailed categorization and the corresponding appraisal of each resource and capability reduced the number of competitively relevant strengths and weaknesses to six resources (financial resources development, information resources, trademarks and service marks, highly trained associates, proprietary information systems, and experience of top management team) and three capabilities (a seamless distribution system, joint ventures with suppliers, and joint ventures with global partners). In addition, there were three strategically relevant disadvantages (narrow financial margins, questionable ability to retain management team, and geographically diverse markets). The competitive relevancy of each strength and weakness was determined by its ratings on the four questions in Figure 4. In order to be competitively relevant strength, a substantial number of distinctive or competitive ratings must be obtained. To be a competitively relevant weaknesses, a substantial number of inadequate and noncompetitive ratings must be obtained.

Stage Three: Investigating the Source of Competitive Advantage

Competitive advantage is ultimately built and maintained by adding value to customers.[19] Value is added by cost leadership, i.e., offering equal quality products or services at a lower cost than competitors, or by differentiation, i.e., offering products or services that are perceived to be unique relative to some important characteristic. Understanding how each competitively relevant resource and capability affects costs and uniqueness is an important aspect of understanding how, or if, each adds value to the services provided.

Once strategic strengths and weaknesses have been translated into terms of resources and capabilities and the potential for creating competitive advantage is accomplished through systematic categorization, it is important to investigate deeper relationships and determine how and where these factors actually add value. This is the critical task of stage three—pinpointing the primary or support value activity that possesses the potential for building or losing competitive advantage. Porter's modified value-chain (Figure 3) is useful again for breaking the organization "into its strategically relevant activities in order to understand the behavior of costs and the existing and potential sources of differentiation."[20] Understanding the value-chain enables decision makers to better understand and control the primary cost drivers and differentiate their services by capitalizing on their uniqueness drivers.

In the case of Ingram Micro, each competitively relevant resource and capability that emerged from the ASSIST process is evaluated below in terms of its ability to contribute to competitive advantage either as a cost or uniqueness driver. Note that only those strengths and weaknesses that were identified as competitively relevant are subjected to more probing investigation. This deeper investigation is conducted to determine where along the modified value chain the strength or weakness adds or subtracts value and if the strategic implication lies in its ability to enable cost leadership or develop perceived uniqueness. The summary investigation is shown in Table 1.

TABLE 1

Strengths and Weaknesses as Potential Sources of Competitive Advantage and Disadvantage

Strength/Weakness	Description	Potential Source of Competitive Advantage/ Disadvantage	Location on Modified Value Chain
S_1 Resource	Capacity to rapidly develop financial resources with growth rates of more than 40 percent and almost 30 percent in net sales and net income respectively.	Uniqueness Driver	Organizational Infrastructure
S_2 Resource	Industry leader relative to investments in information resources, warehousing systems, and administrative infrastructure. In the past five years, Ingram has reduced its general and administrative expenses by more than a percent through the use of leading-edge information technologies.	Cost Driver	Organizational Infrastructure
S_3 Resource	Ability to offer special promotions and incentives.	Not Competitively Relevant (See Figure 4)	Organizational Infrastructure
S_4 Resource	Company possesses a number of trademarks and service marks that are visible and respected throughout the world.	Uniqueness Driver	Organizational Infrastructure
S_5 Resource	Highly trained associates that receive training through the company's extensive in-house training system.	Uniqueness Driver	Human Resources
S_6 Resource	Only wholesale distributor of microcomputers with a centralized global information expertise illustrated by its Impulse system. On a typical business day the company's systems handle 12 million on-line transactions, 26,000 orders, and 37,000 shipments.	Uniqueness Driver	Technology Development
S_7 Resource	Expertise in final assembly.	Not Competitively Relevant (See Figure 4)	Operations
S_8 Resource	Top management team with experience in number of industries relevant to company's operations. Members of the team have substantial international experience in software development, telecommunications, transportation, and shipping.	Uniqueness Driver	Human Resources
S_9 Capability	Ability to offer reseller customers a "seamless" supply system of one-stop shopping.	Uniqueness Driver	Marketing and Sales
S_{10} Capability	Joint ventures with suppliers that allow many of the effects of vertical integration while avoiding the most significant risks.	Cost Driver	Inbound Logistics
S_{11} Capability	Joint ventures and strategic alliances with firms outside the United States leverage company's international management expertise. In addition to the United States, Ingram has almost twenty locations in Europe, three in Canada, seven in Mexico, and three in Asia. More than 100,000 reseller customers are serviced in more than 120 countries worldwide. Over 30 percent of net sales are derived from operations outside the United States.	Uniqueness Driver	Inbound and Outbound Logistics
W_1 Resource	Narrow margins accentuated by downward trend. Gross margin has declined from a little over eight percent to about 6.8 percent over the past three years.	Cost Driver	Organizational Infrastructure
W_2 Resource	Dependent on company's ability to retain and motivate current executive team.	Uniqueness Driver	Organizational Infrastructure
W_3 Resource	Dependence on information system and risk of downtime.	Not Competitively Relevant (See Figure 4)	Technological Development
W_4 Capability	Over reliance on a few suppliers.	Not Competitively Relevant (See Figure 4)	Inbound Logistics
W_5 Capability	Geographical diversity of operations and markets makes effective coordination a challenge even in light of state-of-the art information system.	Uniqueness Driver	Inbound and Outbound Logistics

Stage Four: Evaluating Competitive Advantage Evaluating competitively relevant resources and capabilities in terms of possible generic strategies is the critical task of stage four. The evaluation suggests that Ingram Micro possesses potential competitive advantages because of uniqueness drivers located throughout the modified value chain—inbound and outbound logistics, operations, marketing and sales, as well as organizational infrastructure and technology development. This evaluation indicates that differentiation strategies are the firm's most promising means to competitive advantage. The competitive nature of this industry and the narrow margins of all competitors underscore the need for cost controls. However, cost control is essentially a requirement to compete in the industry and provides no genuine competitive advantage. The strategic implications of the internal organizational analysis is provided in Table 2.

The summary in Table 2 leads us to the conclusion that Ingram Micro possesses resource driven opportunities for differentiation with regard to organizational infrastructure, name identity, access to capital markets (although its debt load is becoming extremely large). These resources, in turn, allow Ingram to leverage its marketing and sales expertise. Ingram also has substantial ability to differentiate itself in the areas of technology development, managerial expertise, customer service, and the promise of a seamless sales and service system. Its worldwide marketing, sales, and technology support network provides it with clear integrative capabilities that represent opportunities for sustained competitive advantage.

Although Ingram possesses numerous uniqueness drivers, it also possesses competitive disadvantages relative to costs and uniqueness. In 1996, for example, Ingram Micro entered the equity market to acquire the resources necessary to split off from Ingram Industries. While this split-off would reduce some of the risk factors associated with being a subsidiary of another firm, it would also entail the loss of funding through intracompany transfers, infrastructure economies, and related factors. As a result, the increasing cost of capital represents the potential strategic weakness of even smaller gross margins. Moreover, the coordination issues inherent in global operations present dangers to cost control and service quality.

Strategic Challenge

The technique outlined in this paper is an efficient and effective aid for assessing an internal organization and relating strengths and weaknesses to achieving competitive advantage. Admittedly, its focus on the modified value chain does not overcome the possibility of long and superficial lists of organizational characteristics. It does, however, encourage thinking about strengths and weaknesses in terms of their strategic relevance, rather than merely auditing functional subsystems of the firm.

The strategic challenge for any organization does not end with the evaluation of strategically relevant strengths and weaknesses. In fact, strategically relevant strengths and weaknesses provide decision makers with only one of several important parts of the strategy puzzle. The challenge is to integrate the understanding of strengths and weaknesses with the opportunities and threats facing the organization and with the strategic preferences provided by a clear, understood, and shared sense of mission and vision.

Ingram Micro is a leader in a growing and developing industry. Microcomputers will, no doubt, continue to be the hardware of choice for individuals and businesses in the foreseeable future. There are, of course, significant threats. Opportunities attract competitors and evolving technologies possess the potential of redefining how both hardware and software are marketed, disseminated, and delivered. Splitting off from the parent company means stepping out into a dangerous competitive environment without the financial and managerial support of a concerned and sympathetic parent. However, independence creates the opportunity to innovate, invent, and experiment in ways that are rarely possible for subsidiary operations.

The greatest strategic potential for Ingram Micro lies in a differentiation strategy. There is a systematic way of arriving at this conclusion. Costs are not unimportant but primarily represent a constraint. The competitive nature of the industry demands cost efficiency. Strategic success for Ingram Micro, however, lies along the path of differentiation through the provision of distinctive services and support. For another company with different strengths and weaknesses in another industry, this analysis could have suggested another strategy.

TABLE 2

Strategic Implications and Competitive Advantage

Strategic Strength/Weakness	Strategic Implication
Strengths:	
S_1 Resource—Uniqueness Driver—Organizational Infrastructure S_2 Resource—Cost Driver—Organizational Infrastructure S_3 Resource—Uniqueness Driver—Technology Development S_4 Resource—Uniqueness Driver—Organizational Infrastructure S_5 Resource—Uniqueness Driver—Human Resources S_6 Resource—Uniqueness Driver—Technology Development S_8 Resource—Uniqueness Driver—Operations S_9 Capability—Uniqueness Driver—Marketing and Sales S_{10} Capability—Cost Driver—Inbound Logistics S_{11} Capability—Uniqueness Driver—Inbound and Outbound Logistics	Ingram Micro's ability to generate financial resources in an industry characterized by low margins in association with the name recognition it possesses because of its trademarks and service marks provide significant opportunities for further differentiation its services and deeper market penetrations Ingram Micro's resources in the areas of state-of-the-art information systems, highly trained sales associates, and experienced management team offers the opportunity for differentiation through the continual introduction of market relevant service innovations, technical assistance, after service sales, and a seamless distribution system. Ingram Micro's financial resources, managerial expertise, and sales resources in combination with its worldwide network of suppliers and strategic alliances along with the information system that can link them provides a unparalleled opportunity for service differentiation in a highly competitive industry where cost advantage is difficult to achieve.
Weaknesses:	
W_1 Resource—Cost Driver—Organizational Infrastructure W_2 Resource—Uniqueness Driver—Organizational Infrastructure W_3 Capability—Uniqueness Driver—Inbound and Outbound Logistics	Ingram Micro's narrow margins and downward trend in margin underscores the difficulty of obtaining a competitive advantage in the industry though cost leadership. Cost control is essential to survival but cost leadership is not a viable path to competitive advantage for the company. Ingram Micro's need to maintain the management team and focus on coordination of internationally diverse operations are potential issues that could erode the opportunity for competitive advantage through service differentiation.

This paper is not intended as an analysis of Ingram Micro. It is meant instead as an illustration of a technique for internal organizational assessment that can be used along with other techniques for external environmental assessment. It addresses Jay Barney's lament about tools for analyzing strengths and weaknesses. However, it is important to emphasize that just as external environmental threats should be used as warning signs and never as excuses to ignore opportunities, so it is with internal weaknesses.

Although organizations possess cost advantages and may successfully differentiate their products and services, resources and capabilities should not be looked on as absolute determinants of competitive abilities. Even the most oppressive resource and capability limitations can be overcome by innovative leaders and heroic employees. In fact, it has been argued that the essential character of new directions in strategic thinking is the acceptance of "an aspiration that creates, by design, a chasm between ambitions and resources." It is further argued that creating this stretch or chasm "is the single most important task senior management faces."[21] Understanding competitively relevant resources and capabilities is important, even critical, for systematic strategic decision making. This understanding, however, should not blind us to opportunities or make us timid in thinking of new and innovative ways of overcoming limitations.[22]

Endnotes

1. Barney, Jay B. 1995. Looking inside for competitive advantage. *Academy of Management Executive,* 9: 49–61.

2. Schwartz, Peter. 1991. *The art of the long view.* New York: Currency Doubleday. Porter, Michael E. 1980. *Corporate strategy: Techniques for analyzing industries and competitors.* New York: The Free Press; and Fahey, Liam & Narayanan, V. K. 1986. *Macroenvironmental analysis for strategic management.* St. Paul, MN: West Publishing Company.

3. Stalk, George, Evans, Philip, & Shulman, Lawrence. 1992. Competing on capabilities: The new rules of corporate strategy. *Harvard Business Review,* 70 (2): 57–69.

4. Denison, Daniel R. 1990. *Corporate culture and organizational effectiveness.* New York: Wiley and Denison, Daniel R. & Mishra, Aneil K. 1995. Toward a theory of organizational effectiveness. *Organizational Science,* 6: 204–223. See also Hall, Richard. 1993. A framework for linking intangible resources and capabilities to sustainable competitive advantage. *Strategic Management Journal,* 14: 607–618.

5. Information on Ingram Micro obtained from *Prospectus* for issuance of Class A Common Stock. September 9, 1996.

6. Porter, Michael. *Competitive advantage: Creating and sustaining superior performance.* New York: Free Press. Chapter 2. See also Porter, Michael E. Porter. 1991. Toward a dynamic theory of strategy. *Strategic Management Journal.* 12: 95–117.

7. Carroll, Glen R. 1993. A sociological view on why firms differ. *Strategic Management Journal.* 14: 237–249 and Azzone, Giovanni & Bertele, Umberto. 1995. Measuring resources for supporting resource-based competencies. *Management Decision* 33: 57–58.

8. Information was collected by two independent readers who were familiar with the historical development of the resource based view of competitive advantage. Both readers had been involved in discussions regarding the need for more precise definitions of resources and capabilities and the role each might play in achieving sustained competitive advantage. The readers developed lists of strengths and weaknesses through independent readings of the *Prospectus* of Ingram Micro. Consensus discussions were held and agreement was obtained on proper classifications. The same evaluators developed consensus on the appraisals of the four questions in the ASSIST model. It is important to note that the researchers limited their use of information to those sources easily obtained by any executive decision maker in order to illustrate how systematic internal assessment of an organization can be conducted using the recommended approach without large investments in information search and research.

9. Barney, Jay B. 1991. Firm resources and sustained competitive advantage. *Journal of Management.* 17: 99–120; Barney, Jay B. & Hansen, Mark H. Hansen. 1994. Trustworthiness as a source of competitive advantage. *Strategic Management Journal.* 15: 175–190; and Brumagim, Alan L. 1994. A hierarchy of corporate resources. In Paul Shrivastava, Anne S. Huff, and Jane E. Dutton (Eds.). *Advances in strategic management: Resource-based view of the firm:* 81–112. Greenwich, CT: JAI Press.

10. Hart, Stuart L. 1995. A natural-resource-based view of the firm. *Academy of Management Review.* 20: 986–1014.

11. Peteraf, Margaret A. 1993. The cornerstones of competitive advantage: A resource-based view. *Strategic Management Journal.* 14: 179–191.

12. Wernerfelt, Birger. 1995. The resource-based view of the firm: Ten years after. *Strategic Management Journal.* 16: 173. *Insert added.*

13. Henderson, Rebecca & Cockburn, Ian. 1994. Measuring competence? Exploring firm effects in pharmaceutical research. *Strategic Management Journal. Special Issue.* 15: 63–84 and Marino, Kenneth E. 1996. Developing consensus on firm competencies and capabilities. *Academy of Management Executive.* 10: 40–51.

14. Amit, Raphael & Schoemaker, Paul J. H. 1993. Strategic assets and organizational rent. *Strategic Management Journal.* 14: 33–46.

15. Collis, David J. 1994. Research note: How valuable are organizational capabilities. *Strategic Management Journal.* 15: 143–152. See, for example. Ulrich, David & Lake, Dale. 1991. Organizational capability: Creating competitive advantage. *Academy of Management Executive,* 5: 77–85.

16. Henderson & Cockburn, Measuring competence, 66 and Amit & Schoemaker, Strategic assets and organizational rent, 35.

17. Black, Janice A. & Boal, Kimberly B. 1994. Strategic resources: Traits, configurations, and paths to sustainable competitive advantage. *Strategic Management Journal* 15: 131–148.

18. Barney. Looking inside for competitive advantage. Note that the "question of organization" was not included because of its similarity with our definition of capability.

19. Prahalad, C. K. & Hamel, Gary. 1990. The core competency of the corporation. *Harvard Business Review* 68 (3): 82 and Markides, Constantinos C. Markides & Williamson, Peter J. 1994. "Related diversification, core competencies, and corporate performance," *Strategic Management Journal.* 15: 149–165.

20. Porter, *Competitive advantage: Creating and sustaining superior performance.* Chapter 2 and Porter, Toward a dynamic theory of strategy, 95–117.

21. Hamel, Gary & Prahalad, C. K. 1993. Strategy as stretch and leverage. *Harvard Business Review.* 72 (3): 75–84.

22. This discussion has been adapted from Hamel, Gary & Prahalad, C. K. 1994. *Competing for the future.* Boston, MA: Harvard Business School Press. Chapter 7 and Hamel, Gary & Prahalad, C. K. 1996. "Competing in the new economy: Managing out of bounds," *Strategic Management Journal,* 17: 237–242.

About the Authors

W. Jack Duncan is professor and university scholar at the School of Business/Graduate School of Management, University of Alabama at Birmingham. He is a fellow of the Academy of Management and a fellow of the International Academy of Management. Duncan is past president of the Southern Management Association and the Southwest Division of the Academy of Management. His articles have been published in the Academy of Management Executive, Academy of Management Journal, Academy of Management Review, Management Science, Journal of Management, *and others.*

Peter M. Ginter is professor and chair of Health Care Organization and Policy, School of Public Health, University of Alabama at Birmingham. He is past president of the Southwest Federation of Administrative Disciplines. Ginter is the author of numerous books, cases, and articles on management and health care issues. His articles have been published in the Academy of Management Review, California Management Review, Journal of Management Studies, Management International Review, Health Care Management Review, *and others.*

Linda E. Swayne is professor and chair of marketing in the Belk College of Business Administration, and coordinator of the Physicians' Institute at the University of North Carolina at Charlotte. She has served as the executive director of the Carolinas Task Force on Health Care and is the author of numerous books, cases, and articles on marketing and health care issues. Swayne is past president of the Southwest Federation of Administrative Disciplines and the Southern Marketing Association.

Looking Inside for Competitive Advantage

Jay B. Barney

Executive Overview

Strategic managers and researchers have long been interested in understanding sources of competitive advantage for firms. Traditionally, this effort has focused on the relationship between a firm's environmental opportunities and threats on the one hand, and its internal strengths and weaknesses on the other. Summarized in what has come to be known as SWOT (Strengths, Weaknesses, Opportunities, and Threats) analysis, this traditional logic suggests that firms that use their internal strengths in exploiting environmental opportunities and neutralizing environmental threats, while avoiding internal weaknesses, are more likely to gain competitive advantages than other kinds of firms.[1]

This simple SWOT framework points to the importance of both external and internal phenomena in understanding the sources of competitive advantage. To date, the development of tools for analyzing environmental opportunities and threats has proceeded much more rapidly than the development of tools for analyzing a firm's internal strengths and weaknesses. To address this deficiency, this article offers a simple, easy-to-apply approach to analyzing the competitive implications of a firm's internal strengths and weaknesses.

The history of strategic management research can be understood as an attempt to "fill in the blanks" created by the SWOT framework; i.e., to move beyond suggesting that strengths, weaknesses, opportunities, and threats are important for understanding competitive advantage to suggest models and frameworks that can be used to analyze and evaluate these phenomena. Michael Porter and his associates have developed a number of these models and frameworks for analyzing environmental opportunities and threats.[2] Porter's work on the "five forces model," the relationship between industry structure and strategic opportunities, and strategic groups can all be understood as an effort to unpack the concepts of environmental opportunities and threats in a theoretically rigorous, yet highly applicable way.

However, the SWOT framework tells us that environmental analysis—no matter how rigorous—is only half the story. A complete understanding of sources of competitive advantage requires the analysis of a firm's internal strengths and weaknesses as well.[3] The importance of integrating internal with environmental analyses can be seen when evaluating the sources of competitive advantage of many firms. Consider, for example,

- WalMart, a firm that has, for the last twenty years, consistently earned a return on sales twice the average of its industry;
- Southwest Airlines, a firm whose profits continued to increase, despite losses at other U.S. airlines that totaled almost $10 billion from 1990 to 1993; and
- Nucor Steel, a firm whose stock price continued to soar through the 1980s and '90s, despite the fact that the market value of most steel companies has remained flat or fallen during the same time period.[4]

These firms, and many others, have all gained competitive advantages—despite the unattractive, high threat, low opportunity environments within which they operate. Even the most careful and complete analysis of these firms' competitive environments cannot, by itself, explain their success. Such explanations must also include these firms' internal attributes—their strengths and weaknesses—as sources of competitive advantage. Following more recent practice, internal attributes will be referred to as resources and *capabilities* throughout the following discussion.[5]

A firm's resources and capabilities include all of the financial, physical, human, and organizational assets used by a firm to develop, manufacture, and deliver products or services to its customers. Financial resources include debt, equity, retained earnings, and so forth. Physical resources include the machines, manufacturing facilities, and buildings firms use in their operations. Human resources include all the experience, knowledge, judgment, risk taking propensity, and wisdom of individuals associated with a firm. Organizational resources include the history, relationships, trust, and organizational culture that are attributes of groups of individuals associated with a firm, along with a firm's formal reporting structure, explicit management control systems, and compensation policies.

In the process of filling in the "internal blanks" created by SWOT analysis, managers must address four important questions about their resources and capabilities: (1) the question of value, (2) the question of rareness, (3) the question of imitability, and (4) the question of organization.

The Question of Value

To begin evaluating the competitive implications of a firm's resources and capabilities, managers must first answer the question of value: Do a firm's resources and capabilities add value by enabling it to exploit opportunities and/or neutralize threats?

The answer to this question, for some firms, has been yes. Sony, for example, has a great deal of experience in designing, manufacturing, and selling miniaturized electronic technology. Sony has used these resources to exploit numerous market opportunities, including portable tape players, portable disc players, portable televisions, and easy-to-hold 8mm video cameras. 3M has used its skills and experience in substrates, coatings, and adhesives, along with an organizational culture that rewards risk taking and creativity, to exploit numerous market opportunities in office products, including invisible tape and Post-It™ Notes. Sony's and 3M's resources—including their specific technological skills and their creative organizational cultures—made it possible for these firms to respond to, and even create, new environmental opportunities.

Unfortunately, for other firms, the answer to the question of value has been no. For example, USX's long experience in traditional steel-making technology and the traditional steel market made it almost impossible for USX to recognize and respond to fundamental changes in the structure of the steel industry. Because they could not recognize new opportunities and threats, USX delayed its investment in, among other opportunities, thin slab continuous casting steel manufacturing technology. Nucor Steel, on the other hand, was not shackled by its experience, made these investments early, and has become a major player in the international steel industry. In a similar way, Sears was unable to recognize or respond to changes in the retail market that had been created by WalMart and specialty retail stores. In a sense, Sears' historical success, along with a commitment to stick with a traditional way of doing things, led it to miss some significant market opportunities.[6]

Although a firm's resources and capabilities may have added value in the past, changes in customer tastes, industry structure, or technology can render them less valuable in the future. General Electric's capabilities in transistor manufacturing became much less valuable when semiconductors were invented. American Airlines' skills in managing their relationship with the Civil Aeronautics Board (CAB) became much less valuable after airline deregulation. IBM's numerous capabilities in the mainframe computing business became less valuable with the increase in power, and reduction in price, of personal and mini computers. One of the most important responsibilities of strategic managers is to constantly evaluate whether or not their firm's resources and capabilities continue to add value, despite changes in the competitive environment.

Some environmental changes are so significant that few, if any, of a firm's resources remain valuable in any environmental context.[7] However, this kind of radical environmental change is unusual. More commonly, changes in a firm's environment may reduce the value of a firm's resources in their current use, while leaving the value of those resources in other uses unchanged. Such changes might even *increase* the value of those resources in those other uses. In this situation, the critical issue facing managers is: how can we use our traditional strengths in new ways to exploit opportunities and/or neutralize threats?

Numerous firms have weathered these environmental shifts by finding new ways to apply their traditional strengths. AT&T had developed a reputation for providing high-quality long distance telephone service. It moved rapidly to exploit this reputation in the newly competitive long distance market by aggressively marketing its services against MCI, Sprint, and other carriers. Also, AT&T had traditional strengths in research and development with its Bell Labs subsidiary. To exploit these strengths in its new competitive context, AT&T shifted Bell Labs' mission from basic research to applied research, and then leveraged those skills by forming numerous joint ventures, acquiring NCR, and other actions. Through this process, AT&T has been able to use some of its historically important capabilities to try to position itself as a major actor in the global telecommunications and computing industry.

Another firm that has gone through a similar transformation is the Hunter Fan Company. Formed in 1886, Hunter Fan developed the technology it needed to be the market share leader in ceiling fans used to cool large manufacturing facilities. Unfortunately, the invention of air conditioning significantly reduced demand for industrial fans, and Hunter Fan's performance deteriorated rapidly. However, in the 1970s, rising energy prices made energy conservation more important to home owners. Since ceiling fans can significantly reduce home energy consumption, Hunter Fan was able to move quickly to exploit this new opportunity. Of course, Hunter Fan had to develop some new skills as well, including brass-plating capabilities and new distribution networks. However, by building on its traditional strengths in new ways, Hunter Fan has become a leader in the home ceiling fan market.[8]

By answering the question of value, managers link the analysis of internal resources and capabilities with the analysis of environmental opportunities and threats. Firm resources are not valuable in a vacuum, but rather are valuable only when they exploit opportunities and/or neutralize threats. The models developed by Porter and his associates can be used to isolate potential opportunities and threats that the resources a firm controls can exploit or neutralize.

Of course, the resources and capabilities of different firms can be valuable in different ways. This can be true, even if firms are competing in the same industry. For example, while both Rolex and Timex manufacture watches, they exploit very different valuable resources. Rolex emphasizes it quality manufacturing, commitment to excellence, and high-status reputation in marketing its watches. Timex emphasizes its high-volume, low-cost manufacturing skills and abilities. Rolex exploits its capabilities in responding to demand for very expensive watches; Timex exploits its resources in responding to demand for practical, reliable, low-cost timekeeping.

The Question of Rareness

That a firm's resources and capabilities are valuable is an important first consideration in understanding internal sources of competitive advantage. However, if a particular resource and capability is controlled by numerous competing firms, then that resource is unlikely to be a source of competitive advantage for any one of them. Instead, valuable but common (i.e., not rare) resources and capabilities are sources of competitive parity. For managers evaluating the competitive implications of their resources and capabilities, these observations lead to the second critical issue: How many competing firms already possess these valuable resources and capabilities?

Consider, for example, two firms competing in the global communications and computing industries: NEC and AT&T. Both these firms are developing many of the same capabilities that are likely to be needed in these industries over the next decade. These capabilities are clearly valuable, although—since at least these two firms, and maybe others, are developing them—they may not be rare. If they are not rare, they cannot—by themselves—be sources of competitive advantage for either NEC or AT&T. If either of these firms is to gain competitive advantages, they must exploit resources and capabilities that are different from the communication and computing skills they are *both* cited as developing. This may be part of the reason why AT&T recently restructured its telecommunications and computer businesses into separate firms.[9]

While resources and capabilities must be rare among competing firms in order to be a source of competitive advantage, this does not mean that common, but valuable, resources are not important. Indeed, such resources and capabilities may be essential for a firm's survival. On the other hand, if a firm's resources are valuable and rare, those resources may enable a firm to gain at least a temporary competitive advantage. WalMart's skills in developing and using point-of-purchase data collection to control inventory have given it a competitive advantage over K-Mart, a firm that until recently has not had access to this timely information. Thus, for many years, WalMart's valuable point-of-purchase inventory control systems were rare, at least relative to its major U.S. competitor, K-Mart.[10]

The Question of Imitability

A firm that possesses valuable and rare resources and capabilities can gain, at least, a temporary competitive advantage. If, in addition, competing firms face a cost disadvantage in imitating these resources and capabilities, firms with these special abilities can obtain a sustained competitive advantage. These observations lead to the question of imitability: Do firms without a resource or capability face a cost disadvantage in obtaining it compared to firms that already possess it?

Obviously, imitation is critical to understanding the ability of resources and capabilities to generate sustained competitive advantages. Imitation can occur in at least two ways: duplication and substitution. Duplication occurs when an imitating firm builds the same kinds of resources as the firm it is imitating. If one firm has a competitive advantage because of its research and development skills, then a duplicating firm will try to imitate that resource by developing its own research and development skills. In addition, firms may be able to substitute some resources for other resources. If these substitute resources have the same strategic implications and are no more costly to develop, then imitation through substitution will lead to competitive parity in the long run.

So, when will firms be at a cost disadvantage in imitating another's resources and capabilities, either through duplication or substitution? While there are numerous reasons why some of these internal attributes of firms may be costly to imitate, most of these reasons can be grouped into three categories: the importance of history in creating firm resources; the importance of numerous "small decisions" in developing, nurturing, and exploiting resources; and the importance of socially complex resources.

The Importance of History

As firms evolve, they pick up skills, abilities, and resources that are unique to them, reflecting their particular path through history. These resources and capabilities reflect the unique personalities, experiences, and relationships that exist in only a single firm. Before the Second World War, Caterpillar was one of several medium-sized firms in the heavy construction equipment industry struggling to survive intense competition. Just before the outbreak of war, the Department of War (now the Department of Defense) concluded that, in order to pursue a global war, they would need one worldwide supplier of heavy construction equipment to build roads, air strips, army bases, and so forth. After a brief competition, Caterpillar was awarded this contract and, with the support of the Allies, was able to develop a worldwide service and supply network for heavy construction equipment at very low cost.

After the war, Caterpillar continued to own and operate this worldwide service and supply network. Indeed, Caterpillar management still advertises their ability to deliver any part, for any piece of Caterpillar equipment, to any place in the world, in under two days. By using this valuable capability, Caterpillar was able to become the dominant firm in the heavy construction equipment industry. Even today, despite recessions and labor strife, Caterpillar remains the market share leader in most categories of heavy construction equipment.[11]

Consider the position of a firm trying to duplicate Caterpillar's worldwide service and supply network, at the same cost as Caterpillar. This competing firm would have to receive the same kind of government support that Caterpillar received during World War II. This kind of government support is very unlikely.

It is interesting to note that at least one firm in the heavy construction equipment industry has begun to effectively compete against Caterpillar: Komatsu. However, rather than attempting to duplicate Caterpillar's service and supply network, Komatsu has attempted to exploit its own unique design and manufacturing resources by building machines that do not break down as frequently. Since Komatsu's machines break down less frequently, Komatsu does not require as extensive a worldwide service and supply network as Caterpillar. In this sense, Komatsu's special design and manufacturing skills in building machines that break down less frequently may be a strategic substitute for Caterpillar's worldwide service and supply network.[12]

In general, whenever the acquisition or development of valuable and rare resources depends upon unique historical circumstances, those imitating these resources will be at a cost disadvantage building them. Such resources can be sources of sustained competitive advantage.

The Importance of Numerous Small Decisions

Strategic managers and researchers are often enamored with the importance of "Big Decisions" as determinants of competitive advantage. IBM's decision to bring out the 360 series of computers in the 1960s was a "Big Decision" that had enormous competitive implications until the rise of personal computers. General Electric's decision to invest in the medical imaging business was a "Big Decision" whose competitive ramifications are still unfolding. Sometimes such "Big Decisions" are critical in understanding a firm's competitive position. However, more and more frequently, a firm's competitive advantage seems to depend on numerous "small decisions" through which a firm's resources and capabilities are developed and exploited. Thus, for example, a firm's competitive advantage in quality does not depend just upon its announcing that it is seeking the Malcolm Baldridge Quality Award. It depends upon literally hundreds of thousands of decisions made each day by employees in the firm—small decisions about whether or not to tighten a screw a little more, whether or not to share a small idea for improvement, or whether or not to call attention to a quality problem.[13] From the point of view of sustaining a competitive advantage, "small decisions" have some advantages over "Big Decisions." In particular, small decisions are essentially invisible to firms seeking to imitate a successful firm's resources and capabilities. "Big Decisions," on the other hand, are more obvious, easier to describe, and, perhaps, easier to imitate. While competitors may be able to observe the consequences of numerous little decisions, they often have a difficult time understanding the sources of the advantages.[14] A case in point is The Mailbox, Inc., a very successful firm in the bulk mailing business in the Dallas-Ft. Worth market. If there was ever a business where it seems unlikely that a firm would have a sustained competitive advantage, it is bulk mailing. Firms in this industry gather mail from customers, sort it by postal code, and then take it to the post office to be mailed. Where is the competitive advantage here? And yet, The Mailbox has enjoyed an enormous market share advantage in the Dallas-Ft. Worth area for several years. Why?

When asked, managers at The Mailbox have a difficult time describing the sources of their sustained advantages. Indeed, they can point to *no* "Big Decisions" they have made to generate this advantage. However, as these managers begin to discuss their firm, what becomes clear is that their success does not depend on doing a few big things right, but on doing lots of little things right. The way they manage accounting, finance, human resources, production, or other business functions, separately, is not exceptional. However, to manage all these functions so well, and so consistently over time is truly exceptional. Firms seeking to compete against The Mailbox will not have to imitate just a few internal attributes; they will have to imitate thousands, or even hundreds of thousands of such attributes—a daunting task indeed.[15]

The Importance of Socially Complex Resources

A final reason that firms may be at a cost disadvantage in imitating resources and capabilities is that these resources may be socially complex. Some physical resources (e.g., computers, robots, and other machines) controlled by firms are very complex. However, firms seeking to imitate these physical resources need only purchase them, take them apart, and duplicate the technology in question. With just a couple of exceptions (including the pharmaceutical and specialty chemicals industries), patents provide little protection from the imitation of a firm's physical resources.[16] On the other hand, socially complex resources and capabilities—organizational phenomena like reputation, trust, friendship, teamwork and culture—while not patentable, are much more difficult to imitate. Imagine the difficulty of imitating Hewlett Packard's (HP) powerful and enabling culture. One of the most important components of HP's culture is that it supports and encourages teamwork and cooperation, even across divisional boundaries. HP has used this socially complex capability to enhance the compatibility of its mini-computers, and electronic instruments. By cooperating across these product categories, HP has been able to almost double its market value, all without introducing any radical new products or technologies.[17]

In general, when a firm's resources and capabilities are valuable, rare, and socially complex, those resources are likely to be sources of sustained competitive advantage. One firm that apparently violates this assertion is Sony. Most observers agree that Sony possesses some special management and coordination skills that enables it to conceive, design, and manufacture high quality, miniaturized consumer electronics. However, it appears that every time Sony brings out a new miniaturized product, several of its competitors quickly duplicate that product, through reverse engineering, thereby reducing Sony's technological advantage. In what way can Sony's socially complex miniaturization skills be a source of sustained competitive advantage, when most of Sony's products are quickly imitated?

The solution to this paradox depends on shifting the unit of analysis from the performance of Sony's products over time to the performance of Sony over time. After it introduces each new product, Sony experiences a rapid increase in sales and profits associated with that product. However, this leads other firms to reverse engineer the Sony product and introduce their own version. Increased competition leads the sales and profits associated with the new product to be reduced. Thus, at the level of individual products introduced by Sony, Sony apparently enjoys only very short-lived competitive advantages.

However, by looking at the total returns earned by Sony across all of its new products over time, the source of Sony's sustained competitive advantage becomes clear. By exploiting its capabilities in miniaturization, Sony is able to constantly introduce new and exciting personal electronics products. No one of these products generate a sustained competitive advantage. However, over time, across several such product introductions, Sony's capability advantages do lead to a sustained competitive advantage.[18]

The Question of Organization

A firm's competitive advantage potential depends on the value, rareness, and imitability of its resources and capabilities. However, to fully realize this potential, a firm must also be organized to exploit its resources and capabilities. These observations lead to the question of organization: Is a firm organized to exploit the full competitive potential of its resources and capabilities?

Numerous components of a firm's organization are relevant when answering the question of organization, including its formal reporting structure, its explicit management control systems, and its compensation policies. These components are referred to as *complementary resources* because they have limited ability to generate competitive advantage in isolation. However, in combination with other resources and capabilities, they can enable a firm to realize its full competitive advantage.[19]

Much of Caterpillar's sustained competitive advantage in the heavy construction industry can be traced to its becoming the sole supplier of this equipment to Allied forces in the Second World War. However, if Caterpillar's management had not taken advantage of this opportunity by implementing a global formal reporting structure, global inventory and other control systems, and compensation policies that created incentives for its employees to work around the world, then Caterpillar's potential for competitive advantage would not have been fully realized. These attributes of Caterpillar's organization, by themselves, could not be a source of competitive advantage; i.e., adopting a global organizational form was only relevant for Caterpillar because it was pursing a global opportunity. However, this organization was essential for Caterpillar to realize its full competitive advantage potential.

In a similar way, much of WalMart's continuing competitive advantage in the discount retailing industry can be attributed to its early entry into rural markets in the southern United States. However, to fully exploit this geographic advantage, WalMart needed to implement appropriate reporting structures, control systems, and compensation policies. We have already seen that one of these components of WalMart's organization—its point-of-purchase inventory control system—is being imitated by K-Mart, and thus, by itself, is not likely to be a source of sustained competitive advantage. However, this inventory control system has enabled WalMart to take full advantage of its rural locations by decreasing the probability of stock outs and by reducing inventory costs.

While a complementary organization enabled Caterpillar and WalMart to realize their full competitive advantage, Xerox was prevented from taking full advantage of some of its most critical valuable, rare, and costly-to-imitate resources and capabilities because it lacked such organizational skills. Through the 1960s and early 1970s,

Xerox invested in a series of very innovative technology development research efforts. Xerox managed this research effort by creating a stand alone research laboratory (Xerox PARC, in Palo Alto, California), and by assembling a large group of highly creative and innovative scientists and engineers to work there. Left to their own devices, these scientists and engineers developed an amazing array of technological innovations, including the personal computer, the "mouse," windows-type software, the laser printer, the "paperless office," ethernet, and so forth. In retrospect, the market potential of these technologies was enormous. Moreover, since these technologies were developed at Xerox PARC, they were rare, Finally, Xerox may have been able to gain some important first mover advantages if they had been able to translate these technologies into products, thereby increasing the cost to other firms of imitating these technologies.

Unfortunately, Xerox did not have an organization in place to take advantage of these resources. For example, no structure existed whereby Xerox PARC's innovations could become known to managers at Xerox. Indeed, most Xerox managers—even many senior managers—were unaware of these technological developments through the mid-1970s. Once they finally became aware of them, very few of the innovations survived Xerox's highly bureaucratic product development process—a process where product development projects were divided into hundreds of minute tasks, and progress in each task was reviewed by dozens of large committees. Even those innovations that survived the product development process were not exploited by Xerox managers. Management compensation at Xerox depended almost exclusively on maximizing current revenue. Short-term profitability was relatively less important in compensation calculations, and the development of markets for future sales and profitability was essentially irrelevant. Xerox's formal reporting structure, its explicit management control systems, and its compensation policies were all inconsistent with exploiting the valuable, rare, and costly-to-imitate resources developed at Xerox PARC. Not surprisingly, Xerox failed to exploit any of these potential sources of sustained competitive advantage.[20]

This set of questions can be applied in understanding the competitive implications of phenomena as diverse as the "cola wars" in the soft drink industry and competition among different types of personal computers.

The Competitive Implications of the "Cola Wars"

Almost since they were founded, Coca-Cola, Inc. and PepsiCo, Inc. have battled each other for market share in the soft drink industry. In many ways, the intensity of these "cola wars" increased in the mid-1970s with the introduction of PepsiCo's "Pepsi Challenge" advertising campaign. While significant advertising and other marketing expenditures have been made by both these firms, and while market share has shifted back and forth between them over time, it is not at all clear that these efforts have generated competitive advantages for either Coke or Pepsi.

Obviously, market share is a very valuable commodity in the soft drink industry. Market share translates directly into revenues, which, in turn, has a large impact on profits and profitability. Strategies pursued by either Coke or Pepsi designed to acquire market share will usually be valuable.

But are these market share acquisition strategies rare or does either Coca-Cola or Pepsi have a cost advantage in implementing them? Both Coca-Cola and PepsiCo are marketing powerhouses; both have enormous financial capabilities and strong management teams. Any effort by one to take share away can instantly be matched by the other to protect that share. In this sense, while Coke's and Pepsi's share acquisition strategies may be valuable, they are not rare, nor does either Coke or Pepsi have a cost advantage in implementing them. Assuming that these firms are appropriately organized (a reasonable assumption), then the cola wars should be a source of competitive parity for these firms.

This has, apparently, been the case. For example, Pepsi originally introduced its "Pepsi Challenge" advertising campaign in the Dallas-Ft. Worth market. After six months of the Pepsi Challenge—including price discounts, coupon campaigns, numerous celebrity endorsements, and so on—Pepsi was able to double its share of the Dallas-Ft. Worth market from 7% to 14%. Unfortunately, the retail price of Pepsi's soft drinks, after six months of the Pepsi Challenge, was approximately one half the pre-challenge level. Thus Pepsi doubled its market share, but cut its prices in half—exactly the result one would expect in a world of competitive parity.[21]

It is interesting to note that both Coca-Cola and Pepsi are beginning to recognize the futility of going head to head against an equally skilled competitor in a battle for market share to gain competitive advantages. Instead, these firms seem to be altering both their market share and other strategies. Coke, through its Diet Coke brand name, is targeting older consumers with advertisements that use personalities from the '50s, '60s, and '70s (e.g., Elton John and Gene Kelly). Pepsi continues its focus on attracting younger drinkers with its "choice of a new generation" advertising campaigns. Coke continues its traditional focus on the soft drink industry, while Pepsi has begun diversifying into fast food restaurants and other related businesses. Coke has extended its marketing efforts internationally, whereas Pepsi focuses mostly on the market in the United States (although it is beginning to alter this strategy). In all these ways, Coke and Pepsi seem to be moving away from head-to-head competition for market share, and moving towards exploiting *different* resources.

The Competitive Position of the Macintosh Computer

Building on earlier research conducted by Xerox PARC, Apple Computer developed and marketed the first user-friendly alternative to DOS-based personal computers, the Macintosh. Most Macintosh users have a passion for their computers that is usually reserved for personal relationships. Macintosh users shake their heads and wonder why DOS-based computer users don't wake up and experience the "joy of Macintosh."

The first step in analyzing the competitive position of the Macintosh is to evaluate whether or not "user friendliness" in a personal computer is valuable; i.e., does it exploit an environmental opportunity and/or neutralize an environmental threat? While user friendliness is not a requirement of all personal computer users, it is not unreasonable to conclude that many of these computer users, other things being equal, would prefer working on a user friendly machine compared with a user unfriendly machine. Thus, the Macintosh computer does seem to respond to a real market opportunity.

When the Macintosh was first introduced, was user friendliness rare? At that time, DOS-based machines were essentially the only alternative to the Macintosh, and DOS-based software, in those early days, was anything but user friendly. Thus, the Macintosh was apparently both valuable and rare, and thus a source of at least a temporary competitive advantage for Apple.

Was the user-friendliness of the Macintosh costly to imitate? At first, it seemed likely that user-friendly software would rapidly be developed for DOS-based machines, and thus that the user-friendly Macintosh would only enjoy a temporary competitive advantage. However, history has shown that user friendliness was not easy to imitate.

Imitation of the user-friendly Macintosh by DOS-based machines was slowed by a combination of at least two factors. First, the Macintosh hardware and software system had originally been developed by teams of software, hardware, and production engineers all working in Apple Computer. The teamwork, trust, commitment, and enthusiasm that these Apple employees enjoyed while working on Macintosh technology was difficult for other computer firms to duplicate, since most of those firms specialized either in hardware design and manufacturing (e.g., IBM) or software development (e.g., Microsoft, Lotus). In other words, the socially complex resources that Apple was able to bring to bear in the Macintosh project were difficult to duplicate in vertically non-integrated computer hardware and software firms.

Second, Apple management had a different conception of the personal computer and its future than did managers at IBM and other computer firms. At IBM, for example, computers had traditionally meant mainframe computers, and mainframe computers were expected to be complicated and difficult to operate. User friendliness was never an issue in IBM mainframes (users of IBM's JCL know the truth of that assertion!), and thus was not an important concern when IBM entered into the personal computer market. However, at Apple, computers were Jobs' and Wozniak's toys—a hobby, to be used for fun. If management's mindset is that "computers are supposed to be fun," then it suddenly becomes easier to develop and build user-friendly computers.

Obviously, these two mindsets—IBM's "computers are complex tools run by technical specialists" versus Apple's "computers are toys for everyone"—were deeply embedded in the cultures of these two firms, as well as those firms that worked closely with them. Such mindsets are socially complex, slow to change, and difficult to imitate. It took some time before the notion that a computer should be (or even could be) easy to use came to prominence in DOS-based systems.[22] Only recently, after almost ten years (an eternity in the rapidly changing personal computer business), has user-friendly software for DOS-based machines been developed. With the introduction of Windows by Microsoft, the rareness of Macintosh's user friendliness has been reduced, as has been the competitive advantage that Macintosh had generated.

Interestingly, just as Windows software was introduced, Apple began to radically change its pricing and product development strategies. First Apple cut the price of the Macintosh computer, reflecting the fact that user friendliness was not as rare after Windows as it was before Windows. Second, Apple seems to have recognzied the need to develop new resources and capabilities to enhance their traditional user-friendly strengths. Rather than only competing with other hardware and software companies, Apple has begun developing strategic alliances with several other computer firms, including IBM and Microsoft. These alliances may help Apple develop the resources and capabilities they need to remain competitive in the personal computer industry over the next several years.

The Management Challenge

In the end, this discussion reminds us that sustained competitive advantage cannot be created simply by evaluating environmental opportunities and threats, and then conducting business only in high-opportunity, low-threat environments. Rather, creating sustained competitive advantage depends on the unique resources and capabilities that a firm brings to competition in its environment. To discover these resources and capabilities, managers must look inside their firm for valuable, rare and costly-to-imitate resources, and then exploit these resources through their organization.

Endnotes

1. The original SWOT framework was proposed and developed by E. Learned, C. Christiansen, K. Andrews, and W. Guth in *Business Policy* (Homewood, IL: Irwin, 1969). Though the field of strategic management has evolved a great deal since then, this fundamental SWOT framework, as an organizing principle, has remained unchanged. See for example Michael Porter, "The Contributions of Industrial Organization to Strategic Management," *Academy of Management Review,* 6, 1981, 609–620; and Jay Barney, "Firm Resources and Sustained Competitive Advantage," *Journal of Management,* 17, 1991, 99–120.
2. Porter's work is described in detail in M. Porter, *Competitive Strategy* (New York, NY: Free Press, 1980), and M. Porter, *Competitive Advantage* (New York, NY: Free Press, 1985).
3. A variety of different authors have begun to explore the competitive implications of a firm's internal strengths and weaknesses. Building on some seminal insights by Edith Penrose [*The Theory of the Growth of the Firm* (New York, NY: Wiley, 1959)], this work has come to be known as the Resource-Based View of the Firm. Resource-based scholarly work includes: Birger Wernerfelt, "A Resource-Based View of the Firm," *Strategic Management Journal,* 5, 1984, 171–180; Richard Rumelt, "Toward a Strategic Theory of the Firm," in R. Lamb (ed.), *Competitive Strategic Management* (Englewood Cliffs, NJ: Prentice-Hall, 1984), 556–570; Jay Barney, "Strategic Factor Markets," *Management Science,* 41, 1980, 1231–1241; and Jay Barney, "Organizational Culture: Can It Be A Source of Sustained Competitive Advantage?" *Academy of Management Review,* 11, 1986, 791–800. The framework developed in this article draws most closely from Jay Barney. "Firm Resources and Sustained Competitive Advantage," *op.cit.*
4. For more detailed discussions of the internal resources and capabilities of these firms, see Pankaj Ghemewat, "WalMart Stores' Discount Operations," Case No. 9–387–018 (Harvard Business School, 1986); S. Chakravarty, "Hit 'Em Hardest with the Mostest," *Forbes,* 148, September 16, 1991, 45–54; and Pankaj Ghemewat, "Nucor at a Crossroad," Case No. 9–793–039 (Harvest Business School, 1992).
5. Different terms have been used to describe these internal phenomena, including core competencies (C. K. Prahalad and Gary Hamel, "The Core Competence of the Organization," *Harvard Business Review,* 90, 1990, 79–93), firm resources (Birger Wernerfelt, *op.cit.,* and Jay B. Barney, "Firm Resources and Sustained Competitive Advantage") and firm capabilities (George Stalk, Phillip Evans, and Lawrence Shulman,

"Competing on Capabilities: The New Rules of Corporate Strategy," *Harvard Business Review,* March–April, 1992, 57–69). While distinctions among these terms can be drawn, for our purposes they can, and will, be used interchangeably.

6. For details, see B. Schlender, "How Sony Keeps the Magic Going," *Fortune,* 125, February 24, 1992, 76–84; L. Krogh, J. Praeger, D. Sorenson, and J. Tomlinson, "How 3M Evaluates Its R&D Programs," *Research Technology Management,* 31, November/December, 1988, 10–14; Richard Rosenbloom, "Continuous Casting Investments at USX Corporation," Case No. 9–392–232 (Harvard Business School, 1990); and Cynthia Montgomery, "Sears, Roebuck and Co. In 1989," Case No. 9–391–147 (Harvard Business School, 1989).

7. This kind of environmental or technological shift is called a Schumpeterian revolution, and firms in this setting have little systematic hope of gaining competitive advantages, unless the competitive environment shifts again, although they can be lucky. See Jay B. Barney, "Types of Competitors and the Theory of Strategy: Toward an Integrative Framework," *Academy of Management Review,* 1986, 791–800.

8. For a discussion of AT&T's attempt to develop new resources and capabilities, see D. Kirkpatrick, "Could AT&T Rule the World?" *Fortune,* 127, May 17, 1993, 54–56. Hunter Fan's experience was described through personal communication with managers there, and in a publication celebrating Hunter Fan's 100th anniversary in 1986.

9. Prahalad and Hamel's 1990 discussion of NEC's attempt to develop the resources needed to compete in the global telecommunications and computer industry is insightful, especially in comparison to Kirkpatrick's discussion of AT&T's efforts in *Fortune.*

10. WalMart's point of purchase inventory control system and the impact of WalMart's rural stores on its performance, are described in Ghemewat, *op.cit.,* 1986. K-Mart's inventory control response to WalMart is described in L. Steven's "Front Line Systems," *Computerworld,* 26, 1992, 61–63.

11. See M. G. Rukstad and J. Horn, "Caterpillar and the Construction Equipment Industry in 1988," Case No. 9–389–097 (Harvard Business School, 1989).

12. Komatsu's response to Caterpillar's competitive advantage is described in C. A. Bartlett and U. S. Rangan, "Komatsu Ltd.," Case No. 9–385–277 (Harvard Business School, 1985).

13. See Richard Blackburn and Benson Rosen, "Total Quality and Human Resources Management: Lessons Learned from Baldridge Award-winning Companies," *Academy of Management Executive,* 7, 1993, 49–66.

14. These invisible assets have been described by H. Itami, *Mobilizing Invisible Assets* (Cambridge, MA: Harvard University Press, 1987).

15. Personal communication.

16. See E. Mansfield, "How Rapidly Does New Industrial Technology Leak Out?" *Journal of Industrial Economics,* 34, 1985, 217–223; and E. Mansfield, M. Schwartz, and S. Wagner, "Imitation Costs and Patents: An Empirical Study," *Economic Journal,* 91, 1981, 907–918.

17. See S. K. Yoder, "A 1990 Reorganization at Hewlett Packard Already Is Paying Off," *Wall Street Journal,* July 22, 1991, Section Ak, 1+. This is not to suggest that socially complex resources and capabilities do not change and evolve in an organization. They clearly do. Nor does this suggest that managers can never radically alter a firm's socially complex resources and capabilities. Such transformational leaders do seem to exist, and do have an enormous impact on these resources in a firm. Managers such as the late Mike Walsh at Tenneco, Lee Iacocca at Chrysler, and Jack Welch at General Electric apparently have been such leaders. However, this kind of leadership is a socially complex phenomenon, and thus very difficult to imitate. Even if a leader in one firm can transform its socially complex resources and capabilities, it does not necessarily mean that other firms will be able to imitate this feat at the same cost. The concept of transformational leaders is discussed in N. Tichy, *The Transformational Leader* (New York, NY: Wiley, 1986).

18. See Schlender, *op.cit.*

19. See Raphael Amit and Paul Schoemaker, "Strategic Assets and Organizational Rent," *Strategic Management Journal,* 14, 1993, 33–46; David Teece, "Profiting From Technological Innovation," *Research Policy,* 15, 1986, 285–305; and Ingemar Dierickx and Karel Cool, "Asset Stock Accumulation and Sustainability of

Competitive Advantage," *Management Science,* 35, 1989, 1504–1511, for a discussion of complementary resources and capabilities. Of course, complementary organizational resources are part of a firm's overall resource and capability base, and thus the competitive implications of these resources could be evaluated using the questions of value, rareness, and imitability. However, the question of organization is included in this discussion to emphasize the particular importance of complementary organizational resources in enabling a firm to fully exploit its competitive advantage potential.

20. Xerox's organizational problems with Xerox PARC are described, in detail, in David T. Kearns and David A. Nadler, *Prophets in the Dark* (New York, NY: Harper Collins, 1992); Douglas K. Smith and Robert C. Alexander, *Fumbling the Future* (New York, NY: William Morrow, 1988); and L. Hooper, "Xerox Tries to Shed Its Has Been Image with a Big New Machine," *Wall Street Journal,* September, 20, 1990, Section A, 1+.

21. See A. E. Pearson and C. L. Irwin, "Coca-Cola vs. Pepsi-Cola (A)," Case No. 9–387–108 (Harvard Business School, 1988), for a discussion of the cola wars, and their competitive implications for Coke and Pepsi.

22. See D. B. Yoffie, "Apple Computer—1992," Case No. 9–792–081 (Harvard Business School, 1992), for a complete discussion of Apple, IBM, and Apple's new strategies for the 1990s.

About the Author

Jay Barney is a professor of management and holder of the Bank One Chair for Excellence in Corporate Strategy at the Max M. Fisher College of Business, The Ohio State University. He received his undergraduate degree from Brigham Young University, and his master's and doctorate from Yale University. He served on the faculties of UCLA and Texas A&M University before joining the faculty at Ohio State in 1994. Professor Barney's research focuses on the relationship between idiosyncratic firm skills and capabilities and sustained competitive advantage.

Wireless Goes Haywire at Motorola

Faulty switches, a tarnished reputation—how bad can it get?

by Roger O. Crockett in Chicago with Peter Elstrom in New York and Gary McWilliams in Houston

Wireless technology is supposed to be Motorola Inc.'s strong suit. But lately the deck seems to be stacked against the electronics giant. Upstarts have beaten it to market—by years—with new digital phones. And its transmission equipment for digital-cellular networks has been plagued by bugs. With its once-indomitable paging business shrinking and formidable competition squeezing its semiconductor division, it's unclear what sector the $30 billion company can depend on for growth. Wails one Motorola executive: "It's the freaking Titanic over here."

And there's an iceberg ahead. By early March, PrimeCo Personal Communications—a wireless service owned by Bell Atlantic, U S West and AirTouch Communications—is expected to cancel a $500 million contract with Motorola for digital network equipment. Rival Lucent Technologies Inc. is expected to get the business, one of the biggest orders in the industry. "To replace a half-billion dollars? Ouch," says telecom analyst Ian Gillott at International Data Corp.

How bad will it hurt? Even before the anticipated loss of PrimeCo, Furman Selz Inc. has already slashed its Motorola 1998 earnings estimate to $2.38 a share from $2.80 and its 1999 estimate to $2.80 a share from $3.80. "The rest of the business is experiencing worse-than-expected performance," says analyst Susan Kalla.

The misfires raise questions about how Motorola, longtime leader in analog-wireless systems, will fare as the industry moves squarely into the digital age. Last summer, faulty base station regulators that direct calls interrupted service on PrimeCo's digital network in Chicago. The network—using so-called CDMA code—typically stayed down from 30 minutes to two hours because Motorola didn't have enough engineers to fix the problem, executives close to the company say. Though it accepts responsibility for the outages, a top Motorola executive disclaimed: "Rarely is software perfect the day it's rolled out."

For Motorola, this is particularly true. It had software problems with equipment it supplied GTE Wireless and Nextel Communications Inc., too. But those companies say they will stick with Motorola. "With any vendor, you run into occasional problems," says John McLean, GTE Wireless' vice-president of technology.

Motorola has been scrambling to bring its digital portfolio up to speed. An aggressive pitch to Sprint PCS last spring landed the company 60% of a $750 million contract to complete the construction of Sprint's digital network. And on Feb. 22, at the Cellular Telecommunications Industry Assn. convention in Atlanta, Motorola announced its first commercial availability of CDMA digital phones.

Catch-Up

Still, Motorola is playing catch-up. Qualcomm Inc., for example, has already released tiny CDMA phones the size of cigarette packs. Motorola isn't expected to have a digital version of its compact StarTac phone until the end of this year.

The lack of competitive phones is quickly leading to lost market share. AT&T Wireless says its new subscribers are choosing digital as much as 85% of the time—because they're cheaper to use, have longer battery life, and more easily accommodate features like E-mail.

Motorola also faces quality questions with its digital phones. Recently, the company had to issue a software upgrade to digital phones in Latin America because the handsets shut down when they received unfamiliar signals from network equipment. BellSouth, SBC Communications, and AT&T Wireless have chosen other than Motorola technology. A BellSouth spokesman says the company would like to have a digital Motorola product in its mix, but none has passed its "shake and bake test."

"Their brand has eroded," adds Gary Cuccio, COO at Omnipoint Communications, an East Coast digital phone carrier. While some customers still accept Motorola gear, "it's not like they have to have the products." How times have changed.

Why Wall Street's Buying Wal-Mart Again

Seemingly lost for the past five years, the Bentonville boys have recovered some of that old Sam Walton magic.

by Nelson D. Schwartz

When Houston's Dennis Plato visits the giant new Wal-Mart near his home, he tries to stick to his shopping list. But he can't always help himself. For example, when he recently stopped in to buy groceries, he walked out with a $30 tree pruner too. "I wasn't planning on the pruner, but it was on sale," says Plato, sounding faintly apologetic. "They put the food in the back of the store so it's hard to get out without buying something else."

In tiny Palestine, Texas, 2 1/2 hours away from Houston, the story is the same. Pat Lewis Krisch, a single working mom with three kids, barely even goes into her local supermarket now that there's a new Wal-Mart supercenter nearby. These days she just tosses everything from toys and aspirin to steak, vegetables, and socks into one shopping cart.

Then there's Dennis Faulkner. The Cumming, Ga., native raises the retailer-customer relationship to a whole new level—the Wal-Mart *date*. First, Faulkner and his wife, Marilyn, have dinner at a nearby restaurant. Then they head to a new supercenter and spend several hours cruising the wide aisles and checking out the weekly specials. "I used to go to Wal-Mart once a month," says Faulkner, a 52-year-old computer systems specialist. "Now it's more like once a week. They've really suckered me in." Faulkner estimates that in the past few months he's dropped nearly three times as much money at Wal-Mart as at rivals like Kroger or Publix.

Don't snicker. The steak-and-spark-plug shoppers aren't the only ones coming back to Wal-Mart; close behind them are the pinstriped hordes of Wall Street. That's right: Wal-Mart is a hot stock again. After sitting out much of the great bull market of the 1990s, WMT shares have nearly doubled in the past year and now trade just below their all-time high. In the past three months alone the stock surged 20%, even as the Dow succumbed to the Asian peril.

What's changed? Earnings, first of all. After years of lackluster performance, the company's 3,400 stores are raking in profits, driven by strong growth at the new supercenters and sizable gains overseas. But Wal-Mart has also brought a bit of its Main Street marketing skills to bear on Wall Street.

"Wal-Mart people are far more accessible than they were just three years ago," notes J. P. Morgan analyst Mark Husson. "There's been a real change in attitude toward Wall Street, and it's made me a lot more comfortable with the stock." That's exactly what Wal-Mart CEO David Glass had in mind. In the past, Glass concedes, "we may not have been as attentive to Wall Street as we should have been. Now our financial people are doing a better job." The new glasnost has certainly worked on Husson. After rating Wal-mart a hold for years, he upped the stock to a long-term buy last summer.

For Glass and other executives at the giant based in Bentonville, Ark., the turnaround is sweet vindication. Under legendary founder Sam Walton, the company grew staggeringly fast in the 1970s and 1980s. By the early 1990s it had become the nation's largest retailer, one of Wall Street's hottest stocks, and a fixture atop FORTUNE's list of most admired companies. People who put $1,000 into Wal-Mart when it went public in 1970 saw that investment grow to nearly $2 million by 1993. Walton became famous as the richest pickup-truck driver in America.

But after Mr. Sam's death in 1992, Wall Street began to worry that Wal-Mart's years as a fast grower were over. Analysts questioned the company's move into the low-margin food business and its new international expansion. Annual earnings growth declined sharply, from 24% in 1992 to near zero in 1995. For many investors the

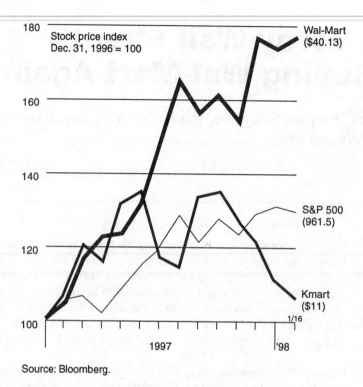

Source: Bloomberg.

darkest moment came in early 1996 when Wal-Mart announced that for the first time in 100 quarters, earnings had actually fallen. A few months later, FORTUNE (April 29, 1996) asked, "Can Wal-Mart Get Back the Magic?"

Well, now we know. But the magic of today's Wal-Mart is quite a bit different from the alchemy practiced in Sam's day. Instead of earnings growth that frequently topped 25% in the rip-roaring '80s, today's Wal-Mart promises consistent profit increases in the 15% range. But with Asia's turmoil hanging over U.S. corporate profits like a noxious cloud, Wall Street is willing to ante up for a little consistency. In fact Wal-Mart—which draws over 90% of its sales from the U.S.—may be one of the few big stocks to benefit from the Asian eruption, as investors flee volatile exporters like Intel and Boeing for the relative stability of a giant retailer.

Wal-Mart's stock has also gotten a boost since management learned to play the Wall Street expectations game. In Sam Walton's time, Wal-Mart was growing so fast that it didn't actually need to court the Street. Walton went so far as to declare in his autobiography, "We couldn't care less about what is forecast or what the market says we ought to do." Walton's successors discovered that ignoring Wall Street can be painful, though, when the stock sank from above $30 in late 1992 to less than $20 in early 1996.

The company's relations with Wall Street were cordial in the 1980s, but during the mid-1990s, "the company frequently over-promised and underperformed," says analyst Don Spindel of A. G. Edwards. Now, Spindel says, Wal-Mart does exactly the opposite, and veteran retail analyst Walter Loeb adds, "Wal-Mart's relationship with Wall Street couldn't be better."

Indeed, the steps Wal-Mart has taken in the past two years read like a how-to guide for companies eager to get back in the good graces of Wall Street. For starters, Wal-Mart cut costs, holding expenses flat even as it pursued pricey expansion plans. In addition, the company reduced the dollar amount of inventory on hand by a cool billion in 1997. Management plans to trim it by another $500 million in 1998, Husson notes. Not only does this allow the company to devote less retail space to storing goods and more to selling them, it also frees up capital for more productive purposes. Taken together, Husson says, these developments helped the company's rate of return on investment to finally start rising in 1997 after a five-year downswing.

A major share-repurchase plan has also impressed Wall Street, says A. G. Edwards' Spindel. Big share buybacks have been popular with investors throughout the '90s bull market, providing a floor for stocks in down periods as well as a signal that execs think their company is undervalued. Wal-Mart came late to the party, but the company's decision last March to buy back roughly $2 billion in stock—the first major repurchase in the company's history—more than made up for it. Another crowd pleaser was Wal-Mart's 30% dividend increase, although earnings are growing less than half as fast.

Finally, there are the little, hard-to-quantify things that play a big role in the care and feeding of Wall Street. Like making executives more accessible. Or providing more detailed information about exactly how stores are doing. And making sure that stores look their best when Wall Streeters come to visit. One analyst says after he recently alerted the company that he was planning to tour an older facility with some big investors, Bentonville brass ordered a quick paint job to brighten the store before the entourage arrived.

This isn't to suggest that Wall Street has been dazzled by a Potemkin village, Arkansas-style. In fact the company's savvy sales job neatly dovetails some very real positives in Wal-mart's operations. Besides the cost cuts and the leaner inventory structure, Wal-mart has continued to build on the technological advantage it has had since Sam's day. Computers at every store track just how fast each item is selling, automatically alerting warehouses when supplies are running low. This allows employees to spend more time with customers, instead of scanning shelves and filling out order forms as they did in the past. All the now technology should help Wal-Mart continue to cut costs in coming years, says Glass. "I'd like us to be much more efficient than we are."

More than cost cuts or technology—or even Wall Street schmoozing—it's the supercenters that are likely to carry Wal-Mart into the next century. Over 100 new 180,000-square-foot emporiums are set to open this year, gradually replacing traditional 90,000-square-foot Wal-mart stores. The older stores are still profitable, but they generate an average of $25 million a year in annual sales, Spindel estimates, compared with $65 million for a supercenter. By 2000, Husson says, supercenters should generate a total of $46 billion in revenues, up from $21 billion today.

The supercenters also give Wal-Mart a crucial entrée into the $450 billion grocery business, which dwarfs the discount-store sector. The company is thinking about more than just customers' convenience here. People shop for food twice as often as they shop for goods. And if they buy their groceries at Wal-Mart, it's a good bet they'll also pick up higher-margin items like CDs, videos—even tree pruners. To be sure, Wal-Mart has plenty of work to do before it can dominate the grocery business the way it commands discount retailing. "Food is definitely a learning curve," Glass admits. "We're improving, but we're not as good in food as I wish we were," he adds, pointing out weaknesses like dull presentation. Even so, groceries are one of the reasons that supercenters are expected to generate nearly $2 billion in operating income in 1998, slightly less than 30% of total profits, according to Prudential's Wayne Hood. Not bad for a division that didn't earn a dime five years ago.

While supercenters provide growth on the domestic front, Wal-Mart has also been expanding successfully overseas. Going global is notoriously tricky in the retail industry, but Glass has finally been able to make real money abroad—$23 million in 1996, an estimated $165 million in 1997, and a projected $250 million in 1998. While overseas profits remain a small fraction of the company's anticipated $3.9 billion in total 1998 income, the rate of annual growth hearkens back to the glory days of the 1970s and 1980s.

Not surprisingly, many of the company's new fans on Wall Street are counting on continued success in Europe, the Americas, and even Asia. "Wal-Mart has a stark choice," warns Mark Husson. "It can become a large, cash-generating all-American company with all the excitement of a utility stock. Or it can go out and play with the big boys overseas." Glass doesn't see the future in such dramatic terms, but he insists the company is committed overseas. Over the next five years, Wal-Mart hopes to get one-third of its profit growth abroad. In 1998 alone, 50 to 60 new stores are set to open overseas.

Whether Wal-Mart's future growth lies in supercenters or international sales is certain to be a key question in the selection of the 62-year-old Glass's successor. The choice, to be made by the board and Rob Walton, Sam's eldest son and the chairman of Wal-Mart, will likely come down to two men—Bobby Martin and Lee Scott. A 19-year Wal-Mart veteran, Scott is a logistics expert who was recently named president of the company's domestic stores division. Martin, on the other hand, heads up Wal-Mart's international unit and has a strong following on Wall Street. "Both men are candidates," says Glass, quickly adding that Tom Coughlin, another domestic stores exec, and Mark Hansen, president of the Sam's Club division, are also in the running.

In the meantime, Glass can take comfort in the fact that Wal-mart stock is once again making investors rich. And what would Sam think of today's Wal-Mart—more sensitive to Wall Street, more reliant on supercenters, and increasingly looking abroad? "He'd love it and recognize it," Glass declares. "All the basic principles are the same. He'd feel right at home."

Why Sears Survived—and Ward and Woolworth's Didn't

by Kevin Mundt

This month has brought grim news for two of the most venerable U.S. retailers. On July 7 **Montgomery Ward** & Co. filed for bankruptcy protection; 10 days later Woolworth Corp. announced that it will close its 400 U.S. five-and-dime stores.

Both Ward and Woolworth's fell victim to sweeping changes in their customers' priorities, as well as to an onslaught of new business designs competing for the same customers. Woolworth did a better job of responding to these changes, diversifying to the point where the doomed five-and-dimes accounted for only a small percentage of the corporation's $9 billion in 1996 revenue. Woolworth established or acquired specialty outlets such as Foot Locker, Kinney Shoes and After Thoughts, an accessory chain. It will survive; **Montgomery Ward** likely will not.

Ward's downfall is best understood in contrast with the story of another American retailing icon, archrival Sears, Roebuck & Co. Fifteen years ago, Ward and Sears were America's largest mall-based retailers. Both enjoyed near-universal name recognition and similar loyal customer bases, predominantly female.

Both were faced with a daunting set of challenges. Beginning in the mid-1980s, both stores' customers became increasingly value conscious; and as women increasingly moved into the work force, they had significantly less time to shop. A host of new competitors rapidly emerged to meet the demand for low cost and convenience: "category killers" like Home Depot and Circuit City, mass merchants like Wal-Mart, and discounters like Costco and Price Club.

Ward was slow to recognize the importance of the changes in the retail market. When it finally did, it misjudged them, in two ways. First, it essentially concluded that customers wanted a cheaper version of itself. It changed its pricing to undercut traditional mall-based competitors like Sears and J. C. Penney. But Ward wasn't able to cut its prices low enough to compete with the mass merchants, so it found itself in a no-man's land. Customers looking for lower prices went to Wal-Mart. Those willing to pay marginally higher prices in exchange for proven brands, better service and a more pleasant shopping experience went to Sears.

Ward's second mistake concerned merchandise selection. Facing tough competition from J. C. Penney and declining overall sales, Ward abandoned apparel and moved strongly into consumer hard goods like electronics. That put Ward in head-to-head competition with the category killers, committing it to a cyclical and lower-margin merchandise mix and further alienating its traditional female customer base.

Everybody was confused. Fewer and fewer consumers could define a clear reason why Ward should be their first stop—a perilous position in retailing. To many customers it wasn't even clear what Ward sold. Thus, one of the company's greatest assets—the **Montgomery Ward** name—was steadily drained of value.

By contrast, Sears responded to the changing market by identifying the customer group that would be critical to its future: 30- to 50-year-old women with household income of $30,000 to $50,000 a year. These baby boomers were of course quite different from their mothers, the previous generation of Sears customers. But they were still the "chief purchasing agents" of their households—and they exerted strong influence even over sales of hard goods like Kenmore appliances and Craftsman tools.

Sears launched a $4 billion renovation project to make its stores more inviting for women. In the process, 12 million square feet of back-office space was freed up for apparel, which Sears recognized as a key merchandise category for its target customers. It built "family-friendly" brand equities in new apparel lines like Canyon River

Reprinted by permission of Kevin Mundt. Mr. Mundt is vice president and director of Mercer Management Consulting and is responsible for the firm's retail and consumer practice.

Blues jeans. It promoted the changes through a smart and successful advertising campaign: "The softer side of Sears." Its focus also helped it make tough but necessary decisions, like killing the Sears catalog in 1993.

Threatened by the same forces as Ward, Sears was able to turn its stores into a unique value proposition for its customers. By identifying its customer base and its priorities, Sears has become one of the few general merchants left in the mall.

Success in today's hypercompetitive retail marketplace requires much more than good customer service in the traditional sense. It is a matter of targeting a base of customers, recognizing their priorities and the trade-offs they're willing to make, and designing the business to capitalize on those choices. If you get this right, it can compensate for a lot of other errors. If you don't, irrelevance and decline are not far behind—no matter what your name is.

Coke Claims Dominance in Mideast and North Africa, but Pepsi Objects

by Nikhil Deogun
Staff Reporter of The Wall Street Journal

ATLANTA—*Coca Cola* Co., in a claim hotly contested by *PepsiCo* Inc., says it now outsells its archrival in the Middle East and North Africa, one of the last bastions of Pepsi's soft-drink dominance.

Coke, which has launched an aggressive and expensive campaign there, contends that its collective market share for the region is 38%, compared with Pepsi's 36%. Coke acknowledges that Pepsi continues to hold a commanding lead in Saudi Arabia and other Persian Gulf countries but argues that its leadership in countries like Egypt and Israel, combined with gains in the Arab heartland, gives it supremacy in the overall region.

A spokesman for PepsiCo, based in Purchase, N.Y., says, "Coke's leadership claim in the Middle East is simply not true." Pepsi says that based on independent research, its market share in those countries is 46%, compared with 38% for Coke. And within the narrower Middle East region of the Gulf peninsula, Pepsi says its share is 71% vs. 22% for Coke.

Fierce Cola War

The Middle East has emerged as one of the fiercest battlegrounds in the never-ending cola wars, with heavy price discounting and massive marketing programs.

Whoever possesses leadership in the region, this much is clear: Coke is making significant inroads in the region and is spending heavily to grab market share. Indeed, Coca-Cola officials say that the soft-drink giant and its bottling partners plan to invest, during the next three years, $200 million in the area, which comprises 15 countries stretching from the Persian Gulf in the east to Morocco in the west. Coca-Cola, which is breaking ground Tuesday on a new $20 million bottling plant in Riyadh, Saudi Arabia, has already invested $400 million, along with its bottlers, in the region since 1993.

"We've invested a ton of money in building infrastructure and expanding availability; we have the momentum in the business," says A. R. C. "Sandy" Allan, chief of Coke's Middle East division.

Coke's 50% Goal

Mr. Allan says he hopes for Coke to capture 50% of the region's soft-drink market in three years.

Until a few years ago, Pepsi had much of the Middle East sewn up. Coke was kept out of many Arab countries because it did business in Israel and was subject to Arab League boycott; Pepsi remained in the region. Over the past few years, Coke has re-entered many of these markets and has been chipping away at Pepsi's leadership. According to industry executives in the region, Coke has led the market in offering bigger cans for the same price and instituting promotional programs, such as giving away mountain bikes.

Michael Bellas, president of Beverage Marketing Corp., a New York consulting firm, says his estimates still show Pepsi in a leadership position in the region. "Coke is gulping up share and closing the gap, but Pepsi is still No. 1," he says.

For its part, Pepsi defends its position. "We've aggressively and successfully fortified our leadership position in the Middle East and will continue to meet any future competitive challenge with equal aggressiveness," a Pepsi spokesman says.

Meanwhile, Samir Ayache, Pepsi's Middle East chief for the past five years, quit earlier this month for "personal reasons," the spokesman says. Mr. Ayache couldn't be reached for comment.

Unprofitable So Far

Of course, Coke's efforts in the region haven't been cheap. Mr. Allan acknowledges that his division isn't making money yet but says he expects it to become profitable in 12 to 18 months. William Pecoriello, an analyst at Sanford C. Bernstein & Co., says he believes Pepsi's Middle East division pulled in profit of about $65 million to $70 million last year.

Disney's Theme-Park Shootout

A host of new competitors has it building like crazy

by Ronald Grover in Los Angeles and Gail DeGeorge in Orlando

The sign out front says it's "The Happiest Place on Earth." These days, Disneyland, *Walt Disney Co.'s* Anaheim (Calif.) flagship, is also one of the most construction-happy places on earth. Workers in bulldozers criss-cross the 100 acres that used to be a parking lot. Outside, streets are being widened, snarling traffic in all directions. Signs tell passersby that a new Disneyland Resort is in the making.

But there's a lot more than that going on. From Anaheim to Central Florida, Disney is expanding its theme-park kingdom with gusto. Faced with stiff competition from a host of rivals that has trimmed its once juicy margins, Disney plans to spend more than $4 billion by 2001 to add two new theme parks, a cruise line, and three regional entertainment chains. On Apr. 22, the Burbank (Calif.) company will open its first new theme park in nine years, the $750 million Animal Kingdom near Orlando. And in May, it will unveil an update of Tomorrowland, an original Disneyland attraction.

Upping the Ante

The burst of spending reflects Disney Chairman and Chief Executive Michael D. Eisner's philosophy that, despite the hoopla about cable TV and handwringing about couch-potato lifestyles, people still hunger to go out for entertainment. "I've never believed what Faith Popcorn said—that people would be 'cocooning' in their homes," says Eisner. "People get sick of sitting around their homes. They need to get out and find new things."

Maybe so. But Disney's four U.S. theme parks are facing their most intense period of competition ever. From the $2.7 billion Islands of Adventure being built by Universal Studios about 20 minutes down Interstate 4 from Walt Disney World to new attractions such as the Wild Arctic helicopter simulation at nearby Sea World to the $35 million in new rides planned for Knott's Berry Farm in Anaheim, everyone is upping the ante.

Those projects all take aim at Disney's most consistent cash cow. Year after year, Disney's parks provide the parent company with huge cash flow and hefty profit margins. Last year, the parks raked in $1.1 billion in operating earnings and a profit margin of 22.7%, compared with 16.8% for Disney's movie studios and 19.8% for broadcasting.

But for much of the past decade, Disney management's attention was focused elsewhere. The company dabbled in regional parks, running into a political buzzsaw with its doomed plan for a historical park in Virginia. It built overseas, suffering through the slow opening of its park outside Paris. And it branched into broadcasting, paying $19 billion for Capital Cities/ABC Inc. in 1995. Meanwhile, Anheuser-Busch Cos. bought four Sea World parks and began pumping in millions of dollars. Universal Studios opened a Florida park in 1990. Even Las Vegas made a play for family vacationers.

The combination of fresh vacation alternatives and a weak economy sent Disney's park attendance skidding in the early 1990s. By 1994, it had fallen 12% from five years earlier, to 39.2 million visitors annually, according to the newsletter Amusement Business. And though theme-park profit margins still beat those of Disney's other units, they've drooped from their far higher 30% of the late 1980s.

Disney has responded with a torrent of cash. The expansions at Universal and elsewhere "made them understand that they're not the only guys on the block," says Abraham Pizam, director of the Dick Pope Institute of

Tourism Studies at the University of Central Florida. "It made them understand that they had to concentrate on quality and add, add, add." Not to mention spend, spend, spend. Today, building one new ride can cost more than $100 million.

Key to the strategy has been expanding operations at the Central Florida and Anaheim strongholds. Florida is the most important, with three theme parks and nearly 18,000 hotel rooms. But that's also where Disney faces its stiffest competition.

Next year, a $2.7 billion expansion of Universal Studios Florida will open. The site includes a second theme park, Islands of Adventure, with Universal's trademark thrill rides, such as Dueling Dragons roller coasters; a 750-room hotel; and an entertainment-and-dining district, Citywalk, that will open later this year. Universal has a sure hit in a dinosaur island modeled after its Jurassic Park movie and is going after Disney's younger fans with rides based on Dr. Seuss characters.

To beat back its rival, Disney will weigh in next month with Animal Kingdom, which features more than 1,000 types of animals, an African safari, and rides based on such Disney properties as The Lion King.

The new attractions include DinoLand USA, featuring a thrill ride called Countdown to Extinction. Universal sees that as a preemptive strike on its dinosaur attraction. "What do dinosaurs have to do with a wild animal park, anyway?" says Cathy Nichols, CEO of Universal Recreation Group. Eisner deflects the charge. "We've been working on a dinosaur movie well before they began Jurassic Park," he says, referring to an animated project.

Will it be enough? The payoff from Disney's spending so far, analysts and competitors agree, is that the company has reinforced its position as the top brand name in the business. Attendance at its U.S. parks grew 12% last year, to a record 53.4 million visitors, while Universal rose 4%, to 14.3 million. And with the additional hotel rooms and restaurants Disney is building, it hopes to extend the average park stay and grab even more guest dollars.

Nowhere is that clearer than in Anaheim, where Disney is using its clout with city officials to build a mini-Disney World. With Disney guaranteeing some of the money, Anaheim is spending $546 million to help the entertainment giant build a resort blocked off from the collection of dives and cheapo motels that ring Disneyland. Disney is building a 750-room hotel, called Grand Californian, to give it 2,350 rooms in Anaheim.

Dry-Docked

Disney has suffered some setbacks. An effort to update Epcot Center in Orlando ran into costly software problems on a ride featuring cars that race at speeds up to 65 mph. That project is at least a year behind schedule. Also, some industry skeptics question Disney's efforts to transfer its brand to smaller regional entertainment centers, such as its new DisneyQuest virtual-reality and entertainment arcades and Club Disney play centers for younger children.

Disney's most public embarrassment has been the four-month delay in the launch of its cruise business because of construction problems. Still, when they finally set sail, the two ships should help Disney fill its parks. They will dock at Port Canaveral, about 90 minutes from Walt Disney World. To meet its targets, Disney needs 70% of the ships' passengers to buy a weeklong package that combines a cruise and a park stay, says a former Disney exec. "The whole strategic value was to get them to the park—that's where Disney makes a lot of money on them," he says.

And that, after all, is the real Disney magic. Recently, Philadelphia ad exec Alex Breder was marching and spending her way through Walt Disney World with children Maggie, 10, and Ian, 8, in tow. Midway through a five-day vacation, Breder figured she had spent upwards of $2,000 for her room at Disney's All-Star Resort, meals, park passes, and trinkets for the kids. "If you're going to spend all that money to get here and stay, you may as well eat and treat yourself well," says Breder.

No doubt the cash registers can be heard ringing all the way back in Burbank. But Disney can't afford to be smug—after all, the Breder family also planned to spend a day at Sea World.

Why Barnes & Noble May Crush Amazon

Selling books online was a neat concept. The nation's leading bookstore is turning it into a cutthroat business. What's a poor startup to do?

by Randall E. Stross

No company has done more to show how the Web overturns conventional assumptions about distribution than Amazon.com. After just two years, this Web pioneer (www.amazon.com) is selling $110-million-a-year worth of books. Investors are impressed: Amazon's shares went public in March and trade at levels that give the company a market capitalization of some $670 million.

The Amazon model is beguilingly attractive: Expensive inventory and bricks-and-mortar warehouses are not needed by the New Age retailer. All one needs, it would seem, is a Website to present the face that greets customers and takes their orders. Other parties handle the capital-intensive aspects of stocking inventory.

Maybe low barriers to entry are a mixed blessing, however: The big guys can just as easily join the fun. Barnes & Noble, the nation's leading bookseller, opened its own online bookshop (at www.barnesandnoble.com) three months ago and has swiftly exposed the tenuousness of Amazon's head start. It turns out that figuring out the sexy new stuff, like Web pages and online order taking, is a lot less difficult than figuring out such drudgery as how to cost-effectively finance, stock, and move the physical stuff, the books.

Anything Amazon.com can do on the Internet, so, too, can Barnes & Noble. "There was a mystique about how difficult it was to get started on the Web," says Steven Riggio, chief operating officer of Barnes & Noble, "but it's quickly fading." Hiring hot designers from Silicon Valley, B&N now offers a Web shopfront that's just as inviting and useful as Amazon's, with easy-to-use subject indexes, online author events every day, book forums, book reviews, and other features. Both Amazon and Barnes & Noble can get any book in print—eventually (so, too, can the smallest bookseller). And both have deals with heavily trafficked Websites—including Yahoo (Amazon) and the New York Times Book Review (B&N)—that send customers their way.

Once you look beyond the Website you begin to see why, in this battle at least, the odds favor the $3-billion-a-year Goliath. The one area in which B&N and Amazon are most easily distinguishable is in how speedily the two can serve their customers, and in that contest, the edge goes to the bookseller with the most books physically on hand. Amazon stocks just a limited number of bestsellers (the company won't disclose how many) but for the most part obtains books from wholesalers or publishers after receiving an order.

B&N, on the other hand, generates such volume in its realworld stores that it has become, effectively, its own giant wholesaler. It deals directly with publishers, cuts out the middlemen, and stocks its central warehouse in New Jersey with 400,000 frequently ordered titles. Consequently, observes Craig Bibb, a Paine Webber analyst, "Barnes & Noble crushes Amazon in speedy delivery."

Barnes & Noble can also afford to give readers books at bargain prices. Since it sells more books than anyone else, it gets the best prices from publishers. Barnes & Noble launched its site with 30% discounts on all hardcovers. Amazon was forced to match the cuts. And the pricing wars have just begun. CUC International, which offers bargains on many goods in return for an annual subscription, recently announced 40% discounts for members at its own online bookstore (www.books.com). Borders, the nation's No. 2 bookseller, is readying its own online service. All this is very bad news for Amazon, which, unlike B&N, cannot afford to run its site as a promotional vehicle for conventional stores. (After all, it has no such stores.) Amazon lost $6.7 million in its last fiscal quarter and admits that profitability is nowhere in sight.

Jeff Bezos, Amazon's endearingly candid founder, agrees that Barnesandnoble.com can duplicate what Amazon has done. The question, he says, is, "Can Amazon.com establish a world-class brand name before Barnesandnoble.com buys, builds, acquires, or learns the competencies they need to be excellent online retailers?" Bezos is expanding the number of titles Amazon stocks. And he is trying to improve delivery time by working closely with wholesalers. While both moves seem promising, both mean that Amazon must pay exactly the kind of tithe it proudly swore it could avoid when it got into the business of selling online.

Barnes & Noble has its own problems. After expanding furiously, it is cutting back on the number of megabookstores it will open in the future. And selling books more cheaply online than it does in stores may eventually cannibalize business and annoy customers. But B&N's fate doesn't rest on its Website. Amazon's does.

How Yahoo! Won the Search Wars

Once upon a time, Yahoo! was an Internet search site with mediocre technology. Now it has a market cap of $2.8 billion. Some people say it's the next America Online.

by Randall E. Stross

Tech stardom started, as usual, amid pizza boxes. For two Stanford engineering students, Jerry Yang and David Filo, the launching pad was an oxygen-depleted double-wide trailer, stocked by the university with computer workstations and by the students with life's necessities—golf clubs, sleeping bags, and enough half-empty food containers to prompt a friend to call the scene a "cockroach's picture of Christmas." It was the first headquarters of Yahoo!, now the most successful company ever spawned by the World Wide Web.

Measured by revenues ($67 million in 1997), Yahoo! would have difficulty making a FORTUNE 10,000 list. Measured by earnings (a $23 million loss last year), it's a failure. Measured, however, by market capitalization, it is the biggest star in the Internet cosmos. With a $2.8 billion market cap, Yahoo! far surpasses beleagured Netscape and keeps company with the likes of health-care giant Humana, cosmetics queen Estée Lauder, and truck-rental giant Ryder System (see charts).

Let's leave aside, for now, questions of whether Yahoo! will be around in ten years or whether there's any way its stock might be a good investment. This much is clear: Yahoo! has won the search-engine wars and is poised for much bigger things.

Its triumph could hardly be less likely. Yahoo! has emerged from a crowded corner of the Web, where at least three other major services help people do the same thing—find things on the Internet. Type in "Pamela Lee" or "IBM" at any of these so-called search sites, and you'll find that others—Infoseek, Excite, and Lycos—tell you about more Websites faster than Yahoo! does. Its technology is not nearly as robust as that of its rivals. Yet Yahoo! gets twice as many visitors as its nearest competitor.

According to a survey by Mediamark Research last year, in a typical month more than 25 million people use Yahoo!. Some months, 40 million people visit. More people go to Yahoo! than to Netscape or AOL. More people search at Yahoo! than watch MTV, Nickelodeon, or Showtime in any given week. More people check out Yahoo! than read the typical issue of *Time, Newsweek,* or *Life.* Simply put, that's why some people think Yahoo! may make wads and wads of money in the future by selling ads. Observes Oppenheimer & Co. analyst Henry Blodget: "I have yet to find a flat surface attractive enough to grab the attention of 40 million pairs of eyeballs but not attractive enough to spend big money advertising on."

Gathering eyeballs has been the company plan since its inception. It turns out that this pack of Net-besotted, Yahoo!ing-their-brains-out, twenty- and thirty-something Web surfers have real business savvy, and their near-flawless execution and brilliant marketing have eviscerated the competition.

Back in late 1993, Dave Filo had a problem. His personal list of favorite Websites had grown beyond 200 "bookmarks," becoming so long as to be useless, especially since his browser—the earliest version of Mosaic— could not sort bookmarks into convenient onscreen folders. He and Jerry Yang wrote some software that allowed them to group their "hot list' into subject areas. They named their little list "Jerry's Guide to the World Wide Web" and posted it on the Web. People from all over the world sent E-mail, saying how much they appreciated the effort. Explains Yang, 29: "We wanted to avoid doing our dissertations."

The two set out to cover the entire Web. They tried to visit and categorize 1,000 sites a day. When a subject category grew too large, subcategories were created, and then sub-subcategories. The hierarchy made it easy for even

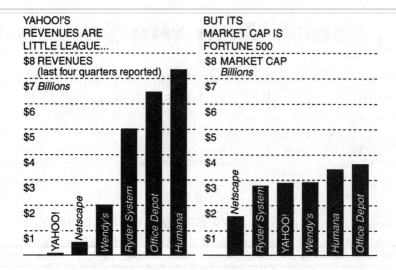

novices to find Websites quickly. "Jerry's Guide" was a labor of love—lost of labor, since no software program could evaluate and categorize sites. Filo persuaded Yang to resist the engineer's first impulse to try to automate the process. "No technology could beat human filtering," Filo, 31 argues.

Though engineers, Yang and Filo have a great sense of what real people want. Consider their choice of name. Jerry hated "Jerry's Guide," so he and Filo opted for "Yahoo!," a memorable parody of the tech community's obsession with acronyms (this one stood for "Yet Another Hierarchial Officious Oracle"). Why the exclamation point? Says Yang: "Pure marketing hype."

The hype worked. Visitors poured in. Both Netscape and AOL offered to absorb Yahoo!, but Yang and Filo decided to take a leave from their studies and strike off on their own.

It was spring 1995, a great time to be a young entrepreneur with an Internet idea. Net mania was just flowering; Netscape hadn't even gone public. Venture capitalists came calling. Kleiner Perkins, the largest venture firm in the Valley, was interested but wanted Yahoo! to merge with Excite (then called Architext), another search engine developed by Stanford grads. Instead, the pair signed with Sequoia Capital, which had helped fund Apple Computer and Cisco Systems. Sequoia put up $1 million for a stake in the company; that stake was worth $560 million at the end of 1997.

Sequoia general partner Michael Moritz claims he never doubted that free Internet services could attract people and advertisers. But four other search sites had the same idea. Back East, Carnegie Mellon spinoff Lycos bragged that its "spider" search software surveyed more Web pages than any other service. In Silicon Valley, Steve Kirsch, an engineer with a strong entrepreneurial record, was pushing his startup, Infoseek. Excite had the KP seal of approval and advanced search technology. Yahoo! had the best name, the worst technology, and a quaint belief that while other companies' machines surveyed Website addresses by the thousands every second, the human touch could somehow win out. Not surprisingly, when Yang, Filo and Moritz talked to professional managers in search of a CEO, some wanted to shake things up. One candidate said, "One of the first things I'd do is change the name." Yang and Filo showed him the door.

The person who did get the job was Tim Koogle, 45, a Stanford-trained engineer who had spent nine years at Motorola. Bringing in "adult supervision" to manage an outfit created by techie kids is another Silicon Valley tradition; almost all venture-capital-backed companies do this at some point. The transition can be rough, especially for the founders, but Koogle made things easy for Yang and Filo. He kept their name. He embraced their concept of wooing advertisers by attracting lots of people with useful information created by humans. Besides getting the most out of the founders, Koogle's main contribution was to steer the company as it added lots and lots of employees.

Supercharged by venture money, all the search companies staffed up in 1995 and 1996. Yahoo!'s competitors recruited executives from conventional media. But the worlds of computer technology and media often collided.

In early 1996, Infoseek's Kirsch, despite his background in engineering, urged his company to invest in a directory compiled by humans. But other top executives at Infoseek were convinced that a more techie approach, with a directory compiled by software, was the way to go. Kirsch lost the battle; the techie approach fizzled. The company underwent a management shuffle, and the strategic zigs and zags left Infoseek far behind Yahoo!

Koogle admits that it was sometimes hard to be the CEO of a tech outfit with a very untechie strategy. At an industry conference he ran into Kirsch, who blustered that Infoseek's searches were "five seconds faster than yours." Alarmed, Koogle ran back to Jerry Yang and asked, "Is he right?"

He was. but what Yang knew, and Koogle came to understand, was that theirs was not a contest about search engines. It was about helping Web users find what they wanted. A powerful search engine may deliver thousands of listings in a flash. But you then have to sift through the dreck. Explains Yang: "If you've got 13 Madonna sites, then you probably don't need a 14th." Yahoo! aims to deliver the best of the Web, not its entirety, in a directory that looks like a book's table of contents. And Yahoo! presents the information on an unadorned page that pops up on your computer screen quickly.

So Yahoo! spends money on people, not computers. Visit Excite, and you'll be shown an enormous glass room housing rows of expensive servers and muscular workstations that quickly deliver loads of results and scour the Web. Yahoo!'s servers are PCs run by a third party.

Its human-created directory was all that distinguished Yahoo! from its rivals as Net euphoria swept the stock market in early 1996. The search companies hit the IPO scene in a pack: Lycos, Excite, and Yahoo! in April; Infoseek in June. Yahoo!'s prospectus was insouciantly candid, pointing out that the company was competing in a crowded field with no proprietary technology. Industry observers were wary. "This is the deal from hell," declared Manish Shah, publisher of *IPO Maven*.

Yet at the close of Yahoo!'s first day of trading, its stock had risen 154% from the offering price, even more than Netscape's first-day leap of 105%. Yahoo!'s market capitalization was $848 million. Chief ontologist Srinija Srinivasan, the person who oversees the directory's categories, describes that day as "just a total rush." But the $35 million of capital that had suddenly flowed into Yahoo! didn't reassure Yang. He recalls feeling "panic—no, not panic, but anxiety." Suddenly, he had shareholders.

The following day, investors took a second look, blanched, and bailed. The stock drifted to less than half the first day's close and stayed there for the remainder of 1996. Reality seemed to set in. Yahoo! needed advertisers, and advertisers were sniffing around but not spending. Manish Shah, it seemed, had been right. Yahoo! really stood for "Yet Another Highly Overhyped Offering."

Yahoo! might never have won out had it not been for Yang's obsession with what he saw as the fundamentals of his business: Give users abundant reasons to visit your service, and promote the hell out of the brand. He recruited Karen Edwards, who had worked on the Apple account at advertising company BBDO, to be the brand's steward. Soon after she arrived, Yahoo! launched $5 million worth of television commercials. It was, says Edwards, "the biggest check Yahoo! had written to date." The nervy ads were directed at people who had heard about the Web but hadn't yet logged on. In a survey it conducted before the first ad, the company asked a cross section of Americans, "What is Yahoo!?" Only 8% correctly identified the company. A sizable percentage said it was a chocolate drink. Those numbers began to change with the ads.

Edwards moved into "guerrilla marketing" mode. She pushed the brand into sports events, rock concerts, magazines, and other conventional locales, as well as some strange ones—she gave free paint jobs to any employee who would splatter the logo over his or her car. One employee had the logo tattooed on his butt.

In addition, the company took every opportunity to turn up the heat on Lycos, Infoseek, and Excite. For example, in early 1996, Yahoo! agreed to pay Netscape $5 million to be one of five search engines to which visitors would be referred when they needed to conduct a search from Netscape's site, the most popular on the Web. Infoseek, which had enjoyed an exclusive franchise on Netscape's pages, now had to share with four others. Confesses Koogle: "We did it to hurt the competition. After the first month, Infoseek's traffic dropped in half." Infoseek's Kirsch confirms the fall.

Yahoo! was not as dependent upon Netscape to feed it traffic. Users were seeking it out on their own. Every time users returned to Yahoo! for a search, the site seemed to offer some new, cool, and free feature. Stock quotes, maps, chat rooms, news, weather, sports, Yellow Pages, and classifieds—combined, all this gave Yahoo! the feel of an online service. Last October the company paid $81 million for Four-11, a service that gives users free E-mail.

The freebies, the branding, and the human touch combined to create a site that was more attractive than any other. In the first quarter of 1996, Yahoo!, Excite, Lycos, and Infoseek had delivered roughly the same number of pages. By the end of the year, Yahoo! was delivering twice as many as second-place Excite. by the third quarter of 1997, Yahoo! visitors were checking out 50 million pages a day—more than the other three combined. Ignoring warnings from his squirming PR adviser, Kirsch concedes the obvious: "It's Yahoo! and everyone else."

Still, the victory doesn't explain why investors have decided to place their Internet bets on Yahoo!, sending the stock up 511% in 1997. Yahoo!'s $2.8 billion market cap gives it a price/earnings ratio, based on analysts' estimates of earnings over the next four quarters, of 171. Intel's, by comparison, is 20. Figures like that send most investors running for cover. So is this highflying Internet company headed for a Netscape-like fall?

Toward the end of last year, advertisers started to make Yahoo! their online buy. by December, Yahoo! had 1,700 paying advertisers, up from just 112 in early 1996. Revenues tripled, to $67 million. Without the onetime charge for buying Four-11, the company would have recorded a profit of $2.5 million for the year instead of a $23 million loss. Advertisers are signing up for relationships that bring in more cash. They're paying hefty sums, for example, to run sweepstakes in which Web surfers fork over their E-mail addresses and some personal information. Co-marketing deals—like the ones the company has engineered with Amazon.com, CDNow, E*Trade, and mortgage broker eLoan—offer new lines of income. If a Yahoo! user takes the time to fill out a questionnaire for eLoan, Yahoo! might get paid something like 30 cents, as opposed to the 2 cents it collects when it displays a simple banner advertisement. Such partnerships already account for 15% of the company's revenues.

What's more, Yahoo! is beginning to be viewed as a key part of the computing establishment. Chief operating officer Jeff Mallett points out that Compaq recently requested the right to preload on its PCs Yahoo! news and weather tickers that will scroll across the bottom of your monitor. Says Mallet: "Companies have come to see us as the hub [of the Web]."

Koogle asks skeptics to consider how much money is spent annually on advertising on TV and radio and in magazines. He puts the total at around $150 billion. "Put big numbers by a leading company serving as a gateway [to the Web], add in a growing market, and you have an interesting story," he says.

Yet even the most optimistic projections of Yahoo!'s revenue growth leave it far short of what that $2.8 billion valuation would call for. What scares the skeptics is the same thing that thrills the believers: Yahoo!'s real competition is no longer Excite or Lycos. The company now finds itself maneuvering against AOL and Microsoft. "There have always been three or four comprehensive branded networks," says Mallett. AOL, Microsoft's MSN online service, and Yahoo!, he says, are the broadcast networks of the Web. Says Volpe Brown Whelan analyst Andrea Williams: "It may be that Yahoo! will grow up to be an NBC. But the possibility that it may stumble in the meantime is not reflected in today's valuation."

Like Yahoo!, AOL and MSN offer users many features, ranging from E-mail to chat to an assortment of content. Microsoft, for instance, recently acquired HotMail, a service similar to Yahoo!'s Four-11. MSN and AOL have far greater revenues—each charges subscribers $19.95 a month, while Yahoo! charges zero—but have had trouble making profits.

Yang and Filo believe they can be profitable without charging subscriber fees. In January, Yahoo! announced a joint marketing deal with MCI. The companies say that by the end of March they will offer a Yahoo!-branded Internet-access service. Get your Internet access from MCI, and you'll be headed Yahoo!'s way. MCI will collect the revenues; Yahoo! gets many more eyeballs and, if all goes well, a cut of the revenues. Mallett says he hopes to convert some of AOL's ten million subscribers. "Maybe they'd like a pure Web play without proprietary connections," he grins. You get the feeling he likes the idea of trying to cut in on some bigger competitors. Investors can only hope his good vibe turns into their good fortune.

The Pure-Play Syndrome

Wall Street once preached the virtues of diversification.
Now the buzzword is focus.
Why did PepsiCo feel obliged to dance to The Street's fickle tune?

by Subrata N. Chakravarty and John R. Hayes

Do Corporate managements pay too much attention to Wall Street? Probably. In seeking to please the analysts, giant PepsiCo is spinning off its $10 billion (revenues) restaurant division, comprising the Pizza Hut, Taco Bell and KFC chains. Call it the pure-play syndrome. The restaurants will be owned by Tricon Global Restaurants, after paying a one-shot dividend of $4.5 billion to the parent company. PepsiCo plans to use the cash infusion for the inevitable stock buyback and for battling Coke in the soft-drink arena.

The spinoff—which takes place this month—is an obvious bow by PepsiCo Chief Executive Roger Enrico to Wall Street's current mantra that companies should "focus" their business. The idea is that investors will pay more for a stock whose businesses are closely related and easy to understand. Enrico's predecessor, Wayne Calloway, had resisted a spinoff, but Enrico has given in. The market cheered—briefly. The day the spinoff was announced, PepsiCo stock rose $3.50, to $35.50, and has since moved four or so points higher, although it lags the rise in the S&P 500.

The spinoff is a done deal, but we suspect it's a lousy one for the company, long term. It violates the sensible rule: "If it ain't broke, don't fix it."

PepsiCo wasn't broken. This year it will earn close to 17% on its invested capital. The stock sells for a quite satisfactory 27 times expected 1997 earnings—a nice premium over the market.

So what's bothering the analysts? Probably the invidious comparisons with Coca-Cola. Even after its recent dips, Coke still commands 37 times earnings. Whereas PepsiCo stock has generally lagged the market the last couple of years, Coke has been a market leader.

Pressed to do something about these sorts of comparisons, Enrico has chosen to throw away the company's best chance for growth.

Boxed-in in the soft-drink business by a triumphant Coke, PepsiCo still had lots of elbow room in the restaurant business.

During 20 years in the restaurant business, PepsiCo built the Pizza Hut and Taco Bell chains practically from scratch into the leaders in their categories, and turned the large but troubled KFC around.

Against these successes, the parent company is outclassed by its principal competitor and has no easy way out of its difficulties. The Coca-Cola Co.'s share of the U.S. soft-drink market has grown from 39.5% in 1985 to 43.1% in 1996, according to the Maxwell Report. Pepsi's products have merely crept from 30.3% to 31%.

Overseas, where Coca-Cola gets 80% of its earnings these days, the two company's fortunes are even more divergent. At a recent analysts' meeting, Craig Weatherup, chief executive of Pepsi-Cola, stated the problem starkly: "The cold, hard facts are, if you exclude Canada, we have never made money in international. . . ." That is an extraordinary record of futility for a company that has been selling a well-known brand overseas for half a century.

Coke is not likely to cut Pepsi any slack. In a study of market shares in 95 countries in 1996 by the trade publication *Beverage Digest,* Pepsi led Coke in fewer than 20 countries. The world is painted Coca-Cola red, with a very few pockets of Pepsi blue. "Coke has the clout to make Pepsi work very hard to get whatever they've decided they don't want," says a former PepsiCo executive, with some sadness.

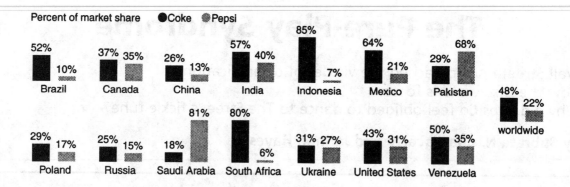

Percent of market share   ●Coke   ●Pepsi

	Coke	Pepsi
Brazil	52%	10%
Canada	37%	35%
China	26%	13%
India	57%	40%
Indonesia	85%	7%
Mexico	64%	21%
Pakistan	29%	68%
Poland	29%	17%
Russia	25%	15%
Saudi Arabia	18%	81%
South Africa	80%	6%
Ukraine	31%	27%
United States	43%	31%
Venezuela	50%	35%
worldwide	48%	22%

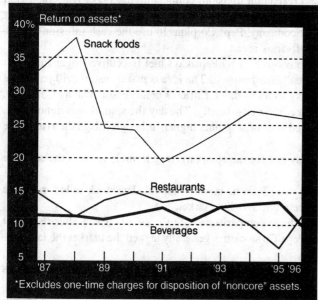

Why dump restaurants?

Return on assets*

40%
35
30
25
20
15
10
5

Snack foods
Restaurants
Beverages

'87   '89   '91   '93   '95 '96

*Excludes one-time charges for disposition of "noncore" assets.

Despite over-investment, restaurants
have often outperformed beverages.

Pepsi's overseas strategy rests on large emerging markets such as China, Russia, Eastern Europe and India, where clear leadership has yet to be established. But Pepsi has lost its leadership position in Russia and much of Eastern Europe since the collapse of the Soviet Union, and trails badly in China. Only in India has it gained any ground, owing to a squabble between Coke and some of its bottlers.

Craig Weatherup says Pepsi will be patient. "The international marketplace demands a degree of discipline and consistency of strategy and execution," he declares. But more than patience is what's needed. Pepsi has fared reasonably well against Coke in the U.S. because it has sometimes out-marketed Coke with clever advertising and promotions. Overseas, however, marketing counts for less than distribution—getting product "within arm's reach of the customer," as the saying goes. "Soft drinks are much less about branding than logistics," says Muktesh Pant, former executive director of PepsiCo's operations in India. "Pepsi spends too much time and effort on advertising. Coke spends time on logistics. They're a more serious company."

It shows in the way the two companies spend. "If you want to invest $100, Coke gives you $150 and tells you to do it right," a former PepsiCo executive says. "Pepsi gives you $20 and tells you to be creative." Put another way, Pepsi sends singer Michael Jackson; Coke sends trucks.

In the restaurant business, Pepsi faces no such competitor. PepsiCo is the world's biggest operator, with 30,000 units, versus McDonald's 22,000 units and Burger King's 9,000.

Over the past five years PepsiCo's restaurant revenues overseas have grown at 22%, compounded, far higher than its revenue growth in beverages or snack foods. In 1995 and 1996 international profits grew 30% and 37%, respectively. Pizza Hut and KFC especially are well accepted overseas. Unlike beverages, in which Coke is entrenched in much of the world and will fight Pepsi every step of the way, PepsiCo's restaurants compete for growth primarily with McDonald's—no slouch, but operating in a different product segment and currently suffering setbacks of its own.

THE KING OF SNACKS

PepsiCo's Frito-Lay division is the company's crown jewel. Frito-Lay dominates the U.S. salty-snack market, with a market share of 54%. Its nearest competitors, Borden's Wise brand and Procter & Gamble, each have only 4%. The other, Anheuser-Busch, threw in the towel last year. It sold its Eagle brand name to P&G and its plants to Frito-Lay.

Frito-Lay has nine of the top ten snack-chip products, with brands like Lay's and Ruffles potato chips, Doritos and Tostitos corn chips and Chee-tos, and extruded product. P&G's Pringles is the only interloper.

Frito-Lay works hard maintaining its position. Its sprawling R&D facility in Plano, Tex. comes complete with a small-scale production plant where new products are made and tested. Marketing people work side by side with the research teams. Researchers incessantly test different oils, flavors, optimal chip thicknesses and the like to ensure that Frito-Lay products worldwide are consistent from bag to bag yet cater to local market tastes. Thus is England there are salt and vinegar potato chips and beef-flavored corn chips. In Japan and China the most popular flavors are seafood. In Mexico and India the chips are more highly spiced.

Although Americans already consume 17 pounds of salty snacks per capita per year, Frito-Lay is constantly trying to find new ways to get us to consume even more. Right now the company is trying to make chips and dips into a convenience meal. "The need for convenience is driving eating habits towards snacking versus sit-down meals at home with the family," says Steven Reinemund, chief executive of Frito-Lay. In a statement that will make nutritionists shudder, he adds: "Some people will sit down with a bag of Tositos and a jar of salsa and make a meal out of that."

For those of you worried about your waistline, Frito-lay now has lower-fat baked chips. Next year it will introduce no-fat chips fried in Olestra, P&G's new fat substitute.

You may hate these junk foods but still admire the way this business is run. Frito-Lay's huge production plant in Irving, Tex. is a revelation in technological innovation.

From raw potatoes to chips on the supermarket shelf, the products remain under the company's control. Brian Foster, a production "team leader," proudly states that on holiday weekends he and other volunteers go to stores to replenish the shelves themselves rather than leave the job to supermarket stock clerks.

That same attention to detail has been transferred overseas. In China, for example, Frito-Lay took two years to get its chips to market because it had to first get the Chinese farmers to grow the perfect chip-frying potato.

Muktesh Pant, who was executive director of PepsiCo's operations in India, says, paying Frito-Lay the ultimate compliment, "Frito-Lay is more like Coke. It is very disciplined."—S.N.C.

Enrico had already addressed the major problem plaguing the restaurant business: its voracious thirst for capital. Largely because of the cost of building and modernizing restaurants, PepsiCo had piled up a considerable burden of debt: about $8 billion at last count, amounting to 53% of total capital. Coke, by contrast, has debt of just 13% of capital.

PepsiCo has long had a strategy of owning a significant percentage of its operating entities: PepsiCo owned over 50% of its restaurants worldwide, compared with around 20% for McDonald's. The story is similar in soft drinks. Where PepsiCo owns about half of its domestic bottlers, Coke owns none. It buys bottlers only to flip them to its aggressive group of "anchor" bottlers—large, well-financed companies, like Coca-Cola Enterprises, in which it often has an equity interest but no assets on its books.

When Enrico took over the restaurant group in 1994, he decided that the investment had gotten out of hand. The restaurants were consuming more cash than they were generating. Enrico's solution: Reduce the investment by refranchising company-owned restaurants (FORBES, *Mar. 27, 1995*).

The results were immediate. Cash flow from restaurants rapidly turned positive. Refranchising generated more than $300 million in cash in the second half of 1995 and over $650 million in 1996. Company ownership of stores has dropped from 51% in 1994 to 45% in 1996. That policy is expected to continue for years to come, even after the spinoff. The restaurants are now gushing cash—$800 million in 1996.

Company ownership did not even result in the higher earnings expected. "The surprise to me is that earnings from franchise royalties have been roughly the same as earnings from the owned restaurants, without the risk of the capital investment," observes Karl von der Heyden, PepsiCo's chief financial officer. Simply put, the multibillion-dollar investment was largely futile. PepsiCo could have had much higher returns by following McDonald's franchising approach.

With a highly positive cash flow, PepsiCo's restaurants are poised for further profitable growth in a world where every year tens of millions of additional consumers are achieving a level of affluence that will make them potential diners-out.

So why get out of restaurants now? Basically, Enrico redefined PepsiCo's business to justify the spinoff. He explains that soft drinks and snacks are packaged-goods businesses, while restaurants are a service business. But with the restaurants spun off, what is left is a superb snack business, an also-ran beverage business—and limited prospects for growth.

The company-owned bottling operations have now been segregated into a separate division. Already Lehman Brothers' Michael J. Branca has pointed out that Pepsi has margins of 21% from sales of concentrate to domestic franchises, compared with margins of 11% from its company-owned bottlers. It is only a matter of time before analysts begin expounding on the shareholder value that could be created by spinning off the bottling operation, as Coke did with Coca-Cola Enterprises.

Will Enrico yield to the pure-play arguments and take this next step? He says no, but he also said no to a restaurant spinoff just three months before he announced it.

And after that, Frito-Lay? Enrico admits it would command a higher stock multiple than PepsiCo as a separate company, but he says that won't happen. "This leg," he says, patting his left thigh, "is Frito-Lay, and this leg [patting his right] is Pepsi-Cola. I gotta have two legs to walk, okay? If those two companies are split apart, so am I. So it ain't gonna happen on my watch, I guarantee you."

Enrico says Frito-Lay is PepsiCo's equivalent of a nuclear deterrent. "With Frito-Lay's market position and cash flow, it provides mutually assured destruction," he says. "If our competitor were to fire every gun he's got and forgo short-term earnings to destroy us, the cash flow from Frito-Lay would keep us going."

He could have said the same thing about the restaurants. In seeking to win short-term stock market gains, Roger Enrico may have broken up a promising marriage. Not to mention throwing away his company's best growth prospects. And just because he was jealous of Coke's P/E ratio.

Is Big Back?

Or Is Small Still Beautiful?

In an age of consolidation, are sleek entrepreneurial companies being overtaken by gas-guzzling corporate Cadillacs? Hardly.

by David Friedman

You want to talk about merger mania? After reaching a record high of more than $1 trillion in 1996, the value of announced company mergers worldwide topped $1.6 trillion in 1997. More than half of that activity—$919 billion in 1997—was in the United States, where there were 10,700 mergers in 1997 and 10,340 in 1996. What's more, from 1988 to 1995, while the average number of companies grew by 10%—from 6 million to 6.6 million—the number of companies with more than 1,000 employees grew by 20%, from 5,000 to 6,000, faster than groups of any other size.

Behind those striking figures are the daily headlines you've certainly read, describing how already-large companies are combining to form truly mammoth ones, many of which seemingly dominate entire sectors. Raytheon's absorption of Hughes Electronics resulted in a single U.S. air-to-air missile maker. Columbia/HCA Healthcare Corp.'s acquisition of Value Health Inc., and Aetna Life & Casualty's marriage with U.S. Healthcare Inc., drastically reduced market competition among health-maintenance organizations.

Add to all that the consolidation from below—the so-called "roll-up" or "poof" companies that combine small operations in areas like printing, waste hauling, and video rentals into bigger, publicly traded enterprises. "Poof!" says one consolidator with a successful record of marketing roll-ups to investment-hungry Wall Street, "you have a company." While recent accounting-rule changes may dampen roll-up activity, efforts to consolidate many traditional types of small businesses, such as drugstores and veterinarians, contribute to the sense that the days of the "little guy" are numbered.

So if industry after industry is being rolled up into just a handful of mammoth companies, and Wall Street is pouring billions into "big-cap" stocks and ignoring the rest, shouldn't the 1990s be thought of as the Age of Big?

Hardly.

Recent consolidations in sectors like tire businesses and railroads have been, at least at first, disastrous. There have been cases in which new train companies couldn't even keep track of where their engines were. And even the well-publicized struggles of small businesses like mom-and-pop druggists may sometimes have been overstated. In 1980, 13 chain-drugstore companies operated 200 or more stores; today there are only 10 chains. In the same period, the number of drugstore chains with more than $75 million in revenues fell from 43 to 33. From 1988 to 1995, the total number of drugstores did fall, but only by 12%, from 50,000 to 44,000. From 1993 to 1995, a period in which small companies really felt competitive heat, payrolls for the smallest drugstores, with just one to four employees, actually increased to 8%, more than the industry average. Consolidation is happening, to be sure, but it hardly heralds the death of independents.

Let's face it: "big" just isn't what it used to be. The U.S. economy is no longer an atomistic, libertarian free-for-all in which the biggest player is likely to be the strongest. Even the largest and smallest businesses must form enduring links—strategic alliances, supply chains, project-specific work teams—to survive in constantly changing markets. Modern production networks comprise truly gargantuan organizations that drawf even the largest merger, but what makes them tick is collaboration, constant learning, and unique compensation and authority structures, not size. Still, it's easy to understand why some might think otherwise.

Big Investors Build Big Illusions

So what accounts for our current merger mania and Wall Street's big-company infatuation? The answer is that mutual-fund money and huge institutional investors have profoundly changed the investment criteria that motivate highly public financial markets. In the past, company performance and skill were the primary factors guiding where money was spent. Today the things that matter are liquidity and name recognition.

When money flooded into mutual funds through retirement, pension, and other savings accounts, fund managers had to find ways of investing huge sums without driving up the price of the stocks they wanted to buy. "You just can't buy small-cap stocks as efficiently as big caps," explains David Shulman, formerly the chief equity strategist for Salomon Brothers and now a general partner at Ulysses Management. The managers also wanted to be able to sell their holdings as easily as possible if they needed to raise cash.

Over the past five years, billions of dollars shifted into the biggest companies' stocks because they had the largest number of shares on the market, as well as brand-name recognition. Since 1994 the proportion of cash invested in "big-cap" index funds—those consisting of only large-company stocks—has risen from just 3% of total mutual-fund investments to 20%. "The market is willing to pay a premium for liquidity and so-called quality," explained one fund manager, John Bogle Jr. of Numeric Investors, to the *Wall Street Journal*. "And that's going to benefit the larger companies."

Merger mania was largely a direct result of Wall Street's preference for liquidity. Companies saw they would be rewarded for meeting the new criteria, and fund money provided the cash to do big deals. As companies' stock prices rose, moreover, they could use their own equity as currency to do their own mergers and acquisitions, trading stock for businesses.

Consolidation and stockprice appreciation began to feed on each other. Through layoffs, recapitalizations, and growing industry market shares, newly merged companies could often dramatically improve earnings and balance-sheet ratios. In the quarter-by-quarter time frame that governs public equity markets, those achievements seemed to justify even greater stock-price appreciation.

Indeed, the prices of holdings favored by most fund managers spiked to stratospheric levels. And in the mid-1990s large-company corporate earnings generally met expected targets. But often, smaller companies offered much better economic fundamentals, and in those cases, Wall Street had to scramble to explain why *only* big-cap investments made sense. More than anything else, it was the need for a story the Street could use to make pricey big-cap investments plausible—coupled with the fact that the media tends to focus on Wall Street but don't always understand it all that well—that launched the "Big Is Back" campaign.

Apart from simple investment liquidity, Shulman points to three other arguments Wall Street promulgated in support of big-cap stocks:

Near-monopoly positions. Large companies like Intel and Microsoft so dominated their markets that they could effectively set prices and ignore pathetically weak competitors.

Globalization. Only the biggest companies could afford to be in several markets at once, an advantage in hedging against a recession in any one country.

Procurement power. Big brand-name companies—such as Boeing, Ford, and Disney—can squeeze suppliers for price concessions and insulate themselves from profit pressures.

All of those attributes were supposed to protect big-cap company earnings and justify stratospheric stock prices, particularly when compared with the attributes of more vulnerable little companies. But in retrospect, there was much to doubt about that story.

For one thing, bigness has little to with access to foreign markets. Fully 96% of exporters are small businesses. Far from suffering under intolerable wage and price pressures, those small companies pay wages comparable with those paid by the biggest companies. And while cornering the market on stock micro-processors or operating systems might well be profitable, increasingly, such products are commodities around which higher-end, more lucrative components and innovations are assembled. That's why the small companies are doing so well, even if Wall Street doesn't recognize it.

So no one should have been surprised when last October, Boeing—the very model of a monopoly, a globalized, oppressive big-cap company—predicted it would lose a record $2.6 billion over the ensuing 15 months. Early in the decade, the company had done exactly what Wall Street said it should do: ruthlessly cut back by 50% the number of suppliers it used, to "streamline" and cut costs. Boeing discovered that that strategy also gutted the skills and production capabilities of its crucial supply chain to the point where it could not meet demand.

"Ten years ago, if we bought rubber hoses, we might have bought them from 10 suppliers, and today we'd buy them from 3," explained Ron Woodard, president of Boeing Commercial Airplane Group, to the *Seattle Times* last October. "There are cost advantages and all that, but there's a downside. If one supplier doesn't come through, you've lost a third of your supply source." Even mighty Boeing had become dependent on small companies throughout its supply chain.

At the same time, despite their supposed advantages, much-hyped companies like Gillette and Coca-Cola failed to meet earnings projections. "The markets began to realize the big guys aren't perfect," recounts Shulman, "and maybe they were overvalued."

Wall Street's "Big Is Beautiful" story further crumbled with the collapse of Asian currency markets last summer, an event that undermined one of the key advantages largeness purportedly conferred: global reach. For three years big-cap stocks had been hyped on the theory that large companies could open offices overseas and take advantage of foreign opportunities more quickly than small companies could. Now, with an Asian meltdown in progress, that same attribute was seen as exposing big companies to a far greater risk, the caprices of overseas markets. "The allure of globalism has been tarnished," wrote Shulman in an October investment report.

Seemingly overnight, Wall Street shifted billions out of once-favored big-cap stocks into smaller domestic stocks, triggering rallies in the Russell 2000 and other small-cap stock indexes. For the first time in three years, small stocks out-performed large ones.

The moral of the story is that the fables Wall Street tells itself, no matter how widely they're publicized, don't necessarily reflect the rest of the economy. "Just about 7,000 companies are publicly traded," says small-business expert David Birch, and those amount to perhaps 15% of the nation's net growth. "Wall Street is a tiny part of what's really going on."

It's Not the Size; It's the Coordination

At a deeper level, while big companies are unquestionably part of the economic landscape, and supply chains are generating even larger production networks, those who study company organization are concluding that 1950s-style "big" can't possibly make a comeback. Size, in fact, seems increasingly irrelevant to business success.

One sign of that new awareness is that the old theory of why companies become big in the first place is in total disarray. In the past, economists claimed that bigness reduced transaction costs. If each person in a production team—a welder and a painter; a graphic artist and a secretary—was an independent company, the time and effort of bargaining over prices, delivery, or quality would overwhelm the whole operation. Worse still, people with special skills no one else could match might threaten to hold up everyone else for more compensation. Big companies, it was thought, solved those problems by bringing everyone under one set of rules that dictated how everyone interacted.

Even when the approach was plausible, it had its limitations. If vertical integration reduces transaction costs and increases efficiency, why shouldn't a single company control the *whole* economy? And when should a particular skill be brought in-house to avoid production holdups, while other skills are purchased on the open market? No one could answer those questions, and no one could convincingly explain why certain companies got big and others didn't.

Today, with the advent of E-mail and high-speed computer networks, it seems absurd to claim that corporate expansion is still driven by companies' fear of holdups and efforts to avoid transaction costs. As industry observers Peter Huber and Jessica Korn wrote in *Forbes* magazine, old-style "corporations grew for negative reasons—to eliminate friction and to compensate for poor communication and the prohibitive cost of negotiating with too many outsiders. Andy Grove and Bill Gates grow their companies to exploit economies of scale and scope and to capture the fecundity and elusive value of teamwork culture. The new corporation isn't an assembly line. It's a human beehive, at its best."

Similarly, the idea of bigness as an antidote to "knowledge blackmail" is inconsistent with how large companies actually decide to "make" or "buy" products and services. Older, 1970s-era studies of auto suppliers, for example, suggested that companies like Ford and GM would be more likely to make something in-house—become vertically integrated—when the product involved demanded a greater level of design and engineering skill. That was consistent with the view that companies got bigger to avoid holdups when sophisticated activities are involved.

But now, two decades later, companies still tend to outsource even those projects demanding greater skills, instead of handling them in-house. "Vertically integrated establishments," a team of Columbia University researchers recently concluded, "are no more likely to be engaged in design work . . . on technically demanding parts than independent firms." Something other than mistrust of other groups' intentions, or friction caused by transaction costs, must explain how companies are organized.

Like Huber and Korn, Columbia University law professor Charles Sabel believes there's a new logic at work that challenges our understanding of how entire industries, not just individual companies, operate. "When you fully articulate any supply chain," he says, "the resulting unit is quite large. And it's completely confusing to many what's going on—it's decentralized but still coordinated."

In contrast to the thinking behind Wall Street's "Big Is Back" campaign, which focuses on the 1950s notion that economies of scale drive corporate earnings, Sabel believes the best modern companies and production networks instead seek "economies of scope": the more they do, the easier it is for them to do something new that builds on past experience. By pooling information and monitoring one another's performance over time, work groups within companies, and even vast production networks, continually increase their ability to understand and solve market problems.

What counts is not size but the ability to learn, apply knowledge to problems other companies face, and convince other prospective team members that a company can hold up its part of the production chain. "In the past," Sabel notes, "the game was being the first in the door with prospective customers or vendors. Now getting a foot in the door is just the first step; not only do you have to qualify, you have to continually show you can solve problems better than others."

The implications Wall Street and others want to draw about a company's prospects on the basis of its capitalization or how many employees it has are particularly misguided. If "big" means having a hierarchy and being efficient when it comes to repetitive tasks, and, on the darker side, engaging in wage, price, and consumer-market exploitation, then being big doesn't guarantee much in today's economy. Solving the riddles of autonomy to stimulate creativity and collaboration so that joint solutions to complex problems can be found is the real key. Size is no indicator of whether a company or an entire supply chain is performing well.

That's the ultimate reason the "Big Is Back" claim is so wrongheaded: it implies that the crude 1950s-era business model is somehow back in vogue. The companies that try to duplicate such practices, no matter how dominant they may appear, will suffer if they disrupt the ongoing development of modern collaboration and coordination approaches. Think of companies like Boeing, which elected to cut back the number of its suppliers and then turned up the heat on product prices for those it continued to do business with.

Aspiring and existing business owners who fear that their dreams will be dashed by a newly merged corporate giant should remember that this is still the age of the entrepreneur. The path to success may be more complicated for a start-up or a growing company than ever before, but bigness has little to do with getting there.

David Friedman's last article for Inc. *was "The Smoke-Filled Tomb" (August 1996). He can be reached at dbfr@worldnet.att.net.*

Up for Grabs?

DEC, a proud company, finally agreed to be bought. Netscape could be next.

by Eric Nee

Remember when Netscape Communications Corp. was the hottest company in America? That was a couple of years ago, and things move at lightning speed today. At a recent $16.88, the stock is down by half from its first day of trading and 80% off its alltime high. Bad news for Netscape shareholders, but good news for anyone who wants to pick up a nice little software company on the cheap.

For about $2 billion you could buy a company that practically created today's Internet, has one of the most visited sites on the Web, has a large and growing corporate Internet software business—and still has the lion's share of the browser market. Netscape had $534 million in revenues last year, $261 million in the bank and no debt.

But Netscape's troubles are all over the media. It's taken on two of the biggest software companies in the world—Microsoft Corp. and IBM Corp.—and it's losing.

Netscape does not have the sales and marketing muscle to go up against these two behemoths. To stay competitive, Netscape is having to spend more and more for each dollar of sales. Year-to-year revenues grew 9% in the fourth quarter, to $125 million, but Netscape spent a heck of a lot more on the effort, with sales and marketing expenses up 58%, to 82 million. As a result of bloating expenses and slowing revenues, Netscape lost $88 million last quarter and is laying off 300 of its 2,600 full-time employees.

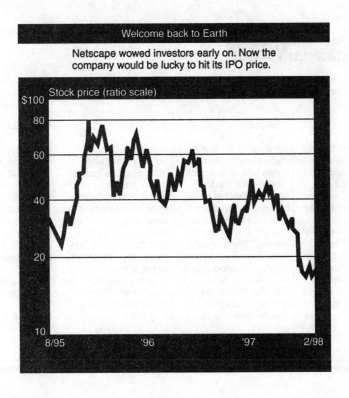

Welcome back to Earth

Netscape wowed investors early on. Now the company would be lucky to hit its IPO price.

Who would want to buy Netscape? Microsoft might want to, but Janet Reno would have a fit. Four other companies get mentioned often as possible suitors—IBM, Oracle Corp., Sun Microsystems, Inc. and Novell, Inc. Each of these companies wants to strengthen its position in the corporate Internet software market, and all would benefit from buying Netscape *(see box, opposite).*

Just as important, Netscape would benefit from being acquired by any of these four companies. Each of them has deeper pockets and a more diverse product line to weather the current pricing battles. One year ago Netscape got 45% of its revenues from browsers. This quarter it will get none because it has been forced to give the browser away free to match Microsoft.

Each of the four companies also has a much larger sales, support and marketing staff, and more experience selling to the corporate world, than does Netscape. The battle in the corporate Internet software market is no longer about being hip or having hot technology. It's about how many sales and support people you can field. IBM, Oracle, Sun and even Novell have lots of them. Netscape doesn't.

Giving shareholders a bit of a premium, you could probably pick up the company for $2 billion or so.

Skeptics think the company isn't worth anything like $2 billion. David Locke, an analyst with Volpe Brown Whelan in San Francisco, agrees. "The stock is overvalued," he says. Locke expects the price to drop even further.

Mary Meeker of Morgan Stanley Dean Witter (which took Netscape public) is more optimistic. She values Netscape's enterprise software and service business at four times revenues, or $1.5 billion, and its Web site at six times revenues, or $500 million. Throw in the brand name and $261 million in cash and you're up over $2 billion.

Netscape Chief James Barksdale would not be interviewed for this article, but others say neither he nor other top management have given up on Netscape's ability to survive as an independent company. That may be true, but Digital Equipment didn't want to lose its independence either, and it was forced by circumstances—and a good offer—to do so. FORBES actually predicted as much in our issue of May 5, 1997 ("Solving the DEC puzzle," *p. 45*). Netscape's Barksdale is a tough guy and proud, but he can't afford to run his company into the ground just to keep the flag flying high.

Just browsing...

Netscape has a good brand, good technology and the added benefit of being a thorn in Bill Gates' side. Here are four Microsoft fighters who might bite at the chance to buy the ailing company.

IBM
Flush with $7.5 billion in cash, an appetite for software acquisitions (IBM bought two firms last quarter) and a desire to be "wired," Lou Gerstner just might pop the question. Despite some overlap in messaging software, Netscape has technology IBM wants, and IBM would love to have it's name pop up on tens of millions of desktops each day.

ORACLE
What better way to stand up to Bill Gates than to buy Netscape? It also makes business sense. Oracle's database business is slowing, and it has little presence in the corporate Internet software market. Oracle bought Netscape's Navio technology, including browser, in August. Maybe this time it'll buy the part of Netscape it should have bought.

SUN
Sun has long toyed with the notion of building a software business. The acquisition of Netscape would give it the opportunity to do so, combining two firms whose names are almost synonymous with the Internet. Sun came close to buying Apple Computer a couple years back. This deal makes much more sense than that one ever did.

NOVELL
This is the wild card, but it's not as crazy as it seems. Novell's chief would love to be in the thick of the Internet battles, and the combination of the two companies would create a strong portfolio of networking software. Novell posted a profit last quarter, which is better than Netscape managed to do, and still has a strong balance sheet.

A New Cat on the Hot Seat

Slowing global markets are shaping up as the first big test for the revamped Caterpillar

by De'Ann Weimer in Peoria, Ill.

For eight years, CEO Donald V. Fites has been working to insulate Caterpillar Inc. from surprises. But on Feb. 22, Illinois members of the United Auto Workers gave him a shock. Although union leaders had finally agreed to a contract to end the company's six-year labor standoff, rank-and-file workers rejected the deal.

The setback comes at a particularly delicate time for the construction and heavy-duty equipment giant. Thanks to booming U.S. markets, a flood of new products, and a hugely successful restructuring that has slashed costs while making global diversification priority No. 1, the Peoria (Ill.)-based company has been on a tear. But with a slowdown in global markets sure to give management plenty of new problems to worry about, Cat had hoped finally to put its bitter labor troubles behind it.

That looks unlikely to happen anytime soon. The union rejection has put an end to talks—and for now, an end to any hope Cat had of being able to hire lower-cost workers at its union plants. Still, if Cat's managers are worried, they're not showing it. Although Fites, 63, wouldn't comment for this article, his executives brush off any difficulties ahead. Overall, the company has "never been in a better position" to weather a tough environment, says Cat Vice-President James W. Baldwin, who oversees the key service and parts business.

Import Scare

For now, Wall street also appears fairly sanguine. Cat's shares tumbled 36%, to 44, in less than a month last fall after news hit that Asia's currency crisis would trim sales by $80 million, but they have since recovered to around 52. The reason: Despite initial fears that collapsing Asian currencies would lead to a flood of cheap products from Asian rivals, it's now clear that most don't have capital to launch an export attack. Manufacturers like Cat "had their stock punished too much" last fall, says Jeffrey P. Davis, chief investment strategist with State Street Global Advisors, which holds 1.6% of Cat's shares.

Of course, that hardly means the horizon is trouble-free. The U.S. market, where Cat sells 49% of its goods, is expected to slow in 1998. And Asia, Cat's fastest-growing market, is suffering a headline-grabbing downturn. Already, American dealers say barely used, heavily discounted Cat equipment has begun to trickle into the U.S. from Asia, as customers dump equipment to raise cash. The slowdown promises the biggest test yet of the "New Cat" the combative CEO has built.

One thing is sure: The reborn company skyrocketed through the upturn with flying colors. Since 1993, when Cat completed its manufacturing overhaul amid soaring demand for construction equipment in the U.S. and developing nations, sales have leaped from $11.6 billion to $18.9 billion, an average of 13% a year. Meanwhile, earnings have risen a stunning 45% annually, jumping from just $626 million to $2.3 billion last year. Investors have also won big: In five years, Cat's stock has more than tripled.

Fites's tumultuous restructuring came in response to a painful industry collapse in the 1980s. Global demand was dropping fast, and the weak yen allowed Cat's biggest rival, Japan's Komatsu Ltd., to undercut prices by 40%. When Komatsu began to gain share, Fites—and Cat—got the scare of their lives.

Fites began by overhauling manufacturing in Cat's core truck and tractor operations. He invested almost $2 billion to modernize his U.S. plants. New state-of-the-art machinery helped Cat slash time out of such mundane tasks as painting, for example, and vastly simplified production. Today, Cat can build 20 different models from the same basic design. The changes—together with the increased use of temporary workers in its nonunion plants—have also greatly improved Cat's flexibility. The company can now change production levels with a week's notice—down from six months at the height of its 1980s crisis. Altogether, Cat's manufacturing time has fallen 75%—one key reason operating margins have exploded, from 5.2% in 1993, to 12.6% in 1997.

Faster production has also allowed Fites to slash inventories. Gone are the long order backlogs and dealer inventories that weighed heavily on Cat's books; today, it refuses orders more than three months in advance. At the same time, Cat has broadened its products. In the last two years, it has introduced 90 offerings—some all-new, some well-targeted line extensions. In 1997, for example, Cat introduced a telescopic handler—essentially a tractor with an arm on it that allows masons to work their way up the side of a building.

Good timing helped with the turnaround, too. As the combination of reduced costs and the end of recession restored the company's financial health, Fites pushed into new markets. He focused on Asia, where infrastructure development created huge demand. Markets in Latin America, Central Europe, Russia and other former Soviet states.

Power Surge

Today, some 51% of Cat sales come from overseas—though Fites wants to hit 75% by 2008. To cut the risk of fluctuating currencies—and trim labor costs—Fites has also pushed much manufacturing abroad. Today, roughly half of Cat's 74 plants are abroad, vs. just 39% of its 38 plants a decade ago. In the wake of the UAW's rejection of the labor contract—which will prevent Cat from hiring new workers at lower wages or demanding more flexible scheduling in union plants—analysts say the percentage of foreign production could go even higher.

Fites has also bulked up in less-cyclical businesses like electric power generation. An offshoot of its long-standing engine business, the move into power gained steam in 1996 when Fites purchased a German maker of engines for generators. Driven by demand for power in developing countries—where governments often don't want to build big power plants—generation has helped boost engines to more than 25% of Cat sales. "They are trending toward smaller, easier-to-operate generators," says Siegfried R. Ramseyer, vice-president of Cat Asia. "This we can do very, very well." He says sales could triple in the next few years.

The company's largest acquisition to date—the $1.3 billion purchase of Britain's Perkins Engines, which closed in February—was directed at another target altogether: the fast-growing $3.6 billion market for compact construction machinery. These machines, typically operated by one person, are the industry's hottest segment. The star of the category: skid-steer loaders, which break up asphalt, move dirt, and do such a variety of useful things that sales are growing a red-hot 11% a year.

Today, Cat is all but absent in the lucrative small-equipment market, but Fites wants a 20% share by 2003. He's counting on big gains from Perkins, which makes engines for skid-steers. Since engines account for 25% of the costs of a skid-steer, Cat figures that trimming those expenses will allow it to undercut rivals while maintaining margins. But Rivals Deere & Co. and Case Corp. are also revving up. "It is going to be a brawl," says industry consultant Frank Manfredi.

Elsewhere, Fites has tapped other new markets by focusing dealers on rental equipment. Initially unpopular with dealers, who must keep rental gear on their books as assets, the change drew lots of smaller customers. The added demand also helped keep prices strong. In 1997, for example, when few companies could do so, Cat raised prices.

But that, as they say, was then, and this is now. The question today is whether Fites can keep up the performance. Speaking to investors at a Boston conference, he promised sustained sales growth of 5% to 7% annually for the next decade. But outside predictions for 1998 are much lower. Analyst Eli S. Lustgarten of Schroder & Co. expects sales to grow only 3.2% in 1998, to $19.5 billion. Operating earnings should nudge up only 1.5%, to $2.3 billion. Although he believes "strategically they are in a very strong position," Lustgarten doesn't expect Cat to avoid the cyclical slowdown. Fites has brought Cat far. But not that far.

Mattel Tailors Toys for Overseas, Plans to Increase Sales Abroad

by Lisa Bannon
Staff Reporter of The Wall Street Journal

Mattel Inc. plans to double its international sales over the next five years as part of a new strategy aimed at worldwide growth, according to Chairman and Chief Executive Jill Barad.

In an interview at the American International Toy Fair in New York, Ms. Barad disclosed that the strategy includes producing toys for individual foreign markets rather than simply adapting U.S. products, revamping the company's management structure to focus more aggressively on overseas sales and linking bonus incentives for employees to international growth targets.

The changes follow a six-month study of Mattel by Boston Consulting Group to determine key markets and product areas for growth. The study identified a potential $6 billion in additional sales growth over the next five years for Mattel by increasing the size of the toy market and Mattel's market share. Two-thirds of that growth should come from Japan and Europe, and less than a quarter from U.S. and Latin America, Ms. Barad said.

If Mattel manages to double its international sales as it hopes, the U.S. market would account for less than 50% of sales, compared with 65% today. "The greatest opportunity exists outside the U.S.," Ms. Barad said. "Only 3% of the world's kids are in the U.S."

In fiscal 1997, Mattel earned $285 million on sales of $4.8 billion. International sales accounted for about $1.7 billion of the total.

Sales Forecast

For 1998, Ms. Barad projected overall sales growth of 10% and annual earnings growth of at least 15%. She declined to break out sales projections for international sales this year. Ms. Barad said she expects world-wide sales of Barbie to increase about 10% in 1998, despite a first quarter of flat or single-digit growth, and dismissed concerns that the famous franchise may be slowing down. Barbie products include dolls, accessories, software and collectors' items.

The renewed focus on international growth comes as Mattel seeks to convince Wall Street that it is evolving away from a toy company associated with fads and volatility and into a more predictable consumer-products company. Wall Street analysts, who were also briefed on the plans this week, generally applaud the new strategy. "Mattel needs to be aggressive in international markets," says Gary Jacobson, an analyst with Jeffries & Co.

The international push marks the latest move by Ms. Barad to strengthen the company, the world's largest toy maker, since taking over as chief executive just over one year ago. Last year, Mattel took a substantial charge and said it was laying off 2,700 employees, or about 10% of its work force, following its merger with Tyco Toys. Mattel stock has risen sharply, outperforming the market, since she took charge.

Four Regions

The process of overhauling the management structure will start later this month. Mattel currently has a U.S. and an international marketing manager. That will now change, so that each product category will have its own managers for marketing and product development in Europe, the U.S., Latin America and Asia. Managers in these four regions will each oversee counterparts in every country in their region.

Ms. Barad said the practice of simply adapting U.S. products for overseas markets has resulted in overpriced merchandise in some places. That's because products were developed without any regard for how their prices would translate into foreign currency. The company has been unable to sell Holiday Barbie—which has been highly successful in the U.S.—in many international markets, for example, because prices were too high.

Barbie alone has potential additional sales of $2 billion, the Boston group's study found. In the U.S., the company sells four dolls per child each year. In Europe, it sells only two, and in Japan only one. To capture that market, Mattel will introduce lower-priced dolls in foreign markets, a line called "Global Friends" that features a different doll for each major global city, and brand extensions such as interactive products and collector Barbies.

In the vehicle market, which includes Matchbox, Hot Wheels and radio-controlled toy cars, the study has identified $1 billion in potential new revenue, especially from Europe and Japan.

China Approves Shell Investment after Ten Years of Discussions

by Craig S. Smith
Staff Reporter of The Wall Street Journal

SHANGHAI, China—Just as the flood of foreign capital into China is beginning to subside, Beijing approved a *Royal Dutch/Shell Group* plan to build a $4.5 billion petrochemical plant, the biggest foreign investment to date.

The plant, a 50-50 joint venture with a Chinese partnership, has been under discussion for 10 years. Shell already has close to $1 billion invested in China through its stake in an offshore oil field and various lubricant plants.

Still, the project has huge symbolic importance for China. The approval comes as the rest of Asia wallows in an economic crisis that has scared off many foreign investors, including some who might have put their money in China.

The country already faces a slowdown in economic growth, and a decline in fresh investment may slow it further from its 8.8% rate of last year. For Shell, the project is an opportunity to use some of its large cash holdings, which at the end of the third quarter of 1997 amounted to 6.7 billion pounds ($11.01 billion).

Spending a 'Cash Mountain'

"It shows that Shell is willing and capable of investing the cash mountain it has built up over the years," said Paul Spedding, an analyst at Dresdner Kleinwort Benson in London. What's more, Mr. Spedding and others approved of Shell's willingness to pursue opportunities in Asia, despite short-term economic concerns in the region.

The new project also comes when Asia's petrochemical industry faces overcapacity and sagging prices. Shell dismissed those worries, saying it remains confident in southern China's long-term demand for its products. "Certainly for an investment of this scale, you need to take a long-term view," said Shell's China spokesman, Jeremy Frearson.

Industry analysts shared that view. "Now could, in fact, be the best time to build it," said Craig Pennington, head of regional energy research at Union Bank of Switzerland in Hong Kong. While work on Shell's plant will begin this year, it won't begin production until 2003, he noted, "and by that time, we're looking for pickup in the cycle."

Shell's project might grow even bigger if China loosens its protectionist grip on the domestic oil industry. The company originally wanted to build a multibillion dollar refinery with the petrochemical plant, but China banned work on new refineries two years ago to protect its existing refineries while they expand and upgrade their facilities. Shell's refinery has been shunted into a "second phase" of the project with no definite time frame.

"We'll build it when refinery margins, economics, costs and prices are favorable," said Mr. Frearson.

Waiting may work to Shell's advantage, analysts said. China sets the price at which refineries sell their products, keeping margins thin. And it forbids refineries from participating in such downstream businesses as gas stations, where margins are fatter.

Renewed Talk of Deregulation

Many oil companies, including Shell, have balked at refinery investments because of the restrictions. In 1995, France's *Elf Aquitaine* pulled out of negotiations for a $2.5 billion refinery near Shanghai because promised deregulation failed to occur.

But talk of deregulation is heating up again. Last month, state-run China Daily's Business Weekly warned China's massive oil industry needs a dose of market economics to stave off collapse. "It is high time [China] combined both upstream and downstream business," the article said.

Shell said it will hold a 50% stake in the petrochemical plant, known as the Nanhai project, while China National Offshore Oil Corp. will hold a 25% stake, China Merchants Holdings 20%, and Guangdong Investment & Development Corp. 5%.

With the project approved, the partners must now finalize a joint-venture agreement, financing terms and the selection of contractors to build the plant.

The plant's annual production capacity will be 800,000 metric tons of ethylene, 450,000 tons of polyethylene, 320,000 tons of mono-ethylene glycol, 240,000 tons of polypropylene, 560,000 tons of styrene monomer and 250,000 tons of propylene oxide. It will be built in Huizhou, a city on China's southern coast near Daya Bay—the site of the country's largest nuclear power plant.

Ericsson's Big Leap
(int'l edition)

Its new boss is stressing software and eyeing acquisitions.

by Julia Flynn in Stockholm, with Peter Elstrom in New York

When Sven-Christer Nilsson was summoned to L.M. Ericsson's Stockholm headquarters for an early-morning chat with CEO Lars Ramqvist last month, he had an inkling of what to expect. After all, Nilsson and 19 other Ericsson insiders had undergone two days of psychological tests as part of Ramqvist's half-year hunt for a successor. Nilsson knew he was in the running for one of the most demanding jobs in Swedish industry. Yet when Ramqvist leaned over the boardroom suite's burled wood coffee table that day and asked him whether he's take the job, Nilsson played it cool—and ultimately took a week to get back to Ramqvist with his answer.

Nilsson will need that kind of self-assurance when he starts as Ericsson's new boss on Mar. 30. Not only will the youthful 53-year-old take over Sweden's largest company but he will also face the crucial task of preserving Ericsson's technological edge in mobile phones, where it vies with Motorola Inc. and Nokia Group for global leadership. With the telecommunications and computer industries converging, Ericsson is in a race to develop advanced networks to help the world's phone companies provide the next generation of multimedia services, from videoconferences to speedy Net surfing over cellular phones. "The challenge will be evolving into a systems and software" provider rather than sticking with Ericsson's traditional role as a hardware supplier to telephone companies, Nilsson explains. "This is a big strategic shift for us."

Lots of Cash

To reach that goal, Ericsson is hitting the acquisitions trail. The company's bankers are already prowling the globe for deals in data communications—the company's "weakest point," Ramqvist told BUSINESS WEEK in a recent interview. The likely target is a company in the U.S., Nilsson adds, because that's where telecom and computers are converging most quickly. Ericsson has begun collaborating on some projects with data-communications companies such as Cisco Systems Inc. and Bay Networks Inc.

With a cash hoard of $3.7 billion and little debt, Ericsson is well positioned to do a deal. "We can make almost any sized acquisition" as far as the money is concerned, Ramqvist boasts. Cisco would be an attractive partner, but with a market capitalization of $66 billion vs. Ericsson's $36 billion, even insiders at the Swedish company admit acquiring the U.S. giant is beyond their reach. A smaller, less costly company still on its way up is a more likely target, Ramqvist notes. Data-networking companies such as 3Com Corp. and Bay Networks would be easier for Ericsson to swallow.

Ericsson is also interested in an acquisition to help diversify its management. Although 94% of the company's $21 billion in sales come from outside Sweden, Ericsson's executive ranks are strictly Swedish. And because of the country's high personal-tax rates, Ericsson has had trouble recruiting talented outsiders to Stockholm.

Ericsson's new CEO will be able to draw on his own experience as he seeks a U.S. partner. Indeed, Nilsson's familiarity with the U.S. was one reason he was tapped for Ericsson's top job. After working for a startup that developed systems for automated teller machines in Sweden, he was recruited to Ericsson in 1982. He jumped quickly from the components division to radio systems to Ericsson's mobile-switching business. For much of the

1990s, he ran the unit that sold cellular networks in the U.S., Ericsson's single largest market, and to other countries adopting the same standard.

That got him deeply involved with handling American customers. Nicolas Kauser, executive vice-president and chief of technology for AT&T Wireless Services, recalls asking Nilsson for Ericsson's help three years ago to develop an indoor wireless phone for big corporate customers. Nilsson came up with the money for the product, Wireless Office Service, which will hit the market this year. "He's very responsive. We went directly to him when we needed help," Kauser says.

Ad Blitz

A far tougher assignment for Nilsson will be filling Ramqvist's shoes. Ericsson's current CEO is a "strong person" and may be a hard act to follow, observes a senior exec from a rival company, adding that Ericsson's large size makes it "harder to generate growth and innovation." Indeed, since Ramqvist became CEO in 1990, Ericsson's stock has jumped fifteenfold. It's now trading at around 40 3/4. Return on equity has soared to nearly 28%, and the company earned a record $2.2 billion in pretax profits last year (chart). The profit surge was fueled by mobile handset sales—up some 87% last year—as Ericsson's heavy R&D investment in establishing the Europe-wide GSM mobile-phone standard has paid off.

Behind Ericsson's success is its youthful and flexible culture. Half of its 100,000 employees are under 30, and around 1,000 jobs a month are shifting to the fast-growing mobile business from Ericsson's troubled fixed-line phone unit, where margins have been squeezed by new rivals. The division has shed a fifth of its workforce and plans to lose an additional 10,000 in the coming two years.

It also looks as if Ericsson's bet on the next mobile multimedia phone may pay off. On Jan. 29, Europe's mobile-phone industry voted to adopt a standard drawing heavily from the one Ericsson had spent more than eight years and millions of dollars to develop. These phones will receive data nearly seven times faster than traditional fixed lines. Over time, analysts expect more users will shift to the high-speed mobile phones, abandoning traditional fixed-line phones. Says Douglas Smith, European technology analyst for Salomon Smith Barney in London: "Ericsson has a very significant head start."

The trick will be keeping it. While running hard to meet demand for its mobile handsets, Ericsson is launching a global advertising blitz to promote its brand name, starting in mid-February. It's also continuing to expand in Asia, despite recent turbulence. China, where Ericsson commands a 50% share of the fast-growing mobile business, is the company's second-largest market, accounting for 9% of sales. Ericsson aims for even higher sales in the region. On Feb. 4, Ramqvist jetted to Malaysia to inaugurate a new factory.

Will Ericsson's new CEO keep up the pace? Nilsson, who spent several weeks last summer on a 10-meter sailboat in the Bay of Biscay, knows something about navigating amid shifting winds. For 3 1/2 days, the boat and its crew were buffeted by gales. "It was hilarious. I never felt unsafe," recalls Nilsson, who enjoyed the thrill of surfing the whitecaps in a small boat. Considering the wild fluctuations of the telecom industry, Ericsson may have found the right captain.

Sleeping with the Enemy

Creating alliances—even with direct competitors—is a risk more small companies are taking as they confront a cruel reality: many market opportunities are impossible for them to pursue on their own.

by Donna Fenn

Consider Ron German's dilemma. The plastics-molding company where he is vice-president of sales and engineering has an opportunity to do some work for a new customer—a very large customer. There's just one problem. Although German's company can mold the part the prospective customer wants, it isn't set up to do the decorating work that the job also requires. A competitor down the road, however, is. German can do one of two things: tell the customer he can do only the molding and risk losing the business, or align himself with his competitor to complete the job and—you guessed it—risk losing the business. "We're scared to death, but we don't have any choice," says German. So the two companies will produce the part together, and German will hope like crazy that the customer won't eventually be lured away by the competitor—his momentary ally—with both molding and decorating capabilities. "It's a big risk," he says.

But it's a risk that more and more entrepreneurs find themselves taking as market conditions compel them to consider a rather cruel reality: while advances in technology, communications, and transportation have created an unprecedented number of opportunities for growing companies, it's now nearly impossible for entrepreneurs to take advantage of those opportunities on their own. Market pressures are forcing small companies to work together in ways that few people could have imagined 10 years ago—and that many still find terribly discomfiting. Today small companies share benchmarking information, seek help from one another to achieve better quality standards, or jointly market their services to customers. And increasingly, they even find themselves working shoulder to shoulder with their direct competitors.

You may be tempted to dismiss it as a trend solely among manufacturing companies, but the fact is that you can find competitors cooperating in nearly every segment of the economy—in service businesses such as insurance and recruiting, among retailers and catalog companies. None of them will say that it's easy. Perhaps like you, many balk at sharing information with their most trusted employees, let alone with companies they perceive as their fiercest competitors. Rightfully, they worry about losing their competitive advantage, diluting their market share, exposing their weaknesses, and damaging their relationships with customers. It's one thing to embrace the latest management trends—opening the books, creating teams, forging strategic alliances—but it's quite another to take the next logical (but most threatening) step by getting into bed with your enemy. Until you find yourself in Ron German's shoes. And you will.

If you doubt it, take a look at the auto industry, where the big manufacturers have methodically and relentlessly winnowed the supplier base. The remaining primary, or "tier one," suppliers are expected to forge more intimate relationships with their customers—the auto companies. At the same time, the suppliers are expected to provide a broad range of services in one-stop-shopping fashion while also meeting specific quality standards, such as ISO 9000 specifications. Companies all the way down the supply chain are being pulled in two opposing directions: specialization and comprehensiveness. The rapid pace of change and increased quality requirements force a company to focus, yet the customers doing the outsourcing are expecting do-it-all solutions. "The suppliers that survive are being asked to provide all kinds of capabilities at reduced costs," says Kenneth Preiss, coauthor of *Cooperate to Compete: Building Agile Business Relationships.* "And that forces them into cooperative relationships with other companies willing to share their core competencies."

In other words, broad but quickly changing market demands can't be met any longer with bricks and mortar, with broad, embedded, inflexible capacity; they must be met by enlisting the skills needed at any given moment to serve a customer for that moment only. And the customers—whether they're large auto companies seeking to outsource or parents shopping for toys—are unforgiving. They don't want to micromanage their supply chains anymore; they want you, dear vendor, to do it for them. So you're out of Playmobil pirate ships? You'd better be able to call the retailer in the next town and have one sent to you—fast. Can't make the mold and produce the part? Find another company to help you do it, or your customer will find someone else who can do it all, leaving you entirely out of the loop. More and more, independence may be prized, but scale is rewarded.

Or so it seems. In fact, it isn't scale that's valued—it's the illusion thereof. Scale, in the traditional sense, has been tried, and it has failed. Remember when vertical integration was all the rage? Large companies that boasted about their ability to manage their processes from beginning to end, totally on their own steam, are now systematically dismantling what they had worked so hard to build. Curiously, they are getting smaller in order to prosper, and are doing so in a way that is transforming our economy. What remains are leaner, more focused versions of their former selves. No longer are they obsessed with scale; they're fixated on scope—the breadth of capability that's achieved by assembling the right players at the right time. They call it "outsourcing" and "strategic partnering." And while entrepreneurs have also embraced those techniques successfully, they're now finding that they, too, must stretch the boundaries of their companies even further—into what once looked like enemy territory.

That's exactly what Harry Brown did. Ten years ago Brown bought an ailing Rustbelt company, Erie Bolt Corp. (now called EBC Industries). He transformed it, mostly by building alliances that are a shining example of what can happen when competitive companies begin to think less about what they make and more about what skills they possess and how they can combine those skills to maximize revenues, reduce costs, and increase quality. Sound a little too idyllic? In the beginning Brown's competitors thought so. "There was resistance at first," recalls EBC president Brown, "but then people saw the success we had." He and his competitors—about 50 of them—jointly market their capabilities to land business they couldn't possibly get alone; they share information about quality systems, consult one another before investing in machinery, use one another's sales reps, and pass on customers to one another. Together they can efficiently serve the customers of the new economy by offering a single point of contact for a variety of products, much the way that our Japanese competitors have done for years.

Do they still compete? Absolutely. For instance, Brown works with a machine shop in Buffalo to produce metal studs because, in this case, combined expertise results in larger profit margins for both companies and a higher-quality product for the customer. But the two bid competitively on jobs that require the manufacturing of special shafts, because each has the ability to make that product efficiently on its own. They let the market—and the numbers—tell them when to choose cooperation over competition and, in the process, create a larger playing field upon which one company's success is less likely to result in another's failure.

Consultants, academics, and economic-development folks know Brown or know of him because he successfully (and unwittingly) created a flexible manufacturing network that many experts believe could—and should—be replicated nationwide. The concept began to take hold in the United States more than a decade ago, when two professors at the Massachusetts Institute of Technology, Charles F. Sabel and Michael J. Piore, published *The Second Industrial Divide.* The book examined the Emilia-Romagna region of northern Italy and its rise to economic prosperity through the creation of networks among small companies. That research inspired captains of government and industry in this country to flock to Italy in search of a model that might help bolster flagging competitiveness in the states.

They came home with visions of a national business agenda that never came to fruition but that, nonetheless, eventually spawned several state and local organizations charged with helping small companies (most commonly, but not exclusively, manufacturers) form networks. "A lot of it turned out to be the marketing of an organizational device," says Sabel, now a professor at Columbia Law School. That "organizational device" took many forms. Like Harry Brown's network, some coalitions of companies were pulled together by a CEO who took on the nearly full-time job of coordinating their efforts. Other groups began to look like hybrid trade associations, while still others actually created separate entities under whose umbrella all cooperative work was organized. Some of those efforts were successful; many were not. What continues to distinguish those that flourish from those that fade is that they not only have found a way to solve the market challenges that brought them together in the first place but have used their collective clout to create new opportunities. Consider the following stories:

- John Anson had been in the equipment-design and -building business for 30 years and was no stranger to the concept of networking. Like many small-business people, he had often called upon friendly competitors to help him out if a job was too big or too complex for his shop to handle. But 4 years ago Anson began feeling pressured by the new demands of outsourcing. "Companies would outsource larger and larger chunks of their business, and I sometimes couldn't handle it alone," he says. When General Electric, a longtime customer, wouldn't even allow Anson to bid on a job because his shop was too small, the Louisville CEO figured it was time for radical measures. He went to his two largest competitors with a plan to complete the $15-million project together; he would coordinate the work while serving as the single point of contact that GE desperately needed.

  Since it landed that contract, in 1993, Anson's network has expanded to include a dozen more companies. The business generated by GE is now worth $60 million, and the networked companies work together on other jobs as well. "It's like combat," says Anson. "You have to use the buddy system." The enemy? Competition from Mexico and the Pacific Rim. "By forming this network, we've given ourselves the opportunity to retain business that would have gone overseas," he says. What's more, Anson's sales have skyrocketed from $3 million to $80 million, and he reckons that the $25 million he's spent on expansion would have been closer to $40 million if it weren't for his network partners. "But it's not just the capital investment that I've saved on," he notes. "It's also the people. I was able to use the talent of the people in those other companies."

- The Oregon Brewers Guild is a group of 40 local microbrewers that network broker Nick Harville, of Gleneden Beach, Oreg., helped assemble three years ago. Originally, the group of brewers banded together to lobby for their common position on legislative issues such as excise taxes and advertising limitations, but they quickly realized that their alliance had marketing power as well. Large breweries had begun creating what Jerome Chicvara, director of sales and marketing at Full Sail Brewing, calls "pseudo craft brews"—a direct assault on the Brewers Guild market. So the guild developed a common quality-assurance label that helps differentiate its members from the knockoffs. "None of them has the financial resources to combat Miller or Anheuser-Busch alone," says Harville.

  Neither would they have the opportunity to test overseas markets on their own. "Our product is still so high-end that the guy on the other end would never want a full container of Full Sail," says Chicvara. "But collectively, we have a portfolio that is very diverse and compelling." Over the past two years Chicvara and seven other guild members have together exported about six shipping containers of beer to Japan, where the appeal of craft brews is just beginning to catch on. They've also wielded their collective clout at home. Last spring they shared a booth and expenses at a Chicago trade show, where Chicvara landed a distribution deal with a 90-store chain in Indiana—not for himself but for four of his competitors.

- Five years ago Bill Hanley, CEO of Galileo Corp., a $34-million Sturbridge, Mass., fiber-optics company, was faced with a dramatic decline in the military contracts that had long constituted the lifeblood of his industry. "When you're faced with a market segment that's shrinking, companies can't start competing with each other more voraciously, or they end up doing each other even more damage," he says. "I viewed the whole industry as being at risk." Hanley's proposal to five of his competitors: come together to promote the Sturbridge area as home to a fiber-optics brain trust. Together they would develop fiber-optics applications for new markets such as the telecommunications and analytical-instrumentation industries, utilities, and hospitals. "We focused on making the pie bigger by marketing ourselves together," says Hanley.

  The group—now comprising 12 companies—formed a separate nonprofit entity called the Center for Advanced Fiber Optic Applications, which markets the combined capabilities of its member companies. Hanley says there are currently a dozen cooperative projects in the works and that "companies are also forming independent alliances on projects outside the center." It seems that cooperation, once mastered, becomes a possibility that one carries into each new business opportunity.

CLOSE ENCOUNTERS OF THE THIRD KIND

Running a "competitor-networked" business isn't like running a small company or a big one—it's a third way of doing business altogether. Here's what we know about competitor networks—and life inside them—after a decade of their existence:

It's Not Easy

"The biggest problem is CEO ego," says Bill Hanley, chief executive of Galileo Corp. "You get five people together who are used to running their own show, and now they have to become part of a team that is interdependent. That's difficult." Hanley says it took 18 months for his group of fiber-optics companies to coalesce and develop trust—18 months of hand-wringing doubt, of wondering, "How much information should I divulge? Could I have this client to myself? Am I jeopardizing my own position in the marketplace?" If there is one phrase uttered most often by CEOs involved in competitor-network relationships, it is this: "It all boils down to trust." Not just trust that your competitor won't steal your secrets or your customers, but trust that forfeiting some of your independence will yield a handsome return.

It Takes a Leader

Show us a successful network, and we will show you a leader who champions it. He or she is the person who drives or coordinates cooperation, the one who refuses to let the others slip back into the old way of doing business. For Harry Brown, that has become a full-time job. "One of the things I've learned is that you can't expect things to flow without day-to-day involvement," he says. Brown's company, $8-million EBC Industries, is usually the lead company on jobs that require input from several of his network partners. Because he accepts liability and responsibility for the final product—in this case, machine parts—he has to make sure that his partners' standards are compatible with his own.

All networks don't function like Brown's, but all were started by individuals with vision. Although CEOs often play that role, a third party can also offer the outside perspective needed to plant the seed. Network brokers, whose very existence is testimony to the growing prominence of this trend, sometimes have a flair for getting overburdened CEOs to see the big picture. And increasingly, state or county economic-development offices promote and aid networking efforts. For instance, Rodney Brown, director of the business and entrepreneurship division of the Kentucky Cabinet for Economic Development, spends 95% of his time helping small companies create manufacturing alliances. "Our role is to turn on the light, then get out of the way," he says.

It Redefines *Competitor*

Rodney Brown recently "turned on the light" for Robin Hunt of H&W Plastic and Charles Rothe of Summit Molding and Engineering, both small custom-molding companies in Kentucky. The two formed a networking arrangement, the Plexus Group, to pursue projects larger than either could manage on its own, in new markets that both would like to penetrate. "What I struggle with most is having to spend a lot of time explaining Plexus to people who know me as H&W Plastic," says Hunt. "They wonder why I would do this with a competitor."

But is Rothe really a competitor? Like so many entrepreneurs who have formed similar relationships, Hunt discovered that a company that looks like a competitor very often appears less threatening when you get a little closer. For example: Rothe's machine are bigger than Hunt's, which means he usually attracts a different kind of job; his expertise is in engineering while hers is in sales and marketing. In short, what they do becomes secondary to the skills and resources they possess.

"What happened in our case is that companies that thought they were going after the same market applications and business segments weren't actually doing that," says Hanley of his fiber-optics network. "We had evolved to serving different segments of the market that were noncompetitive." That realization helped quell the partners' nagging fear of losing customers and compelled them to identify and evaluate their own unique capabilities.

It Makes Specializing Less Risky

"The way the marketplace is developing now, you have to be more specialized, and you have to be fast," says Patricia Stansbury, president of Stansbury Staffing, Inc., a $3.7-million San Francisco-based recruiting and placement firm. That's virtually a universal truth in the new economy. But with specialization comes risk: when you develop a niche, you invariably make painful choices about what you *won't* do. Stansbury's relationship with four competitors eases that pain for everyone involved.

"We'll call each other and say, 'I can't fill this order for my client; can you help?'" she says. "I know they won't go behind my back and try to get the client." Why? Because they need one another too much. Stansbury specializes in graphics, technology, administration, and human resources; another partner is developing a specialty in legal placements; yet another is focusing on conferences and conventions. Their relationship gives them the freedom to specialize because they know they aren't forfeiting their ability to serve a broad range of clients. "It's my relationship with the client that makes all the difference," says Stansbury. "They don't have to call the agency down the street, because I'm doing it for them, and they like that."

It Depends on the Weakest Link

Yes, that's uncomfortable—even dangerous. Your worst nightmare is that your partner's poor quality standards become your problem, jeopardizing your relationship with your most valued clients. It happens. About a year ago Nick Harville, an Oregon network broker, assembled a group of companies to develop wastewater-treatment systems for a particular industry. "On our first project, we found that one of the people in the network was making recommendations for equipment that wasn't up to manufacturer's specs," says Harville. The system didn't work properly, and the group had to absorb substantial retrofitting costs. The offending partner was ousted, and Harville restructured the group. The lesson is obvious but bears repeating: a network or a partnership is only as strong as its weakest link.

But it does also create an uncomfortable interdependence among networked competitors? What happens when such relationships go sour, as some ultimately will, or when they simply dissolve? Harry Brown has seen such things happen; so has Nick Harville. The question often is not whether such a scenario will play itself out, but when and how. In an economy where nearly everyone competes globally and where the only predictable factor is that things will change, one can reasonably expect partners to come and go. "The networks last only as long as the opportunity does," says Harville. How do you know that when your partners leave, they won't take a chunk of your business with them? You don't. But consider what is at stake. "The risk is extraordinarily high if someone cheats," says Hanley. "The group would make it very difficult for that company to participate in the community; a natural process sets that company up for failure." Also bear in mind that an economy driven less by transactions than by relationships fosters an environment in which a loyal customer is less easy to steal. But while "coopetition," the consultant's word for what we're describing, seems to carry with it a set of internal and external checks and balances, it is surely no more risk-free than any other aspect of business. For many, the greater risk is one of lost opportunity.

In the end there are no assurances, no guarantees, no proven formulas for a successful competitor network. "They're all experimenting," says Sabel of Columbia Law School. He worries that people focus too much on the experiment itself and are ultimately blinded to its larger implications. "There's a vision of this network idea that assumes that any form of cooperation is as good as any other form," says Sabel. "But that's just too general. It doesn't put discipline on anyone to change. The real problems have to do with mastering the model of decentralized coordination. You need to be small and flexible in a way that allows you to coordinate with others that are small and flexible." It's like a 6-year-old with a Lego set, meticulously building and rebuilding a model that is a significant expression of ideas and desires that are, nonetheless, ephemeral. There is no expectation of permanence; disassembling comes quickly, with little regret. After all, the marketplace, like a 6-year-old, has a limited attention span, and expects—even rewards—continuous creation and destruction.

Competitor networking is a concept that should revolutionize the way business owners think about producing and marketing a product or service, about capital investment, and about employees, because the proficiency with which CEOs run their own companies will no longer determine how much or how fast those companies grow. Everything will depend on how CEOs manage the process of cooperation within and beyond the boundaries of their companies, the agility with which they recognize a market need, put together the talent to meet it, disperse that talent, and then bring it together again in a way that they—or you—might not have imagined yesterday.

It isn't a particularly tidy way of doing business; it is dynamic and risky, and it defies the labels of "big" or "small." It is a third way of operating—and is as complex, challenging, and mysterious as the other two. Call it competitor networking if you must, but understand that the label is merely a convenient, albeit inadequate, conceit. Before anyone put a name on it or declared it a trend, it was simply the way people like Harry Brown and John Anson did business. It will be the same for Ron German. It will be the same for you.

Donna Fenn (incfenn@aol.com) is a contributing editor at Inc.

A Clash of Philosophies Results in Surprise Switch in Airline Deal

by Wall Street Journal Reporters Scott McCartney, Susan Carey, and Martha Brannigan

Just two days ago, *Continental Airlines* Chairman Gordon Bethune was resigned to losing his job in a *Delta Air Lines* acquisition of his company.

As he headed to New York from Houston for a late-night directors meeting to consider competing bids from Delta and *Northeast Airlines,* the nation's No. 3 and No. 4-ranked airlines, Mr. Bethune busily drafted proposed terms of his own termination.

Meantime, a confident Delta had already conducted job interviews with Continental executives and dispatched senior managers to Houston, Cleveland, London and Mexico City to welcome employees to the "Delta Family."

All of which made the phone call that Delta Chief Executive Leo Mullin got in the wee hours of Monday morning that much more of a shock. It was financier David Bonderman, Continental's controlling shareholder and a company director. He was calling from New York to say that Delta had lost Continental.

"Leo, are you there?" Mr. Bonderman said, according to a person in the room with him at the time.

"Labor?" Mr. Mullin finally replied. "You mean this thing fell apart over labor?"

Thorny questions over the merger of labor forces did prove pivotal in driving Continental into the arms of Northwest, which announced Monday that it had formed a global alliance with Continental. But the labor issue—which centered on preserving seniority for Continental employees in the face of conflicting provisions in Delta's pilot contract—didn't arise purely as a result of Delta's or Continental's loyalty to its work force. Instead, it symbolized a broader clash of egos and philosophies over future control of what would have become the largest airline in the world.

In a statement to employees Monday, Mr. Mullin said that "protection of employee interests was foremost among the issues discussed. The people of Delta provide an extraordinary foundation on which Delta will achieve ongoing levels of future success, and the discussions on the Continental transaction guarded that as the most important priority."

With three Harvard degrees and a reputation as a savvy corporate strategist, Mr. Mullin was adamant about his vision for reshaping the stodgy Delta corporate culture, entrusted to him when he was brought in as CEO of the $13.9 billion airline last August. Meanwhile, as a longtime buyer and seller of companies, Mr. Bonderman, who would have become one of Delta's largest shareholders, was equally determined to protect his investment by putting his own aggressive imprint on that same culture.

The standoff ended in an industry-shaking coup for Northwest, based in St. Paul, Minn., which began pursuing Continental in earnest in November. Monday, Northwest agreed to pay $519 million in cash and stock, or $60.80 a share, for the stake in the nation's fifth-largest airline, owned by Air Partners L.P., the investment group led by Mr. Bonderman and James Coulter, who once worked together managing investments for Texas billionaire Robert Bass.

Northwest and Continental agreed to merge their route networks, frequent-flier programs and marketing, while keeping their employees and airplanes separate. With their complementary operations in the U.S. and Asia—Northwest and Continental currently overlay on only eight routes world-wide—the two airlines will be able to offer complete itineraries from Japan to Latin America, even as far away as Moscow. In 1997, Northwest had revenue of $10.2 billion and Continental had revenue of $7.2 billion.

Northwest will place the Continental shares it acquires—representing 14% of the company but carrying 51% of the voting rights—in a trust, and agreed to give up its voting rights except in limited circumstances. The Class A shares, with voting rights equal to 10 times those of Continental Class B shares, were issued to the Bonderman-led investor group when it brought the airline out of bankruptcy proceedings in 1993. Northwest will pay $300 million in cash and issue 4.1 million new Northwest shares in exchange for the Continental stake.

Executives say Delta isn't likely to try a hostile bid for Continental, especially since Mr. Bonderman told Mr. Mullin he will vote his 51% interest with Northwest. Even when friendly, airline mergers have proved to be tricky and often unprofitable affairs, with the high cost of integration and operating problems canceling cost savings resulting from consolidation. Unhappy employees or scheduling snafus can slow down an airline, causing passengers to seek more-reliable carriers. Delta's Pan Am purchase, for example, almost sank the airline.

The alliance creates a network that rivals *UAL* Corp.'s United Airlines as the largest in the world. And it is likely to force other midsize carriers into the arms of the "Big Three": United, American and Delta. As more corporations and travelers consolidate their flying with a single preferred carrier—for corporate discounts or personal frequent-flier miles—airlines have found they must offer huge global networks to attract the best accounts and busiest road warriors.

What's more, since airplanes are in short supply, carriers face little opportunity for growth unless they can expand through partnerships like Northwest-Continental, which executives estimate will steal $500 million annually in revenue from competitors.

Such partnerships allow for a growth in revenue by merging passengers and winning business away from competitors, without the high cost of integrating labor groups and aircraft fleets. On the flip side, however, there aren't the same long-term cost savings that come from consolidating assets in a merger, and there is the potential for ongoing conflict between the separate-but-equal management teams.

"We firmly believe these types of alliances are the future of our industry," Mr. Bethune says.

US Airways, the nation's sixth-largest carrier, is thought to be the next likely candidate for consolidation or takeover, especially since Chairman and Chief Executive Stephen Wolf has begun winning more productive, economical labor agreements and is revamping the company.

United and *AMR* Corp.'s American both looked at US Air three years ago but deemed it too problematic; both are thought to be more likely US Air partners than Delta, even though the smaller carrier would be vastly more expensive to buy today. Delta would face antitrust scrutiny since it and US Air are heavily concentrated on the East Coast.

"The Street's perception is that Delta is the strategic loser in a Northwest/Continental alliance, because either American or United might be able to do a deal with US Airways that Delta couldn't do," says Samuel Buttrick, an analyst with PaineWebber in New York. "Delta would be left out in the cold."

One winner is Air Partners. It put $66 million of equity into Continental to bring it out of bankruptcy but ran into trouble with a failed attempt to create a low-cost copy of Southwest Airlines dubbed "Continental Lite." Losses from that venture nearly downed Continental, and in January 1995 the company met its payroll only when Mr. Bethune got friends at *Boeing* Co., his former employer, to return aircraft deposits.

But Continental has soared since then, as the airline improved operations and focused on reclaiming business customers, at the same time as the industry staged a big recovery. Continental shares that traded at $3.25 in early 1995 closed Monday at $56.625, up $2.625. Air Partners will walk away from Continental with a total of $780 million, including the latest transaction and earlier stock sales, a spokesman for the group says. Continental had a market capitalization of $175 million when Air Partners stepped in; today, the Houston company is worth more than $3.6 billion.

It was Air Partners' eagerness to cash out its Continental gains that triggered the bidding war.

In late 1996, Continental's Mr. Bethune flew to Atlanta to try to entice Delta to acquire his airline. Those talks soon collapsed amid a lack of interest from Delta, then headed by Ron Allen. After that, Continental President Gregory Brenneman disparaged Delta executives as a "box of rocks" in conversations with industry executives.

Change at Delta

Last May, Mr. Allen was ousted as CEO, and in August, following a long search, he was replaced by Mr. Mullin. A banker turned utility executive—and a newcomer to the airline industry—he moved rapidly to begin shoring up customer service and employee morale, which had suffered under cost-cutting programs. He unveiled an aggressive expansion strategy in Latin America and adopted a plan to refurbish Delta planes and facilities.

But talk of mergers and alliances in the industry continued to grow, and, after learning that Northwest was interested in Continental, Mr. Mullin earlier this month called Mr. Bonderman to explore a merger. Delta named the talks Project Quarry, in an allusion to Mr. Brenneman's "box of rocks" jibe.

Mr. Bonderman, with interests ranging from motorcycles to wineries to food companies, is known to share Mr. Brenneman's concern about Delta management, which he sees as slow and plodding. Eager to protect his investment, Mr. Bonderman insisted from the start that Mr. Mullin hire some of the executives who had helped in the Continental turnaround. Specifically, he wanted Mr. Brenneman and Chief Financial Officer Lawrence Kellner to get similar posts at Delta.

But Mr. Mullin balked at taking the entire Continental slate, and wouldn't put Mr. Brenneman in charge of Delta's operations. He also made clear he wouldn't give up the Delta CEO title, meaning there wouldn't be any room for Mr. Bethune at Delta. "Leo kept saying he wanted to preserve the Delta culture," people involved in the talks say.

Pilot Seniority

Part of that negotiating stance also included Mr. Mullin's determination not to upset his own pilots, who remain bitter about a severe cost-cutting program by his predecessor, Mr. Allen.

Delta's pilots had been pressured into accepting a concessionary new labor contract in the spring of 1996. Then, just two months later, the Delta board abandoned its cost-cutting goals, and pilots felt snookered. Since Delta's pilot contract ensures them a major voice in how pilot groups are integrated and seniority rankings are set in a merger, Mr. Mullin refused to cave in to Continental's demands that its pilots get equal footing in the merged pecking order.

Continental executives argued that, unless the two labor forces were merged based on seniority, as was the case when Delta acquired Western Airlines in 1987 and Pan American in 1991, Continental employees would revolt. Then the merger would become an unwiedy disaster, threatening the value of Mr. Bonderman's investment.

He had reason to be worried. After a breakfast briefing by Continental management on the Delta proposal Sunday morning, Continental pilots began planning a slowdown of the airline that would have begun Monday if Continental's directors had taken Delta's offer, according to persons close to the situation.

Northwest Concessions

Meanwhile, after learning of Delta's bid last Thursday, Northwest scurried to sweeten its offer. It agreed to give up voting rights on the Continental stock except in extreme cases like mergers, giving Continental executives the autonomy they wanted. In addition, Northwest's bid of $60.80 a share in cash and stock was higher than Delta's top bid of slightly more than $57 a share.

Since Northwest was offering to acquire only a limited stake instead of the whole company—and since full implementation of its plan still requires approval from Northwest's pilots—it wasn't hopeful. "I was not confident we had the best deal," says Northwest Chief Executive John Dasburg. "This is not the type of process that inspires confidence."

But as the talks entered their home stretch, Northwest had some subtle advantages that began to emerge more clearly for Continental executives. The carriers have cultures that are more similar than those at the Big

Three airlines. Both tend to run leaner operations. Both have been to the brink before, with Continental going through two bankruptcy-court reorganizations and Northwest nearly headed into Chapter 11 until it won last-minute concessions from its workers in 1993. And at least four senior Northwest executives have worked at Continental. "One of the most dominant tribal strains at Northwest is Continental," remarks one Northwest observer.

Other Alliances

Northwest also has had long experience—both good and bad—in its alliance with KLM Royal Dutch Airlines. And Continental has been an eager and adept arranger of international alliances, and a successful domestic code-sharing partnership with *America West* Airlines. "Alliances are the best way of dealing with a global customer base," says Mr. Dasburg, adding that Northwest has been shopping for a domestic partner for three or four years.

As the negotiations continued, small disputes with Delta began to raise eyebrows at Continental. A 52-page merger model that Delta presented that was rife with cost-cutting ideas and a plan for 5,000 layoffs was troubling. Delta also asked how much it would cost to terminate the naming deal on Continental Airlines Arena in New Jersey's Meadowlands. Since Delta-Continental would be the biggest carrier in New York, Continental executives didn't understand why Delta wouldn't want the naming rights.

But despite such stumbling blocks, the deal still seemed to be Delta's to lose. On Thursday, Mr. Bonderman traveled to Atlanta from a Caribbean vacation and held five hours of talks with Mr. Mullin and Delta Chairman Gerald Grinstein, in an effort to hash out issues involving executive positions after a merger.

Even into the Sunday-night board meeting, where both bidders had been told to deliver their best and final offer, Continental executives presumed Delta would change its stance on labor, especially since almost every merger in the industry has been carried out under the arbitrated seniority system called Allegheny-Mohawk, including Delta's two mergers, both of which involved Chairman Grinstein. Before the Sunday meeting began, Mr. Brenneman, the Continental president, bet Chief Financial Officer Mr. Kellner $100 that Delta would come around on the labor issue, say people in the room at the time. Mr. Bonderman also figured Delta would come around on the labor issue.

Mr. Mullin, on the other hand, never saw the labor dispute as a deal-killer, and thought it should be sufficient for Delta to extend assurances that the Continental employees would be treated equitably, people involved say. He didn't budge.

Halfway through the seven-hour board meeting Sunday night, Continental called Mr. Mullin, who was huddled with Mr. Grinstein and other top executives in offices at Delta's headquarters, and asked, "Is this it?" There was no specific discussion of the labor issues at that point, people involved say.

Finally, a panel of five independent directors considered the two bids because Mr. Bonderman and several other board members had conflicts of interest. The panel recommended the Northwest offer be accepted, and the full board agreed. At that point, Mr. Bonderman placed the call telling Mr. Mullin that Delta's bid had failed.

With mergers and alliances sweeping through the industry, Mr. Bethune, the Continental chairman, was stunned that Delta didn't change the terms of its bid. "Never in my life have I thought stupidity would save anyone," he told his directors, "but it sure saved me tonight."

Monday, Delta officials strived to put the best face on things. In New York Stock Exchange trading Monday, Delta shares closed down $1.6875 at $112.3125; Northwest shares closed in Nasdaq trading up $4.5625 at $55.3125. "Delta has a great strategic platform for growth and prosperity from our strategic base. Continental offered an add-on, not an essential feature," Mr. Mullin said in an interview. "This was an opportunity that came about. It did represent a chance to substantially improve our operation.

"It didn't work out," he added. "The next time it will."

Hewlett-Packard Plans to Market Its Own Strain of Java Technology

by Lee Gomes
Staff Reporter of THE WALL STREET JOURNAL

Hewlett-Packard Co. plans to market its own variant of Java software, breaking with *Sun Microsystems* Inc. and opening a rift in an industry alliance against *Microsoft* Corp.

H-P said it has developed its own specifications and software for running Java programs on a range of electronic devices, including its widely used computer printers. The big Palo Alto, Calif., computer and electronics concern now plans to compete with Sun, creator of the Java programming language, by trying to find customers for its technology. Indeed, H-P has already signed up Microsoft, Sun's nemesis. The Redmond, Wash., software giant has agreed to use the new flavor of Java along with its Windows CE operating system.

H-P's plans, to be announced Friday, are a blow to Sun in its bid to control the evolution of Java and profit by its spread from computers into higher-volume markets. Because Java is designed to run on any operating system, it is regarded as a major weapon for Microsoft's rivals, many of which are Sun competitors that have nonetheless built the Java programming technology into their product plans. The rift signaled by H-P comes just a few days before a Sun-sponsored conference in San Francisco that is expected to attract more than 10,000 Java-software programmers.

Joe Beyers, general manager of H-P's Internet-software business unit, said the company decided to act independently out of frustration over what he called "excessive" licensing fees that Sun was seeking for a consumer-electronics version of Java. Mr. Beyers stressed that H-P's ultimate goal isn't to build a business out of selling Java software, but to pry control of Java away from Sun and place it in the hands of an industrywide group that no single company controls.

Analysts said H-P's introduction of a different strain of Java for appliances and consumer devices, if not reconciled, could create the sort of rival-product camps and software incompatibilities that Java was designed to avoid. Tim Sloan of Boston's Aberdeen Group said H-P's move is a "turning point" for Java, analogous to the first time that *International Business Machines* Corp.'s personal computer was cloned.

Alan Baratz, who runs Sun's Java-software division, dismissed H-P's move as a "publicity stunt" and a negotiating ploy to wrest more favorable terms from Sun. And he predicted H-P will have little marketing success because potential customers may be concerned about supporting a splinter Java faction.

Java has won a wide following among software companies because of technical advantages that allow its programs to run on any Java-equipped computer, regardless of the machine's operating system. Ever since Sun introduced the Java language in 1995, with its "write-once, run anywhere" flexibility, the company has maintained that it could loosen Microsoft's sway over computing, since programmers can look to Sun, rather than Microsoft, for technical direction. But so far, Java has failed to dent Microsoft's growth; in fact, most Java programmers write software for use in Microsoft's various Windows operating systems.

Even Microsoft, however, has licensed Java and included a virtual machine in its Web browser. But it has refused to include all of Sun's modifications in its latest versions. Sun responded by suing Microsoft for allegedly violating the licensing contract, a charge Microsoft denies.

More recently, Java supporters have proposed going beyond computers to use slimmed-down versions of Java for new consumer devices, such as Internet-based telephones and kitchen and living-room appliances that can communicate with each other. H-P envisions, for example, printers that are automatically able to connect to the Internet and order a new printing cartridge. It also has plans for a new breed of consumer devices, such as health-care products for the home.

Mr. Beyers said H-P remains a licensee and supporter of Sun's Java specifications for computers. But after unsuccessfully negotiating with Sun, H-P unilaterally selected a subset of Java that it thought would be appropriate for consumer products. It then wrote its own "virtual machine," a piece of software that could run on those products and execute Java programs; it is the virtual machine that H-P will market to other companies.

A Microsoft spokesman confirmed that it licensed H-P's virtual-machine software for use with Windows CE, an operating system that Microsoft is pushing for hand-held computers, TV set-top devices, factory-automation systems and other fields. Microsoft said the H-P technology is particularly compact, and is useful for classes of devices that its own Java virtual machine can't yet address.

Sun insists that all Java licensees have input in the direction of Java. Sun's contracts, besides assessing royalties, require companies to share any Java improvements with Sun and other licensees. But Sun makes final decisions, a situation that sometimes grates on other companies.

"A lot of companies are unhappy with the degree of control that Sun is trying to have over Java," said David Folger at the Meta Group Inc. of Stamford, Conn. "Now, H-P is offering an alternative, and I bet they'll have a fair degree of success."

Harry Fenik, of Zona Research Inc. in Redwood City, Calif., said H-P's move was inevitable, considering how important Java has become to the computer industry. Big companies such as H-P, said Mr. Fenik, are unlikely to cede control over Java to Sun, since they are often vigorous competitors in the business-computer marketplace. And in particular, they aren't eager to pay Sun a continuing royalty stream for high-volume products such as printers.

Sun's plans for Java in the consumer world are clearly ambitious. At next week's JavaOne conference, various companies plan to show Java running on a wide variety of devices, from gas pumps to coffee pots. "We are heading toward the billions if not tens of billions of devices using Java," said Scott McNealy, Sun's chief executive, in an interview last week.

Mr. Beyers said that because H-P has no license with Sun for a consumer-flavored Java, it has no obligation to make any payments to Sun in connection with its product. Mr. Baratz agreed that H-P had the legal right to make the Java product it announced, assuming H-P is correct when it says that it wrote all the software from scratch. In the Microsoft suit, by contrast, Sun alleges that Microsoft used Sun's technology in a way that violated the licensing contract.

CEO Pay at the Crossroads of Wall Street and Main: Toward the Strategic Design of Executive Compensation

Wayne Grossman and Robert E. Hoskisson

Executive Overview

Incentive or performance contingent compensation plans are rapidly becoming the norm in corporate America, as boards of directors attempt to make executives more accountable to shareholders. However, incentive plans also expose executives to risk, and may also impart a short-term bias on their decision-making processes. This article suggests that the tension between the pressures for accountability and long-term decision making can be managed by aligning firm strategy with an incentive plan that is based on an appropriate performance criteria.

Over the years, few topics have generated as much controversy as executive compensation. At the heart of the controversy is the relationship between executive pay and firm performance. The notion that the rewards given to the custodians of American enterprise should be linked to firm performance is consistent with academic theory and intuitively appealing. Yet, for the most part, academic researchers have been stymied in their search for a meaningful association between executive pay and firm performance.[1] The discussion becomes particularly acrimonious during the annual proxy season, after the business press ferrets out those chief executive officers who received hefty rewards despite declining earnings or substandard stock returns. The apparent lack of a relationship between executive pay and firm performance has led to calls for reform from various organizational stakeholders, including organized labor, public policy makers, and especially shareholder activists. In response to these pressures from organizational constituencies, boards of directors appear to be de-emphasizing fixed salary, and explicitly linking executive rewards to some objective measure of firm performance. Accordingly, performance contingent compensation plans are rapidly becoming the norm in corporate America.[2] Examples of incentive plans include annual bonuses, performance plans, stock options, stock appreciation rights, and restricted stock.[3] However, while the use of incentive compensation plans has been widely lauded by corporate governance pundits, their proliferation has raised some serious issues concerning their potential effects on managerial behavior.

Some critics have charged that linking compensation to objective and explicit performance measures may cause managers to emphasize short-term profitability at the expense of the long-term viability of the firm.[4] Performance contingent incentives may cause managers to forego strategic investment opportunities that are inherently risky because of their long-term payoffs (e.g., product or process R&D and human resource expenditures aimed at developing a highly trained and productive workforce), and focus instead on maximizing short-term profitability and shareholder wealth. In other words, managers may abandon long-term strategies that benefit a diverse group of organizational stakeholders in favor of meeting capital market demands for near-term cash flows. In a classic work entitled, "On the Folly of Rewarding A, While Hoping for B," (recently reprinted in this journal), author Steven Kerr suggested that this results in a misalignment between strategy and executive compensation.[5]

Accordingly, extensive reliance on incentive compensation may be a double edged sword. On the one hand, incentives foster enhanced managerial accountability and promote the alignment of manager and shareholder interests. Alternatively, incentive compensation may be the source of a financially driven managerial myopia that ultimately threatens long-term competitiveness. Therefore, executive compensation is truly at the crossroads of Wall Street and Main. Is the increasing use of incentives in the executive suite an innovation that contributes to efficiency, economic growth, and expanding employment opportunities, or does it merely benefit a small class of already wealthy capital providers?

In order to better understand the potential effect of incentive compensation on executive decision-making horizons, the following discussion briefly outlines the issue's intellectual background. Additionally, we offer some credible suggestions on how those involved in the design and implementation of executive compensation contracts (e.g., boards of directors, compensation consultants, major shareholders, executives, and public policy makers) can better manage the tension between strategy, performance, and compensation.

This tension can potentially be managed by using an appropriate measure of firm performance as a basis for rewarding incentives. Incentive rewards are often based on accounting-based measures (e.g., earning per share, return on equity, or changes in net income), or stock price performance (e.g., capital gains). As discussed below, each of these measures may be different in terms of its ability to evaluate performance strategically. Therefore, the choice of using either accounting- or market-based performance measures to reward executives may have important effects on their decision-making horizons. For example, it may be appropriate for executives in certain firms to focus on short-term operational efficiency where strategy matches this focus. Alternatively, other strategies might require managers to be more forward looking.

Incentive Problems in the Publicly Owned Firm

Combined Ownership and Control

Traditional economics has a highly simplified view of firms, markets, and managers. Individual firms cannot influence the price of their products, since it is assumed that there are a large number of small firms (the "perfect market"). A given firm's cost structure is derived from existing technology, and the cost of a unit of product is largely a function of a firm's scale, or the aggregate number of units produced by the firm.

In this classical model, incentives do not pose a problem. The manager is assumed to be both the owner, or the individual entitled to profits generated from the operation of the firm, as well as the controller of the firm's assets. The principle of profit maximization is assumed to be sufficient to motivate and guide managers because, as owners, they directly benefit from incremental profits. This view is simplified because, in reality, the ownership and control of firms are often separate functions. This is especially the case for large corporations that are traded on the public stock exchanges. Given that such firms tend to drive the controversy over CEO pay) perhaps because compensation data is publicly available), and also account for the lion's share of the economy, it is important to understand how the separation of ownership and control influences incentives.

The Separation of Ownership and Control

The separation of ownership and control is characteristic of the modern public corporation and describes relationships in firms that are owned by a diffuse set of absentee shareholders who through their delegates, the board of directors, retain professional managers to control and manage firm assets. Shareholders maintain the right to receive dividends and capital gains on their stock, and the professional managers receive compensation in return for the decision-making services they render. These professional managers may hold little if any of the firm's equity.[6] These relationships are generally regarded as one way to manage risk. Shareholders are perhaps more capable of bearing risk than managers, since typically, only a small proportion of their total wealth is tied to the fortunes of an individual firm. Despite risk-bearing efficiencies, there are potential incentive problems associated with the separation of ownership and control. Often these have led to calls for reform and regulatory intervention. Even in the latter half of the 18th century, Adam Smith wrote,

---

The directors of such companies however, being the managers rather of other people's money than of their own, it cannot well be expected that they should watch over it with the same anxious vigilance with which the partners in a private copartnery frequently watch over their own. Like the stewards of a rich man, they are apt to consider attention to small matters as not for their master's honour, and very easily give themselves a dispensation from having it. Negligence and confusion, therefore, must always prevail, more or less, in the management of the affairs of such a company.[7]

In recent years, the incentive problem of publicly held firms has been exemplified in the issue of executive compensation. The unprecedented growth in the level of executive compensation has led to calls for reform. For example, a survey of executive compensation published in Business Week reported that Michael D. Eisner, chairman and CEO of the Walt Disney Corporation received approximately $203 million in salary, bonus, and long-term compensation in 1993.[8] A similar survey in 1991 reported that Anthony J. F. O'Reilly, Chairman, President, and CEO of the H.J. Heinz Company received approximately $75 million that year.[9] Considering the rates of growth and increases in shareholder value these companies have achieved in recent years, one might argue that this level of compensation is well deserved. However, in the current era of corporate restructuring and downsizing, pay packages such as these evoke a strong sense of inequity, and calls for reform have increased in intensity. Thus, compensation plan designers may find themselves under certain institutional pressures to explicitly link pay to performance. But when those efforts bear fruit, they are often criticized.

The Double Edged Sword of Pay for Performance

If Incentives Are So Great, Why Don't Firms Use Them?

Despite the intuitive appeal of pay for performance, it seems that boards of directors did not use such compensation as a motivational tool in the past. Research has found the relationship between executive pay and performance to be relatively trivial, when it exists at all. In a comprehensive study of over 2000 CEOs, Michael C. Jensen and Kevin J. Murphy found that CEO wealth changes $3.25 for every $1000 in shareholder wealth.[10] Jensen and Murphy argued that this weak association, is in part, caused by what they term "implicit regulation." Implicit regulation includes strong social forces that prevent boards of directors from paying CEOs "too much," even within the context of high firm performance.

The argument that the level of executive compensation is more closely associated with managerial power than with firm performance has received much more support. Research indicates that pay and performance have a much stronger relationship in firms that have a dominant shareholder that can discipline top managers (e.g., an institutional investor or an individual who owns a significant proportion of the firm's voting stock).[11]

Research also finds that the level of executive compensation is driven more by firm size than by performance.[12] There may be a number of reasons for this. First, large firms tend to be more complex. Therefore, high levels of compensation for CEOs of large firms may be a way of attracting, motivating, and retaining skilled managers who can manage this complexity. A more cynical approach to the relationship between firm size and executive compensation views the manager as an empire builder. In this view, the executive is thought to be acutely aware of the relationship between the size of the firm and both compensation and managerial prestige. Therefore, managers will be motivated to pursue the growth of the firm independent of profitability. Some have suggested that this dynamic causes managers to expand the firm by diversifying into areas that are incompatible with the firm's core competencies, and often results in substandard performance.

There is growing skepticism about the capacity of top executives and boards of directors to adequately police themselves. Michael C. Jensen, a financial economist, recently noted that certain practices—such as loading the board of directors with insiders, or allowing CEOs to also hold the position of chairman of the board—allow executives to take over the system of corporate governance, and engage in self-interested behaviors at the expense of firm shareholders. Jensen argues that this often results in substandard firm performance, and ultimately, threatens long-term, national competitiveness.[13] In response, there is a trend to increase the proportion of independent, outside directors who sit on the board.[14]

Such governance problems would result in executive compensation packages composed primarily of high fixed salaries that are largely independent of firm performance. Packages set under these circumstances presumably have little motivational value. Reformers often argue that corporate governance systems must be reconfigured to emphasize shareholder interests. This might include appointing a majority of outside, independent directors, and adopting pay packages with components—such as stock options, restricted stock, or stock appreciation rights—that directly link executive compensation to shareholder wealth. Although the use of such capital market oriented plans may be intuitively appealing, it assumes that stockholders are the primary (if not exclusive) constituency of top management. However, the potential costs associated with such plans may be why boards have been reluctant to use them in the past.

Incentives, Risk Bearing, and Strategy

Perhaps one reason firms fail to link executive pay to performance is that such policies may adversely affect managers' willingness to pursue risky strategies, and therefore may contribute to shorter decision-making horizons, or to managerial myopia. Under incentive plans, managers directly bear the costs of suboptimal decisions made in good faith. Therefore, incentive plans may provide managers with a disincentive to invest in long-term strategies with uncertain outcomes. Risky strategies might include investing in research and development projects to introduce new products or processes, the pursuit of new market opportunities, or the development of human resources.

Interestingly, it has also been suggested that top managers' risk-bearing concerns have also led to strategic misdirection of firms. The added risk that incentive plans impose on managers may have caused them to venture into lines of business that are unrelated to, and potentially incompatible with their firm's traditional core competency.[15] Shareholders can manage investment risk at a relatively low cost by diversifying their investment portfolio. However, managers' fates are often tied to the fortunes of a single firm. When the firm goes out of business or declares bankruptcy, the manager's reputation may be severely damaged, making it difficult to secure an equivalent position. Thus, managers must bear a certain level of risk associated with their employment. Some have suggested that this has led to efforts to stabilize earnings over the economic cycle through strategies of unrelated, or conglomerate diversification.[16] The performance of many conglomerates has been less than stellar, and may have led to the capital market-driven restructuring wave that recently swept over corporate America.

Accordingly, boards of directors may have been reluctant to explicitly link executive pay to firm performance in order to prevent dysfunctional outcomes (e.g., cutting back on necessary R&D or suboptimal levels of conglomerate diversification). Boards of directors may be sensitive to potential risk-bearing concerns, and this may be one reason why the relationship between executive pay and firm performance has been so elusive (at least in the past). Yet, boards of directors cannot ignore institutional pressures that demand increased accountability and justification for executive compensation packages. For example, a recent study has found that firms that adopt incentive plans often don't use them. The firms may only want to provide the appearance of holding managers accountable.[17]

To design *and use* incentive compensation contracts to manage the apparent tension between strategies that require a different performance emphasis, organizations should base compensation on a measure of firm performance that is consistent with overall firm strategy. Firms should also consider tailoring the reward schedule by using forms of deferred compensation.

Considering Firm Strategy

The Problem with Performance

Much of the criticism leveled at incentive compensation is aimed at the performance standards to which executive pay is tied, usually accounting earnings and stock returns. Plans linked to accounting earnings include annual bonuses and performance plans. Performance plans often reward managers on the basis of long-term (i.e., three to five year) growth in annual earnings per share. Alternatively, stock grants, restricted shares, and stock options reward managers more for stock price performance. Both accounting- and market-based incentives have been criticized for their effect on managerial decision horizons.

Accounting-based incentives have been criticized for their emphasis on the short term. Many expenditures that benefit the firm over the long-term are treated as expenses in the determination of current accounting earnings. Such expenditures include those for research and development that are necessary for product and process innovation, those for advertising and promotion aimed at developing new markets, and those for continuing employee education and development. When executive pay is contingent upon accounting earnings, these expenditures may reduce executive pay. Accordingly, rewarding executives on the basis of accounting earnings may provide a disincentive for them to make these long-term expenditures.[18]

Stock market-based incentives have also been criticized for their potential effect on decision horizons. Because of their own short-term reward schemes, institutional investors such as mutual funds, insurance companies, and pension plans pressure managers for high levels of current performance.[19] Furthermore, stock price is influenced to a great extent by factors outside managers' control, including the general level of inflation interest rates, and perhaps capital market speculation.[20] Executives may therefore try to compensate for the high levels of environmental risk imposed upon them by incentive plans by reducing the risk factors they have control over. For example, they may cut back on risky projects, or diversify a firm's portfolio of business units.[21]

The criticisms of financial measures of firm performance have led to calls for a more careful consideration of firm goals and strategies when rewarding managers.[22] Increasingly popular is the "balanced scorecard" approach, which adds alternative criteria to those financial measures traditionally used to evaluate and reward managers.[23] These criteria include customer satisfaction, internal processes, as well as innovation and learning.[24] While this approach has intuitive appeal and shows much promise, its use to evaluate and reward CEOs is problematic. First, these criteria are difficult and potentially costly to measure. Second, one of the duties of the CEO is to interact with the board of directors and the capital markets. However, firms may be reluctant to disclose performance criteria because these measures are so relevant, and may yield proprietary information.[25] The SEC's 1992 revised disclosure rules for executive compensation require firms to specifically comment on the association between firm performance and CEO compensation, including a description of each performance measure used, whether quantitative or qualitative.[26]

Despite the criticism that both accounting and market measures have received, they continue to be used when incentive plans are implemented, perhaps because each can be determined at low cost, is objective, is highly visible, and, at least superficially, is easy to understand.[27] The question remains whether these measures can be used more effectively. For some firms, one performance measure may be more informative than the other. That is, it might measure firm performance with less extraneous noise and impose fewer uncontrollable risk factors on top executives. It may therefore be important for boards of directors, compensation consultants, and executives to understand how accounting and market performance measures behave within the context of overall firm strategy.

Accounting Performance and Firm Strategy

Economists have criticized the accuracy of accounting based rates of returns, despite their widespread use to measure firm performance. Two shortcomings of accounting based rates of return are that they do not reflect economic substance, and that they are historical, or backward looking. They may not reflect economic substance since there are significant and important differences between cash flow and earnings (e.g., depreciation, accruals, and deferrals). They are historical because they tend to measure the net effect of past transactions. Because of the uncertainty surrounding the outcomes of executive decisions, accounting earnings do not consider the effects that decisions have on future cash flows. For example, accounting standards require that many expenditures that, in substance, are investments for the future be treated as expenses in the determination of annual earnings (e.g., R&D expenditures). These shortcomings have led economists to criticize accounting returns as largely irrelevant for measuring firm performance.[28] Alternatively, because capital markets are considered to be more forward looking (at least in theory), it is often suggested that stock price performance is a more accurate manifestation of firm performance.

However, there are certain advantages associated with accounting performance, particularly if firm strategy is considered. Therefore, incentive compensation plans responsive to changes in accounting performance may be useful in firms pursuing strategies consistent with the properties mentioned above. Because they measure past performance, accounting earnings may be useful in firms with cash flows that tend to be stable between periods. In such firms, innovation and the requisite risky investments may not be necessary to create and sustain a competitive advantage. Past performance may be a good predictor of future performance.

Accounting measures may also be especially useful for firms whose operational efficiency and cost containment are critical success factors necessary to create and sustain a competitive advantage. Unlike stock market returns, which are aggregated, accounting returns can be broken down into a much finer level of detail, including specific components of revenue and expense. Accordingly, accounting returns may be more useful than aggregate stock market returns when costs and efficiency are of primary importance.

Finally, because accounting returns are allocable to lines of business, they may be useful in certain types of diversified, multibusiness firms. Many techniques have been developed by the accounting profession to allocate revenue and expense to various lines of business in order to determine their contribution to overall firm performance. Additionally, advances in information technology, and the advent of activity based costing have improved the accuracy of the allocation process.[29]

Since accounting returns may measure firm performance well under stable conditions, provide fine-grained information on efficiency, and are allocable, they may effectively evaluate the performance of top executives of firms in which these properties are useful. Accounting-based incentive plans, including annual bonuses and various performance plans may be useful for firms pursuing the following strategies.

Cost Leadership Strategies

Firm strategy can generally be analyzed at the business and corporate levels. Business level strategy deals with decisions about how to complete in a given product market or industry.[30] Corporate level strategies are decisions typically made in multibusiness firms about which particular product or geographic markets to compete in. Michael Porter suggest that there two generic business level strategies—cost leadership and differentiation.[31] Firms following cost leadership strategies attempt to achieve a competitive advantage by providing customers with a quality product at a less expensive price than rivals. It is achieved through vigorous pursuit of economies of scale, tight cost and overhead control, and cost minimization in areas like R&D, service, sales, and advertising. A significant focus on cost containment is required. A product with few frills or a highly standardized product are amenable to cost leadership strategies.

In firms that focus on cost control, both net accounting earnings and their costs potentially provide managers with meaningful information. When cost information is used in conjunction with budgeting procedures, it can be used to set specific goals useful to direct activity toward meeting overall strategic targets (i.e., cost leadership). Accounting-oriented incentives can therefore focus attention on operational efficiency, so important to achieving a cost leadership position.

Slow- and Standard-Cycle Resource Profiles

Business level strategies can also be described in terms of the resources firms invest in. This resource-based view suggests that the key role of strategists is to sustain the profitability of resources under their control. Success often breeds imitation, and in time, even the most innovative of firms may see its advantage erode as competitive dynamics evolve. Thus, strategy involves not only deploying resources profitably, but also ensuring that this profitability is enduring.[32]

It has been suggested that firm resource profiles roughly fall into three categories—slow-cycle, standard-cycle, and fast-cycle.[33] Slow-cycle resources are strongly shielded from competitive pressures. They are not readily imitated by competitors. Examples of such inimitable resources include technologies that are protected by patents, enduring brand names, and capabilities based on unique human resources. The competitive advantages associated with slow cycle resources tend to erode slowly. Firms that tend to rely on such resources can be protected by regulation (such as a patent or a franchise granted by the government to operate a public utility), or simply because such resources are complex and difficult to imitate (for example, consumer preference behavior with respect to loyalty for a particular brand is not easy to understand and imitate). Slow cycle firms tend to operate in sheltered, monopoly-like markets. Relationships are typically stable and long-term in nature, with relatively low rates of capital investment.

Standard-cycle resource profiles support products and services that are characterized by mass production technologies. Products are often standardized and produced at high volume. Economies of scale are often important, and therefore production tends to be concentrated among a few large rivalrous firms (e.g., an oligopoly). Such products are more amenable to imitation than those produced by slow-cycle firms and accordingly, standard cycle firms tend to compete on both price and product attributes. Capital investment tends to be more intense than in slow cycle firms as these rivalrous firms must continually protect brand image though advertising and promotion, or develop more efficient and less costly production techniques. The automobile and consumer products industries tend to be dominated by standard cycle type firms.

Finally, fast-cycle resource profiles support products characterized by rapid technological obsolescence and competitive pressures. These types of products are very dynamic and focus on innovation (e.g., biotechnology or electronics). Markets are continually being redefined as firms strive to out compete one another on technological bases. In the words of the noted Austrian economist Joseph Schumpeter, rivalry can be described as a process of "creative destruction."[34] Paradoxically, profitability is not sustained by innovation in fast-cycle firms, but rather is instantly eroded as technological diffusion occurs. The electronics industry is an example of a fast-cycle industry. Innovative firms briefly profit on as they are able to charge a premium price for technological advances. However, prices rapidly fall as competitors adopt these innovations, and production efficiencies are developed.

Accounting-based performance incentives may be useful in both slow- and standard-cycle firms. As discussed above, accounting earnings are a reflection of past cash flows. In slow-cycle firms, cash flows tend to be stable between periods, and therefore accounting earnings may accurately reflect substantive economic performance. Additionally, cost containment and efficiencies are vital to success in standard-cycle firms. Therefore, because accounting earnings comprise more fine-grained cost data, they may be useful in assessing the efficiency of standard-cycle firms. Linking top executive pay to accounting earnings in slow- and standard-cycle firms may create an effective incentive to get them to act strategically, and pursue a high level of performance consistent with overall strategy.

Unrelated Diversification Strategies

Unrelated diversification strategies (conglomerates) are corporate level strategies in which a particular firm may have business units that have little if any synergy between them. Top managers of conglomerates often rely on tight financial controls, including reliance on budgets, strict adherence to return on investment targets, and compensation plans that link business unit manager's rewards to business unit performance. The relatively intense use of financial control is perhaps the most cost-effective way to manage these firms because top managers cannot be expected to be intimately familiar with operating details of vastly different business units. The identification of a particular business unit's contribution to the overall bottom line is vital to the success of these firms, and the fact that accounting earnings are allocable make them especially useful in this regard. Additionally, because of information processing limitations of top management, the business units that conglomerates tend to manage successfully are in mature industries, where cash flows are relatively stable or predictable between periods.[35] Therefore, accounting-oriented incentive plans may be useful in the unrelated diversified firm.

A distinction should be drawn between the evaluation and reward of top corporate executives in conglomerates and of business-level or divisional managers. Because stock market returns measure the performance of an entire firm, they may not be appropriate for evaluating and rewarding divisional managers. This may be particularly true for firms with a portfolio of highly autonomous, unrelated business units. However, given that top corporate executives have responsibility for the strategic direction of the entire firm, it may seem appropriate to reward them on the basis of stock price performance. However, evaluating and rewarding corporate and business level managers on entirely different performance parameters may create incompatible goals, unrealistic expectations on the part of corporate level managers, and, in general, lead to intra-organizational conflict between headquarters and the divisions.[36]

Highly Leveraged Capital Structures

The late 1980s saw a profound change in the capital structures of some major U.S. firms. Many firms significantly reconfigured their capital structures to include a higher proportion of debt financing. This was often accomplished through the leveraged buyout (LBO). In LBOs, a group of buyers (often takeover specialists such as Kohlberg Kravis Roberts, or a firm's top management team) purchases a particular company from existing stock-holders often at a substantial premium. In order to finance the purchase of outstanding stock, bonds are issued that are collateralized on firm assets and that also pay a significant above-market interest rate. These so-called "junk bonds" were very controversial because they were highly risky from an investment standpoint, and because they enabled takeover groups to acquire companies with little if any equity interest in the transaction.

Some have suggested, however, that the heavy use of debt associated with leveraged buyouts was efficient in certain circumstances. Highly leveraged capital structures may serve as an effective control for firms operating in mature industries, where there is little opportunity for profitable reinvestment. Firms operating in such environments are likely to generate substantial amounts of free cash flow. Unlike dividends, which are subject to managerial discretion, interest payments must be made on a timely basis. Thus, the high yield debt associated with leveraged buyouts may effectively discipline top management teams and force them to remit free cash flows to capital providers rather than diverting them for their own use.[37]

Given the mature environments in which these firms may operate, the historical nature of accounting earnings may make accounting-based incentives a relatively accurate measure of firm performance. Efficiency and cost containment are also likely to be very important for the success of debt constrained firms. Therefore, because they include detailed cost information, accounting earnings may be a useful basis for incentives in highly leveraged firms.[38]

Stock Market Performance and Firm Strategy

Stock market based incentives have been criticized for imposing a short-term bias, or managerial myopia, on executive decision-making because of pressures from institutional investors, speculation, and factors beyond managers' control. However, the efficient markets hypothesis is in sharp contrast to the view that capital markets are short-term and myopic, and forms the basis of modern investment theory.[39] In general, the efficient markets hypothesis holds that all information concerning the future cash flows of the firm, whether long- or short-term, is immediately reflected in share price. Therefore, changes in share price reflect changes in a firm's underlying fundamental value, or in its capacity to generate cash flow in the future, and represent the capital market's evaluation of firm strategy.

Projects that are risky, but are perceived by the capital market to have positive cash flow potential, are appropriately valued by the market. The level of risk is simply incorporated into the firms' cost of capital. It has been argued that the highly liquid and responsive U.S. capital markets actually foster innovation and risk taking by facilitating the rapid and correctly valued flow of capital toward risky endeavors. Several studies document the positive association between share price and R&D expenditures.[40] Unlike accounting-based measures where R&D is expensed, R&D expenditures tend to be capitalized in share price. Therefore, considerable controversy exists as to whether market-based incentives contribute to innovation or induce managerial myopia.

Some of these controversies can be addressed by considering firm strategy. If long-term expenditures such as R&D are reflected in share price, then the utilization of stock market-based incentives may be more effective in certain contexts. Incentive contracts such as stock options, stock grants, or restricted shares might be effective for firms pursuing more long-term strategies requiring high levels of innovation and investments that may not be reflected in accounting records. For firms following the strategies set forth below, true economic performance might depart significantly from accounting returns. Market-based incentives might therefore provide a more effective basis for rewarding these strategies.

Differentiation

Firms that follow a differentiation strategy attempt to achieve a competitive advantage by charging a premium price for products with unique attributes that provide value to customers. Examples of such attributes include brand image, superior service, or innovation. These unique attributes often require substantial investments in intangible resources. For example, a unique brand image often requires high levels of advertising and promotion. Superior service might require a great deal of investment in human resources such as training or continuing education. Innovation might require high levels of research and development expenditures. Most of these investments are required to be expensed in the determination of accounting earnings. However, as discussed above, the capital markets may capitalize some of these costs in stock price. Therefore, linking compensation to stock market performance might reward executives for making those investments that facilitate the development of unique product attributes.

Fast-Cycle Resource Profiles

Firms facing rapid technological change and innovation may be well suited to market-based incentives (e.g., biotechnology, computers, telecommunications, and software). Because they face environments of creative destruction, fast-cycle firms must continually renew and sustain their innovative trajectory. Many of the long-term expenditures that these firms must make in order to secure a competitive advantage may be reflected in share price. In contrast, accounting standards require that these be expensed. Innovation, therefore, may be effectively rewarded by market-based incentives in firms operating in fast-cycle environments.

High Growth Industries

Certain industries may be undergoing a period of rapid, demand-driven growth. However, consumer demand is often capricious and difficult to forecast. There may be little consensus on the future growth patterns in such entrepreneurial firms. Stock prices reflect the diverse opinions of multiple investors as to the future growth potential of these firms,[41] and may be more informative than accounting measures, which are oriented toward the past and associated with formal bureaucratic control procedures.[42]

Related Diversification Strategies

Related diversification is a strategy in which a firm has a portfolio of business units that operate in similar industries. In general, related diversified firms pursue efficiencies through synergy, or the sharing of resources across business units. Research indicates that firms that pursue related diversification strategies tend to invest in more research and development expenditures than unrelated diversified firms.[43] Presumably, such firms are more technologically intense.

Because capital markets tend to capitalize research and development expenditures in stock price, market-based measures might also be appropriate in related diversified firms. Changes in stock price might effectively measure top executives' ability to identify new technological opportunities, direct resources towards their development, and manage the potential synergy that may be obtained through the transfer of technologies across business units. Managing synergy across divisions using complex, transfer pricing schemes has been shown to be counter-productive for division heads and other managers.[44]

Restructuring Strategies

In recent years, transactions such as mergers and acquisitions, spin-offs, and hostile takeovers have resulted in the dramatic restructuring of corporate America. Some have suggested that these transactions have been precipitated by over-diversification, as well as by the failure of internal governance devices. Over-diversification often leads to poor performance as top managers move away from the firm's core competencies and implement inappropriate control systems.[45] Internal governance systems such as the composition of the boards of directors or compensation plans may fail as bureaucratic incentives induce top managers to load the board with insiders rather than independent, outside directors, and to secure pay packages that are largely decoupled from firm performance.[46] Ineffective governance often leads to declining performance, depressed share price, and capital market induced restructuring as management becomes unresponsive to market forces. Performance often declines and share price becomes depressed. Often, firms restructure by down-scoping, or spinning-off business units that have been ineffectively managed under one corporate umbrella.

Spin-offs present opportunities to improve the governance system over former business units. Top managers of spun-off units (formerly divisional managers) can now be awarded incentives that are clearly predicated on the unit's performance. Where appropriate, market-oriented growth incentives may serve to revitalize business unit innovation and performance.[47] As mentioned earlier, however, this may depend on the amount of debt versus equity that makes up the capital structure. Leveraged buyouts may require an emphasis on accounting-based incentives whereas a spin-off or new issue of stock to facilitate the separation may require an emphasis on market-based incentives.

Deferred Compensation and Firm Strategy

Tomorrow's Payoff for Today's Performance

In addition to aligning performance measurement with a firm's strategy, compensation plan designers might also consider implementing a deferred compensation plan, which rewards current performance at some point in the future. Deferred compensation arrangements can be explicit contractual elements of the total compensation package that vest over time (e.g., pensions, restricted stock, performance plans, or stock options). Deferred compensation can also be implicit (e.g., wages and salaries that increase with employee tenure at a rate that is faster than any increases in performance).

Deferred compensation plans are often adopted as a tax planning vehicle for executives. In general, individuals are taxed when they receive income rather than when it is actually earned. Deferred compensation provides a legitimate and convenient way for executives to postpone the payment of tax on income which is earned, but not yet received. However, there may also be strategic factors associated with deferred compensation that warrant further consideration.

Deferred compensation can be viewed as a bonding mechanism. Executives forego income during the initial stages of their tenure with a particular firm, in return for a higher level of income as their careers progress. Initially, executives might be underpaid relative to firm performance, but, as their careers progress, they might become overpaid. The initial underpayment serves as a bond posted by the executive to be recouped upon attaining long-term performance. In effect, this provides executives with an incentive to manage for the long term, rather than engage in opportunistic behaviors that boost short-term performance.[48]

Stock options serve as an example of this bonding mechanism. Boards of directors might grant an executive a number of stock options on a particular date. This may be the board's way of rewarding an executive for decisions anticipated to benefit the firm in the future. However, the executive will not constructively benefit from this grant until he or she exercises the option. Therefore, the executive might only benefit from the grant of stock options if the stock appreciates during the period between the date the options are granted and the time when they are ultimately exercised. The difference between the exercise price and the market value of the stock at the date of exercise can be thought of as the value of the bond.

Considering Firm Strategy

This bonding mechanism has important implications for firm strategy. Deferred compensation arrangements that tend to tie executive fortunes to the long-term well-being of the firm might also serve to extend their decision-making horizons. As discussed previously, a long-term outlook might facilitate the pursuit of strategies requiring higher levels of innovation, creativity, or market responsiveness. Thus, much like market-based incentives, deferred compensation arrangements might contribute to those firms pursuing a differentiation strategy, with fast-cycle resources, in high-growth environments, pursuing related diversification strategies, or restructuring. Deferred compensations arrangements might be less amenable to firms operating in mature environments with few opportunities for profitable investment (e.g., those firms pursuing a cost leadership strategy, with slow- and standard-cycle resource profiles, pursuing unrelated diversification strategies, and with highly leveraged capital structures.)

It should also be noted that, in practice, the compensation reward schedule and the performance measure used to award incentives are not mutually exclusive. Compensation plans tend to vary by both the time period in which awards are received and the performance measure used. For example, performance plans can be both deferred (e.g., based on a five year period) and based on accounting measures (e.g., five year growth in earnings per share).[49] As discussed above, stock options can also be considered a form of deferred compensation, yet they are largely predicated on market performance.

The potential interaction between the reward schedule and performance measures provides compensation plan designers with greater opportunities to tailor executive compensation packages to specific firm strategies. Given the complexity of most firms' strategies, this is a potentially important feature of incentive plans. Firm strategy may not always be neatly categorized as being either long- or short-term. Some firms might require a focus on operational efficiency and an intermediate decision horizon of say, three to five years. In such cases, firms might adopt a long-term performance plan based on accounting measures (e.g., growth in earnings per share over the period) but that defers rewards until after the measurement period. This might be appropriate for firms that require incremental (e.g., product enhancements such as new features or improvements), rather than radical types of innovation (e.g., firms with products or services that are relatively well-established, but could benefit from continuous improvement through either product enhancements or process innovation).

The ability to fine tune an incentive plan in terms of the performance measure used or the timing of rewards may also be useful for more complex corporate-level diversification strategies. Although it appears that successful unrelated diversified firms tend to operate in mature environments,[50] it is possible that strategic business units may be more disparate in terms of their required decision-making horizons. An unrelated diversified firm might, for example, have a business unit that does business in a more high-tech environment. Such a firm might base the majority of the CEO's compensation on accounting performance in order to foster a decision-making horizon that is appropriate for the predominant portion of its portfolio. However, it might also include a market-based component of compensation to reflect the proportion of its total portfolio that is in a more innovation-intensive environment. Another alternative might be to base rewards on accounting performance but to defer their award (for an example of this type of incentive customization, see the discussion of Textron below).

Toward the Strategic Design of Executive Compensation

Some Examples

In summary, some tension exists between the need to constrain potential opportunism in the executive suite and the need to encourage appropriate risk taking. Compensation plan designers must carefully consider the influence that incentive plans have on executive decisions, and whether these decision horizons are consistent with firm strategy. Several firms appear to be measuring performance and rewarding executives strategically.

Genentech

A recent article in the *Wall Street Journal* documented some controversial pay practices in the biotechnology industry. Because of problems in developing and commercializing new products, biotech stock prices dropped an average of 32 percent in 1993 and 29 percent in 1994. However, CEO pay in the industry during 1993 averaged around $260,000. In 1994, the pay packages of the industry's 10 highest paid CEOs averaged $664,200, while share values declined an average of 18 percent for these 10 firms. The discrepancy between executive compensation and stock price performance may be driven by new pay and recruiting practices in the industry, where there is an ostensible trend to professionalize top management teams by recruiting talent from major pharmaceutical concerns.

These executives were brought in to help commercialize products and guide the companies through the maze of regulations that must be complied with in order to market a drug. To attract them, the smaller, more entrepreneurial firms had to adopt pay practices that were more in line with the larger, more mature pharmaceutical firms. These practices include high fixed salaries and cash bonuses.[51] However, many of the companies' innovative projects have been encountering greater than expected commercialization problems. Investors have become somewhat vexed at high salaries and bonuses with little or no revenues or earnings. This problem could have been avoided if the industry, which can be categorized as a fast-cycle or high growth industry, had adopted more market-based incentives. Indeed, the article points out that during the early days of biotech, the pay packages of senior executive were more equity based.

Genentech is a biotech company that has maintained a more market-based incentive scheme with some moderate success. In 1994, the company's CEO, G. Kirk Raab, earned $1.045 million, more than anyone in the industry. During approximately the same period, Genentech's stock appreciated approximately 4 percent. Viewed in isolation, this gain in value appears quite modest. But considering that the stock value of companies of the 10 highest paid executives in the industry fell an average of 18 percent, this gain is quite respectable. The following statement appears in the company's 1992 proxy:

> As determined based on surveys performed for the [Compensation] Committee, the salaries for executive officers adopted by the Committee are in the low to mid-range of base salaries as compared to pharmaceutical companies. Bonuses are in the low-range as compared to pharmaceutical companies, while stock options are in the high-range compared to pharmaceutical companies. In biasing the compensation mix toward stock options, the Committee has sought to fix executive incentives to the creation of shareholder value as measured by the equity markets.[52]

General Electric and Textron

General Electric and Textron are pursuing unrelated diversification strategies and emphasizing accounting returns in the evaluation and reward of their managers. General Electric successfully manages a diversified portfolio of eight industrial and 24 financial service units. A recent *Wall Street Journal* article quotes the company's chairman, Jack Welch as saying investors value GE's ability "to deliver strong, consistent earnings growth in a myriad of global economic conditions." The quest for consistent earnings extends even to the company's acquisition strategy. James Parke, the chief financial officer of GE Capital, the company's financial service arm, recently stated, "Of course we're buying earnings when we do an acquisition." Dennis Dammerman, chief financial officer of General Electric, the parent company, echoed this view by stating, "I see nothing wrong with someone saying, 'Look, I have an earnings objective for the year, and to achieve that earnings objective maybe I need to go make an acquisition.' That's fine if the individual can come up with a good acquisition."[53]

General Electric's basis for rewarding its CEO appears consistent with the reported emphasis on earnings. The company's 1994 proxy statement indicated that, "The [Compensation] Committee continued to consider this level of payment appropriate in view of Mr. Welch's leadership of one of the world's top companies in terms of *earnings,* balance sheet, share owner value and management processes (emphasis added)."[54]

Textron has four major lines of business: aircraft, and aircraft parts; tanks and tank components; accident and health insurance; and personal credit institutions. For the year ended December 1995, the company earned a respectable 14.04 percent return on equity. In 1995, earnings per share were up approximately 15 percent over the prior year. Textron's 1992 annual proxy states that president and CEO J. F. Hardymon received $650,000 in fixed salary, an $850,000 bonus award, a long-term incentive plan payout of $324,000, and 50,000 stock options granted near year end. The rationale for the bonus was that Textron's earnings per share before the impact of 1992 accounting changes (an improvement of 13% over the previous year) exceeded the planned increase, as did the growth in Textron's free cash flow.[55]

Hardymon's incentive package illustrates how firms with more complex corporate level diversification strategies use both performance measures and deferral mechanisms to reward executives. The largest component of his compensation ($850,000) is clearly predicated on short-term accounting performance. However, the $325,000 long-term incentive plan payout is 75 percent based on the growth in earnings per share over a three-year cycle (25 percent based on other discretionary measures). Finally, stock options are both market-based and deferred. The long-term incentive plans and stock options may reflect some of Textron's business units that are more technologically sophisticated (e.g., aircraft and aircraft parts).

Conclusion

While reform of incentive compensation plans might enhance executive accountability, may also constrain executive discretion. However, executive discretion and creativity might be precisely what is needed to succeed given the pace of technological change and the shift toward a more knowledge intensive, service-based economy.

We suggest that compensation plan designers take the following steps to manage the apparent tension between strategy, compensation, and performance:

- Identify the firm's strategy and a decision-making horizon appropriate to it. The appropriate decision-making horizon can be determined by identifying the key success factors necessary to achieve and sustain a competitive advantage. For example, high levels of current cash flow and operational efficiency are potentially key success factors for a cost leader. Long-term customer loyalty and innovation are probably key success factors for a firm pursuing a differentiation strategy.
- Identify an appropriate measure of firm performance. If current cash flow and operational efficiency are key success factors, then accounting performance is probably the best measure. If innovation is a key factor, then market based measures are probably most appropriate.
- Link CEO pay to the appropriate performance measure. If short-term, accounting performance is the goal, then firms might adopt an annual bonus scheme. If longer term market performance is the objective, then a firm might grant restricted shares or stock options.
- Consider the timing of rewards. A deferred compensation plan may be appropriate for companies pursuing intermediate- or long-term strategies.

Strategically designed plans may help align the goals of managers and stockholders, as well as contribute to a particular firm's competitive advantage. Well-designed compensation plans may also serve to restore public confidence in the top management teams of large public corporations. Given the contributions these organizations have made to economic growth and innovation, this would seem to be a worthwhile endeavor.

Endnotes

1. Jensen, M. C. & Murphy, K. J. 1990. Performance and top management incentives. *Journal of Political Economy*, 98:225–264.
2. Bennett, A. 1989. A great leap forward for executive pay. *Wall Street Journal*, April 24:B1; Byrne, J. A. & Bongiorno, L. 1995. CEO pay: ready for takeoff. *Business Week*, April 24:88–94.
3. In recent years, there has been a proliferation of different executive compensation plans, including annual bonuses, performance plans, stock options, stock appreciation rights, and restricted stock. *Annual bonuses* are cash payments that are often based upon a percentage of a corporation's net income for a given year. *Performance plans* are often based on longer-term performance objectives (e.g., the compounded growth rate of earnings per share over a five year period). The initial value of the units in a performance plan can be based on either share value at the date of the initial grant (performance shares) or some fixed dollar amount (performance units). *Stock options* grant employees the right to acquire company shares at a specified 'exercise' price (the exercise price is often the market value of the stock at the date the option is granted) over a period of time (e.g., ten years). If the stock appreciates during that time period, the employee potentially gains the difference between the exercise price and the current market value. *Stock appreciation rights* are similar to stock options in that executives benefit from the appreciation in share value above a particular exercise price. However, stock appreciation rights do not require that executives actually purchase the stock. Rather, executives simply receive, in cash, the appreciation in share value. Finally, executives are frequently granted *restricted stock*. These are grants of stock that are conditional upon certain events such as the attainment of corporate performance objectives or executive length of service requirements.
4. Rappaport, A. 1978. Executive incentives vs. corporate growth. *Harvard Business Review*, July–August: 81–88; Hill C. W. L, Hitt, M. A. & Hoskisson, R. E. 1988. Declining U.S. competitiveness: Reflections on a crisis. *Academy of Management Executive*, 2:151–160.

5. Kerr, S. 1995. On the folly of rewarding A, while hoping for B. *Academy of Management Executive*, 9:7–14.

6. Chandler, A. D. 1977. *The visible hand: The managerial revolution in American business*. Cambridge, MA: Belknap Press.

7. Smith, A. 1976. *An inquiry into the nature and causes of the wealth of nations, p. 265*. Chicago: The University of Chicago Press.

8. *Business Week* 1994. Executive compensation scoreboard. April 25:70.

9. *Business Week*. 1992. Executive compensation scoreboard. May 4:142.

10. Jensen and Murphy, 1990, op. cit.

11. McEachern, W. A. 1975. *Managerial control and performance*. Lexington, MA: D.C. Health; Allen, M. 1981. Power and privilege in the large corporation: Corporate control and managerial compensation. *American Journal of Sociology*, 86:1112–1123; Arnould, R. J. 1985. Agency costs in banking firms: An analysis of expense preference behaviors. *Journal of Economics and Business*, 37:103–112; Gomez-Mejia, L. R., Tosi, H. & Hinkin, T. 1987. Managerial control, performance, and executive compensation. *Academy of Management Journal*, 30:51–70; Dyl, E. A. 1988. Corporate control and management compensation: Evidence on the agency problem. *Managerial and Decision Economics*, 9:21–25.

12. Baumol, W. J. 1959. *Busiess behavior, value, and growth*. New York: Harcourt, Brace, & Court.; McGuire, J. W., Chiu, J. S. Y., & Elbing, A. O. 1962. Executive incomes, sales, and profits. *American Economic Review*, 52:753–761; Cosh, D. H. 1975. The remuneration of chief executives in the United Kingdom. *Economic Journal*, 85:75–94; Mees, G. & Whittington, G. 1975. Directors' pay, growth, and profitability. *Journal of Industrial Economics*, 24:1–14; Finkelstein, S. & Hambrick, D. C. 1989. Chief executive compensation: A study of the intersection of markets and political processes. *Strategic Management Journal*, 10:121–134; Lambert, R. A., Larcker, D. F., & Weigelt, K. 1991. How sensitive is executive compensation to organizational size. *Strategic Management Journal*, 12:395–402.

13. Jensen, M. C. 1993. The modern industrial revolution, exit, and the failure of internal control systems. *Journal of Finance*, 48:831–880.

14. Financial economists tend to emphasize the monitoring, or control role of the board of directors. In their view, the influence of outside, independent directors prevent executives from engaging in self interested, opportunistic behaviors that detract from shareholder value. Greater proportions of outside directors will therefore contribute to long-term performance. However, it should be noted that some academic research suggests that boards play more of a strategic role in their relationship with top executives. For example, it has been suggested that outside directors are an important link between firms and their external environments. Outside directors may provide access to scarce, yet vital resources. This is especially true in environments that are hostile or very unstable. Thus, in terms of long-term firm performance, this "resource dependence perspective" views outside directors as having a more strategic role. See Pfeffer, J. & Salancik, G. R. 1978. *The external control of organizations: A resource dependence perspective*. New York: Harper & Row.

   Others have commented on the potentially positive impact of inside directors on long-term performance. For example, some have argued that inside directors possess more in-depth, firm specific knowledge than outside directors. Thus, it has sometimes been suggested that inside directors facilitate the pursuit of more complex and risky strategies due to their specialized firm and industry knowledge. Therefore, inside directors may actually contribute to long-term performance rather than detract from it in the case of firms pursuing more innovative and risky strategies. See Baysinger, B. D. & Hoskisson, R. E. 1990. The composition of boards of directors and strategic control: Effects on corporate strategy. *Academy of Management Review*, 15:72–87, as well as, Hoskisson, R. E. & Turk, T. A. Corporate restructuring: Governance and control limits of the internal capital market. *Academy of Management Review*, 15:459–477. Thus, the relationship between the composition of board composition and long-term firm performance is potentially complex, and may depend on numerous internal and external strategic contingencies. See Zahra, S. A. & Pearce II, J. A. 1989. Boards of directors and corporate financial performance: A review and integrative model. *Journal of Management*, 15:291–334.

15. Hill, Hitt, and Hoskisson, 1988, op. cit.
16. Amihud, Y. & Lev, B. 1981. Risk reduction as a managerial motive for conglomerate mergers. *Bell Journal of Economics,* 12:605–617.
17. Westphal, J. D. & Zajac, E. J. 1994. Substance and symbolism in CEOs' long-term incentive plans. *Administrative Science Quarterly,* 39:367–390.
18. Rappaport, 1978, op. cit.
19. Hill, Hitt, and Hoskisson, 1988, op. cit.
20. Porter, M. E. 1992. Capital disadvantage: America's failing capital investment system. *Harvard Business Review,* 70:65–82.
21. Amihud and Lev, 1981, op. cit.
22. Kerr, 1995, op. cit.
23. McWilliams, B. 1996. The measure of success. *Across the Board,* February: 16–20.
24. Kaplan, R. A. & Norton, D. P. 1992. The balanced scorecard—Measures that drive performance. *Harvard Business Review,* January–February: 71–79.
25. Kaplan, R. A. & Norton, D. P. 1992. Putting the balanced scorecard to work. *Harvard Business Review,* January–February: 71–79.
26. See Banerjee, A. 1995. Changes in SEC disclosure rules for executive stock options: Implications for valuation. *Journal of Accounting, Auditing, and Finance,* 10, p. 333.
27. Kerr, 1995, op. cit.
28. Fisher, F. M. & McGowan, J. J. 1983. On the misuse of accounting returns to infer monopoly profit. *American Economic Review,* 73:82–97.
29. Johnson, H. T. & Kaplan, R. S. 1987. *Relevance lost: The rise and fall of management accounting.* Boston: Harvard Business School Press.
30. In the discussion that follows, we assume that business level strategies are implemented in a single product or relatively non-diversified firm.
31. Porter, M. E. 1980. *Competitive strategy.* New York: Free Press.
32. See Wernerfelt, B. 1984. A resource-based view of the firm. *Strategic Management Journal* 5:171–180; Barney, J. B. 1986. Strategic factor markets: Expectations, luck, and business strategy, *Management Science,* 36:1231–1241; Dierikx, 1. & Cool, K. 1989. Asset stock accumulation and sustainability of competitive advantage. *Management Science,* 35:1504–1510; Barney, J. B. 1991. Firm resources and sustained competitive advantage. *Journal of Management,* 17:99–120; Conner, K. R. 1991. A historical comparison of resource based theory and five schools of thought within industrial organization economics: Do we have a new theory of the firm? *Journal of Management,* 17:121–154; Grant, R. M. 1991. The resource-based theory of competitive advantage: Implications for strategy formulation. *California Management Review,* 33:114–135.
33. Williams, J. R. 1992. How sustainable is your competitive advantage. *California Management Review,* 34:29–49.
34. Schumpeter, J. A. 1934. *The theory of economic development.* Cambridge, MA; Harvard University Press.
35. Dundas, K. M. & Richardson, P. R. 1982 Implementing the unrelated product strategy. *Strategic Management Journal,* 3:287–301.
36. Due to the problems associated with bureaucratic measurement techniques and accounting performance, it has long been recognized that getting divisional executive to think for the long-term poses a significant problem for compensation plan designers. See Crystal, G. S. & Hurwich, M. R. 1986. The case for divisional long-term incentives. *California Management Review,* 29:60–74. This article presents several useful techniques for factoring the opportunity cost of capital into divisional executives compensation plans. However, each of these techniques rely to some extent on a division's bureaucratically determined contribution to profit rather than the more decentralized market determined returns. Accordingly, whether or not these more sophisticated divisional incentive plans actually extend divisional managers' decision horizons remains an interesting question.

Another interesting question pertains to the effect of rewarding CEOs and their divisional managers using different measures of performance. Research has found that accounting and stock market returns are statistically associated, but the relationship is relatively small. See Jacobsen, R. The validity of ROI as a measure of business performance. *American Economic Review,* 77:470–478. One could readily imagine the pressure to increase divisional earnings put on divisional managers by a CEO whose compensation is highly dependent upon stock options, but the firm's price to earning multiple (P/E ratio) is relatively low.

37. Jensen, M. C. 1986. Agency costs of free cash flow, corporate finance and takeovers. *American Economic Review,* 76:323–329.

38. This view of leveraged buyouts is highly controversial. High levels of debt may constrain managerial discretion beyond that which is optimal. Indeed, under conditions of discontinuous environmental change, managerial discretion and creativity may be precisely what is needed to ensure the long-term viability of the firm. Additionally, highly leveraged capital structures may be very costly for certain firm stakeholders such as employees who are often dislocated by LBO induced restructuring. See for example Fox, I. & Marcus, A. 1992. The causes and consequences of leveraged management buyouts. *Academy of Management Review,* 17:62–85.

We do not advocate the wholesale implementation of highly leveraged capital structures. We do however, suggest that much like compensation systems, debt may be an effective control in a narrow set of circumstances. More specifically, highly leveraged capital structures and accounting based incentives might contribute to the strategic mission of firms in mature environments.

39. Fama, F. F. 1970. Efficient capital markets: A review of theory and empirical evidence. *Journal of Finance,* 70:383–417.

40. Johnson, L, D. & Pazderka, B. 1993. Firm value and investment in R&D. *Managerial and Decision Economics,* 14:15–24; Hirschey, M. & Weygandt, J. J. 1985. Amortization policy for advertising and research and development expenditures. *Journal of Accounting Research,* 23:326–335; Chan, S. H., Martin, J. D., & Kensinger, J. W. 1990. Corporate research and development expenditures and share value, *Journal of Financial Economics,* 26:255–276.

41. Allen, F. 1993. Strategic management and financial markets. *Strategic Management Journal,* 14:11–22.

42. Lambert, R. A. & Larcker, D. F. 1987. An analysis of the use of accounting and market measures of performance in executive compensation contracts. *Journal of Accounting Research,* 25:85–129.

43. Hoskisson, R. E. & Hitt, M. A. 1988. Strategic control systems and relative R&D intensity in large multiproduct firms. *Strategic Management Journal,* 9:605–621; Baysinger, B. D. & Hoskisson, R. E. 1989. Diversification strategy and R&D intensity in large multiproduct firms. *Academy of Management Journal,* 32:310–332.

44. Eccles, R. G. 1985. *The transfer pricing problem: A theory for practice,* Lexington, MA: Lexington Books.

45. Hoskisson, R. E. & Hitt, M. A. 1994. *Downscoping: How to tame the diversified firm.* New York: Oxford University Press.

46. Jensen, 1993, op. cit.

47. Rather than directly restructuring, some firms have issued separate classes of stock which each predicate dividends on the performance of a particular division (e.g., General Motor's GMH and GME classes). This may be one way of increasing the market oriented intensity of managerial incentives.

48. Lazear, E. P. 1979. Why is there mandatory retirement? *Journal of Political Economy,* 87:1261–1284. Lazear, E. P. 1981. Agency, earnings profiles, productivity, and hours restrictions. *American Economic Review,* 71:606–620.; Main, G. M. 1990. The new economics of personnel, *Journal of General Management,* 16:91–103.

49. Ibid., Note 3.

50. Ibid., Notes 36 and 44.

51. *Wall Street Journal.* 1995. Biotechnology: Are biotech CEOs earning their keep? March 28:B1.

52. Genentech, 1992 Annual Proxy.

53. *Wall Street Journal.* 1994. Managing profits: How general electric damps fluctuations in its annual earnings. November 3:A1.
54. General Electric Co., 1994 Annual Proxy.
55. Textron, Inc., 1992 Annual Proxy.

About the Authors

Wayne Grossman is assistant professor of management at Kansas State University, where he teaches strategic management and business, government, and society at the undergraduate and graduate levels. He received his PhD in strategic management from Texas A&M University and is also a certified public accountant.

His research interests include corporate governance, corporate-level strategy, technology and innovation management, and business and public policy.

Robert E. Hoskisson is the Rath Chair in Strategic Management at the Michael F. Price College of Business, the University of Oklahoma. He received his PhD from the University of California, Irvine. His research focuses on topics in technology strategy, international and product diversification, corporate restructuring and privatization, corporate governance and cooperative strategy. He has served on the editorial review board of the Academy of Management Journal, *including one term as consulting editor. His publications have appeared in the* Academy of Management Journal, Strategic Management Journal, Academy of Management Review, *and* Journal of Management. *He has co-authored* Downscoping: How to Tame the Diversified Firm *(1994, Oxford University Press) and a textbook,* Strategic Management: Competitiveness and Globalization *(1997 2nd edition, ITP West Publishing).*

They Don't Bite the Hand That Feeds Them

by David Leonhardt in Oak Brook, Ill.

Coca-Cola Co.'s largest customer is McDonald's Corp. Sonnenschein Nath & Rosenthal has been the hamburger chain's lead law firm for decades. DDB Needham Worldwide Inc. and Leo Burnett Co. are two of its longtime ad agencies. And Dean Foods Co. supplies the Arches with pickles.

What else do these firms have in common? Each has an executive, retired executive, or director on the McDonald's board. In fact, by current standards of corporate governance, only 4 of McDonald's 15 directors can be called independent—meaning they don't work for the company, do outside business with it, or have a McDonald's exec sitting on their own board.

"Not Even Close"

That's not all: Cross-directorships, in which directors serve on each other's boards, are common, too. Gordon C. Gray, for example, chairman of a Canadian mining company and an independent director, also sits on the board of a subsidiary of Stone Container Corp., a McDonald's packaging supplier whose CEO, Roger W. Stone, is a fellow McDonald's director.

Thanks to pressure from shareholders and regulators, Corporate America over the past decade had raised the quality of its boards and increased its directors' accountability. But that trend has passed McDonald's by. "They are not even close to keeping up with corporate-governance standards that most other companies their size meet," says Anne Hansen, deputy director of the Council of Institutional Investors in Washington. Adds Warren Bennis, a University of Southern California professor who studies leadership: "For a company that size, it's stunning." The National Association of Corporate Directors recommends "a substantial majority" of a company's directors be independent. And many shareholder groups discourage cross-directorships; governance experts say they can lead directors to look out for each others' interests, rather than those of shareholders.

McDonald's denies that the many relationships between its board members and the company are a problem. "We have always had a board that was fairly heavily peopled by inside directors. I am not troubled by that at all," says CEO and Chairman Michael R. Quinlan. He argues that insiders bring detailed knowledge of McDonald's to the board. And director Robert N. Thurston, a former Quaker Oats Co. executive, calls it an active board that "can stick our noses anywhere we want to." To suggest that directors are hampered by company ties "discounts the independence and the pride and the intelligence and the fortitude of the people on the board," he adds.

The proper question, though, may not be whether the directors have integrity—there is no evidence they don't—but whether, as a group, they bring the type of broad experience and objectivity that a company facing a watershed requires. Despite the hamburger chain's lackluster performance in the past few years, its board has done little to agitate for change, say people who follow the company. "This board is so stale, it's hard to imagine it asking the right questions," Bennis says. Or, as one major shareholder puts it: "If McDonald's is one of your largest customers, I don't think you're going to challenge the CEO too much."

Compare the McDonald's board with those at another globally branded company. Nine of Coca-Cola's 13 directors are independent. The board includes former Senator Sam Nunn, former baseball Commissioner Peter V. Ueberroth, former Delta Air Lines CEO Ronald W. Allen, and superinvestor Warren Buffett.

In fact, inspect almost any company with a brand similar in strength to McDonald's, and you will find more outside directors, a shorter average term, a younger board, and greater diversity of experience. Inspect McDonald's, on the other hand, and you will find a disproportionate number of directors who rely on the company for one kind of paycheck or another.

A Close-Knit Group

Along with five current or former executives, McDonald's 15-member board is packed with directors who have links to the company and each other. At right, their ties and the year they joined the board

HALL ADAMS JR.
64, former CEO of Leo Burnett & Co., a McDonald's ad agency (1993)

GORDON C. GRAY
70, A Canadian mining executive; sits on another board with Stone (1982)

DONALD R. KEOUGH
71, former president of Coca-Cola Co., a major McDonald's supplier (1993)

ENRIQUE HERNANDEZ JR.
42, CEO of California-based provider of security guards (1996)

DONALD G. LUBIN
64, partner at McDonald's Chicago law firm, Sonnenschein, Nath & Rosenthal (1967)

TERRY L. SAVAGE
53, Chicago-based television and print journalist (1990)

ANDREW J. McKENNA
68, CEO of Schwarz Paper Co., a McDonald's supplier. Director of Aon Corp. (with former McDonald's CEO Fred Turner) and Dean Foods, another McDonalds's supplier (1991)

ROGER W. STONE
63, CEO of Stone Container Corp., a McDonald's supplier that also owns stake in supplier of take-out bags. Jack Greenberg, president of McDonald's USA, sits on Stone board (1989)

B. BLAIR VEDDER JR.
73, former COO of agency that became McDonald's lead ad agency (1988)

ROBERT N. THURSTON
65, Former Quaker Oats executive (1974)

Disney Holders Use Annual Meeting to Protest Lack of Independent Board

by Bruce Orwall
Staff Reporter of THE WALL STREET JOURNAL

KANSAS CITY, Mo.—*Walt Disney* Co. shareholders for the second straight year used the company's annual meeting to send a strong message of discontent about the independence of Disney's board of directors. About 35% of voting shareholders supported a resolution urging the company to reconfigure its board to achieve greater independence.

The resolution, put forward by the College Retirement Equities Fund, the powerful equities arm of the huge pension fund TIAA-CREF, asked the Burbank, Calif.-based entertainment company to revamp its board so that a majority has no management ties and key panels consist entirely of independent directors. While a majority vote would be needed to force Disney to change, the support for the CREF resolution sends a strong message to management. It is more than double the average of 16.9% of the votes cast for similar resolutions at 13 companies in 1997.

Despite its record of delivering strong returns for shareholders since Chairman and Chief Executive Michael Eisner took over in 1984, Disney has been under attack lately over the composition of its board.

Numerous Disney directors have close personal and professional ties to the company, and the 16-member board includes two former Disney chairmen and three corporate executives.

'An Accurate Perception'

The strong support for the resolution "really reflects public perception, and an accurate perception, of the Disney board," said Richard M. Schlefer, director of corporate governance for CREF. He said CREF challenged Disney because it thinks the company should be a corporate model, not a laggard. And he said CREF believes that "no company is immune to problems somewhere down the line. You don't wait until you have a crisis to determine that you've got the wrong board."

Disney's senior executive vice president, Sanford M. Litvack, who is also a board member, indicated that Disney doesn't agree with CREF's definition of an independent director, and after the meeting said that the company won't yield to it in the future. Nonetheless, he told shareholders that the company will try to be responsive to such concerns in the future. "We do understand that in this area, perceptions are important," he said.

Disney showed early in the meeting that its attempts at reconciliation with shareholders only go so far. Mr. Eisner began the session by introducing each director and calculating the growth in Disney's stock price since they joined the board. Although most observers attribute Disney's success to Mr. Eisner, he passed on credit to board members, whom he said "are the ones who assume ultimate authority" for the company.

A More Sensitive Face

Nonetheless, Disney has tried to turn a more sensitive face toward its critics in the wake of last year's annual meeting, a five-hour slugfest in an Anaheim, Calif., hockey rink, when an unusually high 13% of voting shareholders withheld their votes for the re-election of several directors. This year's session was moved to Kansas City—ostensibly because the Midwestern city was the place where Walt Disney made his first cartoons in 1922.

The result was a more orderly two-hour session attended by 1,400, not 10,000, and absent the boos and harsh questioning that pelted Mr. Eisner last year. Holders last year were also upset with the severance package granted to former Disney President Michael Ovitz and the rich new contract Mr. Eisner had just been awarded.

Disney met in the past year with influential investor groups such as TIAA-CREF and the California Public Employees' Retirement System, and even put forward an amendment to the company's bylaws calling for annual election of all board members. That measure was approved with 60% of the votes cast.

But the outcome of the quieter meeting was in some ways worse, as the CREF vote approached the all-time biggest vote-getter for such a resolution—the 45.8% of the votes cast for a union-backed measure at Dillard's Inc. last year.

Mr. Schlefer said the high vote against Disney will probably result in CREF and other organizations being more assertive in seeking independence on company boards. CREF itself has filed six such resolutions recently, including the Disney resolution. It has withdrawn one, but four others are pending and may come to shareholder votes.

Motorola Plans Restructuring, Forming Two Major Divisions

Electronics Giant Will Create Units for Consumer, Industrial Customers

by Quentin Hardy
Staff Reporter of THE WALL STREET JOURNAL

Motorola Inc. is planning a major corporate restructuring that will merge about a half-dozen businesses into two huge divisions, one geared to consumers and the other to industrial customers, people familiar with the company say.

The operations that build infrastructure products for paging, two-way radio and cellular telephones will be combined into one division. Motorola will also create a separate division for sales of consumer devices such as cellular-telephone handsets and pagers, said the people. The Schaumburg, Ill., company's big semiconductor operation, which was revamped last year, will remain separate, as will the much smaller automotive and space groups.

Currently, Motorola operates its paging, cellular and two-way radio operations as separate company "segments," each of which has its own infrastructure and consumer sectors. Each segment also has its own technology-development and sales forces. Last year's sales by the three segments totaled $20.6 billion, out of $29.8 billion in revenue at Motorola. The reorganization is likely to directly affect thousands of Motorola employees.

'No Secret' at the Company

Motorola officials wouldn't confirm details of the planned changes, which are expected to be announced within the next several weeks. "We've made no secret inside the company that we are looking at our structure," said Albert Brashear, Motorola's director of corporate communications. He added, "No one at Motorola would be surprised if [the restructuring] looked like that . . . but more discussion has to take place." The reworking of the three segments into consumer and industry-oriented divisions reflects both technological and competitive changes that have jarred Motorola in recent years. In addition, they reflect efforts by Christopher Galvin, who became chief executive officer of Motorola in 1997, to make his organization less internally combative and more cooperative.

At a meeting of some 500 Motorola corporate officers last year, where changes such as the restructuring were first discussed, Mr. Galvin told his troops that the time had come to end Motorola's "warring tribes" culture, where different sectors would attack each other's products and procedures. The culture was credited with giving Motorola well-engineered technologies, but also led to internal feuding and suspicion.

"Chris told us to get comfortable with change or move on," according to one person who attended the meeting.

Driving the Changes

The chief force for changes at Motorola, however, may be technology itself. Wireless businesses such as police radios, cellular phones and pagers for bike messengers once seemed distinct. Now they overlap. For example, Motorola's land mobile-radio segment, which produces two-way radios, makes a dispatch-style device for Nextel Communications Inc. that can also handle cellular-phone calls and accept alphanumeric and text messages similar to pagers.

The Nextel integrated offering was Motorola's greatest success last year, in terms of growth. Land-mobile sales were up 23%, to $4.9 billion, while overall company sales grew by just 7%. Cellular-product sales grew by 10%, to $11.9 billion last year, while messaging segment sales fell 4%, to $3.8 billion.

But Motorola hasn't changed as rapidly as the technology, and the different sectors have often repeated painful lessons. The digital technology behind the Nextel equipment, for example, required a massive overhaul of software operations at land-mobile, similar to overhauls later required in the development of digital cellular infrastructure and handsets.

Leaders of the Divisions

Merle Gilmore, who led the land-mobile segment while it developed the Nextel product and who now heads up Motorola's operations in Europe, is expected to take over one of the two new reconfigured divisions. The other candidate hasn't yet been determined, although likely candidates include Jim Norling, president and general manager of Motorola's messaging, information and media segment; Fred Kuznik, president of its cellular subscriber sector, and Jack Scanlon, general manager of the cellular and space business.

The explosion of wireless devices like cellular telephones has put Motorola more firmly into consumer markets, after years of sales to business users. Its share of cellular-handset sales has fallen in recent years, bested by more snazzy offerings by competitors such as Finland's Oy Nokia, and Telefon L.M. Ericsson of Sweden. Several other savvy consumer-product companies, such as Sony Corp. of Japan and Philips Electronics NV of the Netherlands, are also making renewed runs at the U.S. market.

Motorola's overall share of the U.S. cellular-handset market stood at 34.1% last year, according to consulting firm Herschel Shosteck Associates Ltd., compared with 55% in 1995. Nokia's share meanwhile, increased to 24.4%, from 13.6%, while Ericsson had a 14.4% share in 1997, up from 2.4% in 1995. Motorola officials dispute those figures, but won't provide their own market-share numbers.

Arthur Andersen Responds to Call for Break Up of Firm

Dow Jones Newswires

CHICAGO—The accountants at Andersen Worldwide are willing to let the consulting unit break away from the firm, but they want the consultants to pay a hefty price for leaving.

The accountants plan to argue that Andersen Consulting is bound by contract to pay close to $11 billion if it wants out. It also should give up the highly-recognizable Andersen name, a source close to Andersen Worldwide said Monday.

"If Andersen Consulting wants to fly the coop, to go out on their own, so be it," said the source, who spoke on condition of anonymity. "But we intend to get our fair share, what is equitable."

Under terms of the contract between the units, any entity leaving must pay 150% of their annual revenues to the remaining firm.

More than 1,000 partners of Andersen Consulting, the world's largest business consulting group, voted in December to split away from the Arthur Andersen accounting firm after an acrimonious nine-year history. The consultants requested that an arbitrator appointed by the International Chamber of Commerce resolve the legal issues involved.

With just 30 days to respond to the consultants' claims that Arthur Andersen committed "serious breaches of contract" by expanding into consulting and poaching its staff, documents filed with the arbitrator indicate the accountants are trying to delay a split and make Andersen Consulting pay a heavy price for leaving.

Arthur Andersen also would seek damages for equity in the company that is being lost and for the return of technology created jointly for the units, the source said. Andersen Consulting argued that since Arthur Andersen breached the contract, its breakup provisions are no longer valid.

"Any assertions that the (breakup) provision would even come into play is something I believe that Andersen is putting forward to distract from the core issue—that they breached the contract by getting into consulting," said Jon Conahan, managing partner for strategy at Andersen Consulting.

If the arbitrator were to rule that a breach never occurred, Andersen Consulting would remain with the firm and the breakup issue would be moot, Conahan noted. If the arbitrator rules the other way, the entire contract would likely be thrown out, he said.

Conahan also accused Arthur Andersen of delaying tactics.

Since Arthur Andersen is a worldwide accounting firm composed of 130 member firms—each semi-independent and subject to regulations of their host countries—partners from each were sending letters that could force Andersen Consulting to file separate claims for all 30, delaying the arbitration process.

Further, some of the firms contend they would not be bound by the French arbitrator's decision under provisions in their contracts that call for resolving disputes in Switzerland.

Arthur Andersen Managing Partner Jim Wadia, reached by telephone on Monday, declined to comment on the firm's strategy.

Conahan said Andersen Consulting agreed last week to give Andersen Worldwide and Arthur Andersen another 30 days to respond to the allegations against it but believes all member firms are bound by French arbitration under a 1991 agreement.

The bitter rift between the firm's accounting and consulting partners began almost from the time Andersen Worldwide, the parent of the firms, was restructured into the two units in 1989.

Since 1989, Arthur Andersen's overall revenues have grown at a compounded annual rate of 13%, although its accounting practice has grown on average less than 8 percent. Andersen Consulting's revenues have grown at a compounded annual rate of 20%, and the consultants have complained they were paying too much to the consultants over the year—including millions used to launch competing businesses.

An aggressive sales and marketing campaign by the accounting branch also has blurred the distinction between the two, a breach of their contracts, Andersen Consulting contends. Under terms of the contract between the units, any entity leaving must pay 150% of their annual revenues to the remaining firm.

For the fiscal year ended Aug. 31, Andersen Consulting posted worldwide revenues of $6.1 billion, a 25% rise from the previous year. Arthur Andersen took in $5.2 billion, a gain of 13%.

The action comes at a bad time for Andersen Worldwide, which is losing status as the world's largest accounting and consulting firm with the mergers of Ernst & Young with KPMG Peat Marwick and Price Waterhouse with Coopers & Lybrand.

Achieving and Maintaining Strategic Competitiveness in the 21st Century: The Role of Strategic Leadership

R. Duane Ireland
Baylor University

and

Michael A. Hitt
Texas A&M University

Abstract

Competition in the 21st century's global economy will be complex, challenging, and filled with competitive opportunities and threats. Effective strategic leadership practices can help firms enhance performance while competing in the next century's turbulent and unpredictable environments. The purpose of this work is to describe six components of effective strategic leadership. When the activities called for by these components are completed successfully, the firm's strategic leadership practices can become a source of competitive advantage. In turn, use of this advantage can contribute positively and significantly to the firm's achievement of strategic competitiveness and earning above-average returns in the 21st century.

> "It is possible—and fruitful—to identify major events that have already happened, irrevocably, and that will have predictable effects in the next decade or two. It is possible, in other words, to identify and prepare for the future *that has already happened.*" Peter Drucker, 1997.

Grounded in the insights and understanding that experience provides, conventional wisdom holds that it is very difficult to predict the future with high degrees of accuracy. In fact, Drucker even goes so far as to suggest that "In human affairs—political, social, economic, or business—it is pointless to try to predict the future, let alone attempt to look ahead 75 years."[1] This difficulty notwithstanding, the capability implied by the opening comment from Peter Drucker is encouraging. Stating this a bit differently, it is our belief that it is both possible and productive for firms to identify and prepare for a future *that has already happened.* Thus, although it is difficult for organizations to predict their future accurately, examining events that have already taken place allows them to know how to prepare for a future whose state has been influenced.

Based on this approach, we present a description of the strategic leadership practices that will contribute to corporate success during the 21st century. More precisely, our position is that the *global economy* is a major irrevocable event whose existence has already had a major influence on today's strategic leadership practices and offers insights about practices that should be used in the future. By examining appropriate and often innovative strategic leadership practices currently being used successfully by visionary organizations, it is possible to identify and understand practices that will be effective in the next century. This analysis is important, because strategic leadership may prove to be one of the most critical issues facing organizations in the next century. Without effective strategic leadership, the probability a firm can achieve superior or even satisfactory performance when confronting the challenges of the 21st century's global economy will be greatly reduced.[2]

Herein, strategic leadership is defined as a person's ability to anticipate, envision, maintain flexibility, think strategically, and work with others to initiate changes that will create a viable future for the organization.[3] When strategic leadership processes are difficult for competitors to understand and hence, to imitate, the firm has created a competitive advantage.[4] Because the creation of sustainable competitive advantage is the universal objective of all companies,[5] being able to exercise strategic leadership in a competitively superior manner facilitates the firm's efforts to earn superior returns on its investments.

Our paper proceeds as follows. First, we describe briefly the global economy and the new competitive landscape that has been created by it. Following this material is a discussion of strategic leadership. Viewed first from the lens of strategic leadership theory, we conclude this analysis with a description of the general nature of strategic leadership that is emerging in response to the global economy. Next, we discuss six key effective strategic leadership practices—determining the firm's purpose or vision, exploiting and maintaining core competencies, developing human capital, sustaining an effective organizational culture, emphasizing ethical practices, and establishing balanced organizational controls—that can contribute to the firm's competitive success. In the article's final section, we offer recommendations that if followed, will increase the probability that the firm's use of strategic leadership will facilitate its efforts to be globally competitive in the 21st century. The recommendations are integrated summaries of guidelines offered in other parts of the article.

The Global Economy

There is virtually uniform agreement that the complexity, turbulence, and extraordinary changes during the 1980s and 1990s are contributing to the rapid development of an ultracompetitive global economy. Joseph Gorman, TRW's CEO, suggests that a transformational change is occurring, from regional economies and industries to global ones.[6] A key reality of our time, the commercial interactions that are taking place in the global economy are becoming the dominant force shaping relationships among nations. The fact that ". . . the proportion of trade among nations as a share of global income has increased from 7 percent to 21 percent since the end of World War II demonstrates why the globalization of commercial markets has an important effect on individual countries."[7] Thus, in the global economy, products are shipped anywhere in the world in a matter of days; communications are instant; and, new product introductions and their life cycles have never been shorter with six months the norm in some high-tech industries.[8]

The incredible breadth and depth of the global economy's effects are shown by the suggestion that in the 21st century, nation-states will lose their sovereignty, technology may replace labor, and corporations may come to resemble amoebas—collections of workers that are subdivided into dynamic, ever-changing teams to competitively exploit the firm's unique resources, capabilities, and core competencies. Thus, some analysts argue with conviction that the large number of structural changes occurring simultaneously in the international system are resulting in economies and communications systems that are more integrated. For example, it has been predicted that by 2150, all or most of the global economy will be part of a ". . . single market, perhaps complete with a single currency and monetary authority."[9] However, others believe that the political structures supporting various economies and their communication systems will remain somewhat fragmented and may even be reduced to ethnic units during the 21st century.[10] Combined, predicted changes such as these may culminate in corporations that would be unrecognizable to many employees and world citizens today.[11] Moreover, the global economy may create a need for individual citizens to maintain separate loyalties—one to their own unique traditions and institutions, the other to the characteristics of a rapidly evolving international culture.

The New Competitive Landscape

The global economy has created a new competitive landscape—one in which events change constantly and unpredictably.[12] For the most part, these changes are revolutionary, not evolutionary in nature. Revolutionary changes happen swiftly, are constant, even relentless in their frequency, and affect virtually all parts of an organization simultaneously.[13] The uncertainty, ambiguity, and discontinuity resulting from revolutionary changes challenge firms and their strategic leadership to increase the speed of the decision-making processes through which strategies are formulated and implemented.[14] In the global economy, knowledge work and knowledge workers are the primary sources of economic growth—for individual firms and for nations. Thus, in the 21st century, the ability to build, share and leverage knowledge will replace the ownership and/or control of assets as a primary source of competitive advantage.[15]

However, certain conditions of the new competitive landscape, including the expectation that the world's economy will grow substantially during the first 20 years of the next century, also create opportunities for companies to improve their financial performance.[16] Organizations in which strategic leaders adopt a new competitive mindset—one in which mental agility, firm flexibility, speed, innovation, and globalized strategic thinking are valued highly—will be able to identify and competitively exploit opportunities that emerge in the new competitive landscape. These opportunities surface primarily because of the disequilibrium that is created by continuous changes (especially technological changes) in the states of knowledge that are a part of a competitive environment. More specifically, although uncertainty and disequilibrium often result in seemingly hostile and intensely rivalrous conditions, these conditions may simultaneously yield significant product-driven growth opportunities.[17] Through effective strategic leadership, an organization can be mobilized so that it can adapt its behaviors and exploit different growth opportunities.[18]

Next, we describe two perspectives of strategic leadership. following the description of "strategic leadership theory"—a theory that has influenced the study and practice of strategic leadership since the early 1970s—is the presentation of a perspective of strategic leadership whose emergence is being influenced significantly by the global economy.

Strategic Leadership

In the 1960s and early 1970s, it was thought prominently that situations facing the firm were the primary determinant of managerial behaviors and organizational outcomes. Compared to the influence of conditions in the firm's external environment, managers were believed to have little ability to make decisions that would affect the firm's performance.

The "Great Leader" View of Strategic Leadership

In 1972, John Child, a prominent organization theorist, argued persuasively that an organization's top-level managers had the discretion or latitude to make choices that would, indeed, affect their firm's outcomes.[19] In particular, because top managers have the responsibility for the overall performance of their firms, these individuals are in unique positions to have the strongest effect on the firm's strategic management process. In Child's view, strategic leaders, who were armed with substantial decision-making responsibilities, had the ability to influence significantly the direction of the firm and how it was to be managed in that pursuit. Strategic leadership theory holds that companies are reflections of their top managers, and, in particular of the chief executive officer, and that ". . . the specific knowledge, experience, values, and preferences of top managers are reflected not only in their decisions, but in their assessments of decision situations."[20]

Substantial numbers of CEOs have adopted the notion that strategic leadership responsibilities are theirs alone. One of their primary tasks is to choose a vision for the firm and create the conditions to achieve that vision. Thus, as a result of the *significant choice options* available to the CEO as the firm's key strategic leader, this individual often worked as the "Long Ranger" when shaping the firm. Isolated from those being led, the firm's key strategic leader commanded his/her organization primarily through use of top-down directives.[21] Particularly when these choices resulted in financial success for the company, the key strategic leader was recognized widely as the "corporate Hercules."[22]

Appropriate for its time, the theory of strategic leadership described above contributed to organizational success. But, the environmental conditions in which this theory was used have changed dramatically because of the global economy. In the past few decades, environmental conditions were *relatively* stable and predictable as compared to both the current and predicted states of these conditions in the 21st century.

The relative stability and predictability of the past few decades resulted in manageable amounts of uncertainty and ambiguity. Change was often treated as linear in nature in many industries; major competitors were largely domestic, not global companies; and, organizations were structured in hierarchical configurations that were supported by selection and promotion practices. However, conditions associated with the global economy's new competitive landscape, including those of shorter product life cycles, ever-accelerating rates and types of change, and the explosion of data and the need to convert it to useable information prevent single individuals from having all of the insights necessary to chart a firm's direction. Moreover, some believe that having strategic leadership centered on a single person or a few people at the top of a hierarchical pyramid is increasingly counterproductive.[23] Thus, bounded or constrained by their abilities as individual decision makers to deal with rapidly increasing amounts of data and the general complexity of the global economy, top managers are now challenged to discharge their strategic leadership responsibilities differently.[24] Insightful top managers recognize that it is impossible for them to have all of the answers, are willing to learn along with others, and understand that the uncertainty created by the global economy affects people at the firm's apex as well as those working in lower-level organizational positions.[25]

The "Great Groups" View of Strategic Leadership

In the 21st century, the *nature* of the organization in which effective strategic leadership practices occur will be different. In the view of noted business thinker Charles Handy, a public corporation should and will be regarded not as pieces of property owned by the current holders of its shares, but as a *community*. More properly thought of as *citizens* than *employees,* people involved with an organizational community remain together to pursue a common purpose. A community is something to which a person belongs and that belongs to no one individual. The community's citizens have both responsibilities to pursue the common good and rights to receive benefits earned through its attainment.

In an organizational community, strategic leadership is distributed among diverse individuals who share the responsibility to create a viable future for their firm. Charles Handy argues that many citizens will need to serve their communities as leaders and they will need to be dispersed throughout the firm.[26] When allowed to flourish as involved leaders, people spark greatness in each other. As Italian author Luciano De Crescenzo noted, "We are all angels with only one wing, we can only fly while embracing each other."[27]

Combinations or collaborations of organizational citizens functioning successfully have been labeled "great groups." These collaborations usually feature managers with significant profit and loss responsibilities, internal networkers (people, ". . . often with no formal authority, such as internal consultants or human resources professionals and frontline workers, who move about the organization spreading and fostering commitment to new ideas and practices"), and community citizens with intellectual capital that stimulates the development and/or leveraging of knowledge.[28] Members of great groups rely on one another to create an environment in which innovations occur regularly and knowledge is generated and dispersed constantly. Consistent leadership between and among all of the firm's great groups results in innovative strategic thinking and rapid acceptance of organizational changes that even when difficult, are required to enhance firm performance. Top managers who facilitate the development of *great groups*—groups in which strategic leadership takes place among a range or people with different talents— have shifted the locus of responsibility to form adaptive solutions to issues from themselves to the organization's full citizenry.[29]

As knowledge sharing and developing entities, great groups have several characteristics.[30] First, members of great groups have accepted their responsibility for firm outcomes. Involved and committed, these people understand the significance of their work and their responsibility to each other.[31] Second, great groups seek to learn from multiple parties, including contractors, suppliers, partners, and customers. Group members are committed to the position that "No matter where knowledge comes from, the key to reaping a big return is (for the group) to leverage that knowledge by replicating it throughout the company so that each unit is not learning in isolation and reinventing the wheel again and again."[32]

The third great group characteristic concerns information and knowledge. Increasingly, the information great groups gather to form knowledge and to understand how to use knowledge already possessed must come from events and conditions outside the organization. In Peter Drucker's view, it is primarily information from outside that allows a business to decide ". . . how to allocate its knowledge resources in order to produce the highest yield. Only with such information can a business also prepare for new changes and challenges arising from sudden shifts in the world economy and in the nature and content of knowledge itself. The development of rigorous methods for gathering and analyzing outside information will increasingly become a major challenge for businesses and for information experts."[33] Great groups respond positively to Drucker's challenge and are learning how to interpret external information in competitively relevant terms. In the 21st century, it will be increasingly vital for the firm's strategic leadership processes to adopt this perspective regarding the acquisition and use of information flows.

Another characteristic of great groups is their maintenance of records of individuals' knowledge stocks. With these records, people can find others quickly who possess the knowledge required to solve problems as they arise. Maintaining and using these records demonstrates these groups' ability to work smarter through their collective insights and the skills resulting from them.[34] Finally, great groups understand that the firm's method of strategic leadership results in a constantly changing configuration of responsibilities. Across tasks, every member of great groups serves, at different times, as a leader, peer, or subordinate. The operationalization of this understanding results in mutual influence relationships among the firm's top managers and all organizational citizens, including those with formal managerial responsibilities.[35]

Perhaps the most important "great group" in an organization is the top management team (TMT) that is formed by the CEO. The top management team is a relatively small group of executives, usually between three and ten people. These individuals are at the apex of the organization and provide strategic leadership.[36]

Because of the complexity of the new competitive landscape, both in its structure and dynamism, the collective intellect generated by a top management team is necessary for effective strategic leadership to occur in the firm. A philosopher's view demonstrates this point: "None of us is as smart as all of us."[37] The large number of organizational stakeholders, alone, makes it necessary to depend on a team of top executives for strategic leadership. However, perhaps the global economy, more than any other factor, has created the need for the top management team to effectively exercise strategic leadership in organizations. The knowledge needed to understand and operate in many global markets is substantial, thereby requiring a team effort. In fact, global firms such as Asea Brown Boveri (ABB) believe that it is necessary to have a culturally diverse TMT to successfully operate in such markets. This is particularly important because of the emphasis on gaining external knowledge, as identified earlier. Such knowledge is necessary to develop a collective vision for the organization and to gain the multiple constituencies' commitment to pursuit of the vision.

Because of multiple stakeholders with competing interests, there is need for a heterogeneous TMT, one with members having different knowledge sets and skills.[38] While the CEO remains the top leader, s/he must use these different knowledge sets and skills to successfully manage the organization. Viewing the other members of the TMT as partners allows the CEO to do this effectively. But, beyond this, top managers should treat all employees as partners. This is especially true in flatter, matrix type organizations—an organizational form that will be used increasingly in 21st century firms. In such organizations, top managers manage across traditional boundaries (e.g., functions), building the horizontal organization in the process.[39]

Even though the operational details of effective strategic leadership (including the increasing use of top management teams) are continuing to change as the global economy evolves toward the 21st century, it is important to note that as the firm's top manager, the CEO remains accountable for the entire firm's performance. In fact, this critical responsibility cannot be delegated to others. In the final analysis, those monitoring the top manager's performance (i.e., the Board of Directors), will hold the CEO accountable for guiding the firm in ways that best serve the interests of owners (e.g., shareholders) and other stakeholders. Even in the 21st century's global economy, the ultimate accountability for use of effective strategic leadership practices rests with the firm's "chief leader"—the CEO. As such, tomorrow's organizations will still require a "great leader" to be successful. Among other abilities, great leaders are able to share responsibility for leading and managing business units. The great leader mindset is one through which the top manager decides to share widely information and ideas with others and to seek mutual influence among all who have accepted the responsibility to contribute to the formation and achievement of the firm's direction. Thus, as the following discussion suggests, the breadth and depth of those the CEO will choose to involve in the pursuit of effective leadership practices in 21st century firms will be much different as compared to today.

The Great Leader's (Top Manager's) Strategic Leadership Role in 21st Century Organizations

As noted above, the top manager's ultimate responsibility for organizational outcomes will not be questioned in the 21st century. Clearly, it is the CEO and perhaps the relatively small number of upper level executives comprising the top management team that will remain accountable for being able to develop the firm so that it can adapt and succeed in both present and future times.

Linked with discharging this responsibility successfully is the top manager's ability to understand organizational outcomes desired by the firm's stakeholders (e.g., shareholders, financial institutions, customers, suppliers, employees, and local communities). Building relationships with stakeholders yields information about their expectations and facilitates efforts to balance often competing stakeholder interests. Discussions related to building these relationships focus on issues such as the nature of competition facing the firm and the values that guide the corporation's orientations and actions, among others.

What will be different in 21st century companies is *how* top managers discharge their strategic leadership responsibilities. No longer viewing their leadership position as one with rank and title but rather as a position of significant responsibility to a range of stakeholders, and instead of seeking to provide all of the "right" answers, 21st century top managers will strive to ask the "right" questions of community citizens they have empowered to work as partners with them. As the person responsible for selecting the firm's architecture, the top manager can choose to form a community of colleagues rather than a company of employees who are led primarily through the constraints of traditional hierarchical configurations.

To fulfill their responsibilities through interactive and shared leadership practices, the top managers must affect the behaviors of many stakeholders, but especially those of organizational citizens. Working often as a coach, it will be vital for the 21st century's top manager to create the organizational community described above. When created through the leadership and support of the top managers, an organizational community is one in which citizens' creative energy is released, their self-confidence is enhanced,[40] and they are inspired to assume responsibility for leading themselves through the work of great groups. Successful organizational communities unleash the genius of all. Sharing among inspired and committed citizens facilitates the emergence of the collective magic that creates intellectual capital and knowledge. As such, an effective strategic leader "finds glory in the whole team reaching the summit together."[41]

Perspectives from two international executives capture the nature of the top manager's strategic leadership responsibility in 21st century firms. John Browne, CEO of British Petroleum Company, believes that the top manager must stimulate the organization rather than control it. In this role, the top manager provides strategic directives, encourages learning that results in the formation of intellectual capital, and verifies that mechanisms exist to transfer intellectual capital across all of the firm's parts. Moreover, Browne believes that "the role of leaders at all levels is to demonstrate to people that they are capable of achieving more than they think they can achieve and that they should never be satisfied with where they are now."[42] Heinrch von Pierer, President and CEO of Siemens AG, has suggested that some skills used today by top managers to lead their organizations will become even more important in the 21st century. In von Pierer's words, "As we move into what will be a century of unprecedented challenges, successful leaders will rely even more intensely on strengths that have become crucial in recent years: speed of decision, flexibility, capable delegation, teamwork, the ability to build for the long term while meeting short-term needs—and vision. Increasingly, networked and globalized thinking will be essential for coping with the accelerating pace of change."[43]

Based on the evidence discussed above, we believe that 21st century strategic leadership should be executed through interactions that are based on a sharing of insights, knowledge, and responsibilities for achieved outcomes. These interactions should occur between the firm's great leaders—the top managers—and its citizens. These interactions take place as the firm satisfies the requirements associated with six key effective strategic leadership practices.

Although considered individually, it is through the configuration of all six activities that strategic leadership can be effective in the 21st century organization.

Determining the Firm's Purpose or Vision

As indicated above, the CEO is the person who is, in the final analysis, held accountable for the firm's performance. Because of this accountability, and the authority vested in their organizational position, CEOs must play the primary role in establishing the firm's purpose or vision. To fulfill this responsibility successfully, the CEO often involves the top management team in this process, as well as other organizational citizens. Nonetheless, the task of determining the direction of the firm rests squarely on the CEO's shoulders, Joe Gorman, TRW's CEO, argues that the notion that the top manager should not be responsible for forming the firm's purpose is ". . . sheer and utter nonsense." More specifically, Gorman believes that the top manager, often working in concert with the TMT, must provide general guidelines as to where the firm intends to go and the key steps to be taken to reach that end.[44] As demonstrated by the following comment, J. Tracy O'Rourke, CEO of Varian Associates, Inc., endorses Gorman's view: "Clearly, if you're going to do well over time, you have to have some ability—yourself or in combination with others—to come up with a vision . . . and then follow it up with believable and implementable action plans. In most corporate structures, the only person who can do that is the CEO."[45] The perspective held by Gorman and O'Rourke is supported by the results of a recent survey of 1,450 executives from 12 global corporations. The most important of 21 competencies these executives said would be crucial skills for global leaders to possess in the future was the ability to "articulate a tangible vision, values, and strategy" for their firm.[46]

Various definitions of purpose or vision have been offered. However, the one advanced recently by John Browne, British Petroleum's CEO, captures the attributes of an effective organizational purpose for 21st century firms. Browne argues that as a description of *who* the firm is and *what makes it distinctive,* purpose indicates what a company exists to achieve and what it is willing and not willing to do to achieve it. Browne also believes that a clear purpose ". . . allows a company to focus its learning efforts in order to increase its competitive advantage."[47] Visions that facilitate development of this type of focus make sense to all organizational citizens, stretch citizens' imaginations but are still within the bounds of possibility, are understood easily, and create a cultural glue that allows units to share knowledge sets.[48]

As described previously, viewing an organization as a community elicits greater involvement from all citizens. In 21st century firms with effective strategic leadership practices, this involvement, with respect to the firm's purpose or vision, will be most apparent at the implementation level. Once the CEO and the TMT have set the general organizational purpose, all other citizens, including the TMT, will be empowered to design and execute strategies and courses of action to accomplish that end.[49] Empowered organizational citizens working individually or as members of great groups in pursuit of the firm's purpose will be able to provide valuable feedback to the CEO and the TMT. This feedback will help the top executives develop the type of insights required to revisit the purpose regularly to verify its authenticity.

Recent decisions made at Rockwell International are an example of how the 21st century's successful CEOs can invite involvement from citizens to achieve the firm's purpose. The firm's new vision is for the company to become "The world's best diversified high-technology company." The CEO and TMT believe that several actions are necessary for this vision to be reached. Included among these actions are the aggressive pursuit of global growth, the execution of leading-edge business practices, and the manufacture and distribution of products that will allow the firm's customers to be the most successful in the world in their business operations.

Critical to efforts to achieve the firm's vision is the intended active involvement of Rockwell employees (organizational citizens). At locations throughout the world, employees are to be challenged to take determined actions that will help the firm achieve its purpose. To select appropriate actions, employees/citizens are being formed into "great groups." Each of the 23-implementation teams (or great groups) that have been organized is being asked to identify strengths and weaknesses of its unit. Once known, each unit is to develop recommendations that when accomplished will allow it to become the best in the world at completing a particular task or set of activities.[50] This pattern—wherein organizational citizens work as members of a community that is seeking to fulfill a purpose that serves the common good—will be linked with effective strategic leadership practices in the 21st century.

Occurring now but expected to be an even more prominent feature of the 21st century's global economy, the blurring of industry boundaries stimulates the emergence of new and sometimes aggressive competitors with significant resource bases. These changes in the composition of competitive arenas will create interesting challenges for firms' strategic leadership processes in terms of understanding other companies' purposes or visions. The announced entrance in early 1998 of the Korean giant, Samsung Group, into the world's automobile manufacturing industry demonstrates this challenge.

Although as of mid-1997 Samsung had never built and delivered to a customer a passenger car, it was in the midst of a $13 billion investment to allow the firm to manufacture 1.5 million cars annually. the vision suggesting these commitments and actions was for Samsung Group's automaking unit to rank among the world's top ten automakers by 2010. Expressing an operational demonstration of this vision are the words displayed on a billboard located outside of Samsung's new automobile manufacturing facility in Pusan: "Our dream and Korea's future."

Samsung Group's ambitious auto manufacturing goal surprised at least some industry analysts who noted that as the 21st century approached, the global auto industry was awash with excess production capacity—a problem not expected to abate in the foreseeable future. One noted industry observer suggested that "The world is not waiting breathlessly for a Samsung car . . . There's no logical opening in the marketplace where Samsung can step in and fill a vacuum. Its sales will have to come out of someone else's hide."[51] Beyond this, evidence was emerging in mid-1997 that at least some of South Korea's chaebols (or conglomerates) were encountering difficult performance challenges. In the main, analysts suggested that these difficulties were a product of too much diversification at too rapid a pace. A dominant chaebol, Samsung's future competitive intentions could be affected by these general problems.[52]

However, even in light of a daunting set of general environmental and specific competitive challenges, some believe it would be a serious mistake to underestimate Samsung's ability to make its vision a reality. In the words of Richard Pyo of Credit Suisse First Boston in Seoul, "Many people say that Samsung's plans are crazy and too risky, but the Korean economy has developed on gambles."[53]

As this example suggests, every automobile manufacturing company's strategic leadership is challenged to analyze carefully Samsung Group's ability to achieve its vision related to positioning in the world's auto marketplace. To respond successfully to this challenge, both the top managers (strategic leaders) and organizational citizens (through their work in great groups) in companies competing against Samsung Group's auto unit should use significant amounts of external information to select appropriate competitive responses.

Exploiting and Maintaining Core Competencies

Core competencies are the resources and capabilities the firm possesses that give it a competitive advantage over its rivals. The relatively unstable market conditions resulting from innovations, diversity of competitors, and the array of revolutionary technological changes occurring in the new competitive landscape have caused core competencies rather than served markets to become ". . . the basis upon which firms establish their long-term strategies."[54] In the 21st century, an ability to develop and exploit core competencies will be linked even more positively and significantly with the firm's success.

It is only the unique combinations of a firm's resources and capabilities that are valuable, rare, costly to imitate, and for which there are no equivalent strategic substitutes that can be rightly identified as core competencies.[55] In addition, it is only when uniform agreement exists within the organizational community about which resources and capabilities are indeed core competencies that appropriate actions can be designed to exploit them in the marketplace.[56] The large retailer Nordstrom Inc., for example, is thought to have core competencies in its customer service and ability to package merchandise in ways that provide unique value to customers. Dell Computer Corporation's distribution system is a key competitive advantage. Competencies in the general area of marketing and specific applications of special skills in advertising campaigns and its global brand name are recognized as core competencies for Philip Morris. In each of these cases, following agreement about their identification as core competencies, strategic leaders work tirelessly to apply the competencies in ways that will improve company performance.

The sharing of knowledge (or intellectual capital) that is unique to a particular organization will influence significantly the choices strategic leaders make when seeking to use core competencies in novel, yet competitively-relevant applications. Moreover, it is through the reciprocal sharing of knowledge and the learning that results from it that a firm's core competencies are nurtured effectively.

In general, knowledge is shared and learning occurs through superior execution of the human tasks of sensing, judging, creating, and building relationships.[57] The criticality of knowledge for firms seeking competitive advantage in the global economy is shown by the following comment about Owens Corning's positive financial performance in the recent past: Owens Corning success ". . . is a story about the competitive logic of the new economy: In the past year a series of moves in sales and marketing, information systems, and manufacturing and distribution have come together in a coherent strategy that is transforming this Midwestern maker of humdrum materials into a global competitor whose real business is knowledge."[58] Indeed, with only rare exceptions, in the 21st century, a firm's productivity will lie more in its collective intellect—that is, in its collective capacity to gain and use knowledge—rather than in its hard assets such as land, plant, and equipment.[59]

As a set of problem-defining and problem-solving insights that fosters the development of idiosyncratic strategic growth alternatives, the competitive value of core competencies increases through their use and continuing development.[60] In this sense, a firm's privately held knowledge is the foundation of its competitively valuable core competencies; as such, it is increasing in importance as a driver of firms' strategic decisions and actions. The most effective strategic leadership practices in the 21st century will be ones through which strategic leaders find ways for knowledge to breed still more knowledge. The management of knowledge can increase a firm's effectiveness and efficiency because while physical assets such as land, machinery, and capital may be relatively scarce on a global basis, ideas and knowledge ". . . are abundant, they build on each other, and they can be reproduced cheaply or at no cost at all. In other words, ideas don't obey the law of diminishing returns, where adding more labor, machinery or money eventually delivers less and less additional output."[61]

Thus, it will be a through the development of firm-specific knowledge bases and their formation into core competencies that firms will be able to solve the complex competitive challenges of the 21st century's global economy. Johnson & Johnson's CEO is a strategic leader who believes in developing and nurturing his firm's knowledge base. Asked to describe factors that account for his company's success, the CEO suggested that his company is ". . . not in the product business. (It) is in the knowledge business."[62] However, knowledge cannot breed knowledge and core competencies cannot be emphasized and exploited effectively in the global marketplace without appropriate human capital.

Developing Human Capital

Human capital is the knowledge and skills of a firm's entire workforce or citizenry. Top managers who view organizational citizens as a critical resource on which many core competencies are built and through which competitive advantages are exploited successfully contribute positively to their work as strategic leaders. Given the array of issues discussed in this article, it will be even more critical for top managers to recognize the importance of human capital and support its continuous development during the 21st century.

In the global economy, significant investments will be required for the firm to derive full competitive benefit from its human capital. Some economists argue that these investments are ". . . essential to robust long-term growth in modern economies that depend on knowledge, skills, and information."[63] Thus, continual, systematic work on the productivity of knowledge and knowledge workers enhances the firm's ability to perform successfully. In addition, citizens appreciate the opportunity to learn continuously and feel greater involvement with their community when encouraged to expand their knowledge base. On-going investments in organizational citizens result in a creative, well-educated workforce—the type of workforce capable of forming highly effective great groups.

The importance of educational investments in citizens is being supported in a growing number of corporations. Andersen Consulting, for example, allocates 6 percent of its annual revenue on education and requires each professional employee to complete a minimum of 130 hours of training annually. Intel Corp. spends $3,500 per year per person on education. General Motors Corp. and General Electric are examples of a growing number of companies that have appointed people to a Chief Knowledge Officer position. In commenting about these actions, Warren Bennis suggests that "This institutionalization of education is not some fringe, feel-good benefit. It is tangible recognition that education gives the biggest bang for the corporate buck." Evidence for this assertion is provided by the results of a recent study, wherein researchers discovered that companies that invest 10 percent more in education receive an 8.5 percent increase in productivity. In contrast, companies boosted their productivity by only 3 percent as a result of a 10 percent increase in capital expenditures.[64]

The global economy allows firms to earn a financial premium through use of competitively superior practices in terms of the location, selection, and subsequent development of human capital. One key reason is that skilled labor is expected to be in short supply during the first part of the 21st century, at a minimum. For example, a net million new jobs in high technology will be created over the next decade with almost no increase in the supply of human resources to fill these jobs.[65]

The results of a survey of human resource managers conducted by the American Management Association revealed that 47 percent of the respondents worked in firms that faced skilled labor shortages. Interestingly, 54.7 percent of the same group of respondents also believe that the shortages in skilled personnel will be worse in 2000 and beyond. Another indicator of this shortage is the projection that as of mid-1997, at least 190,000 information technology jobs were vacant in U.S. companies alone. The fact that the number of college graduates earning undergraduate degrees in computer science declined by 43 percent between 1988 and 1997 suggested more serious labor shortages in the 21st century with the growing demand for information technology management specialists.[66]

There are several unintended negative consequences associated with skilled labor shortages. One of these concerns differences in work ethics and commitments. Evidence indicates, for example, that talented, dedicated, and motivated employees often become frustrated and dissatisfied when asked to work continuously with those without equivalent skills and commitments. The reactions of a successful financial analyst to some of her initial work-related experiences describe this situation: "I could not fathom, let alone accept, the extreme variations in work ethic, attention to detail, and commitment to job and company. All my prior work and school experience had been with creative, energized self-starters. It took me months, if not years, to value the diverse work styles and varying motivators of the work force I encountered."[67] Thus, a challenge to the work of tomorrow's strategic leaders is to find ways to encourage each employee to fulfill her or his potential. Especially when faced with labor shortages, the organizational community's common good can be reached only when each member of the great group is committed to full participation.

Greater workforce diversity is another issue that will confront 21st century strategic leaders as they seek to develop their community's human capital. Increasingly, organizational communities will be comprised of individuals from multiple countries and cultures—cultures that may have unique and idiosyncratic value structures. To gain the benefits this diversity promises, CEOs and TMTs should develop a global mindset; a mindset through which individuals are able to appreciate the beliefs, values, behaviors, and business practices of companies competing in a variety of regions and cultures. Among other benefits, a global mindset help organizational citizens to better understand the realities and preferences that are a part of the region and culture in which they are working.

To sensitize themselves to the diversity of other cultures, Peter Brabeck-Letmathe, CEO of Nestle SA, believes that it is increasingly important for top managers to speak at least two or three languages.[68] Cross-border and culture transfers among organizational citizens will be used prominently in the 21st century as will other actions (e.g., the use of experts to help people understand the nuances of other cultures) that are intended to help people bond together in the pursuit of the firm's purpose. Similar to ABB today, many firms' TMTs will be culturally diverse. Critical to the success of all of these efforts will be the ability of the firm's top managers to form a community of citizens rather than a band of employees working for a firm. As noted earlier, organizational communities are social constructions of people who remain joined together because the common good they pursue serves as a cultural glue.

As explained next, the firm's human capital plays a critical role in efforts to develop and sustain an effective organizational culture.

Sustaining an Effective Organizational Culture

Organizational culture refers to the complex set of ideologies, symbols, and core values shared throughout the firm. The growing importance of culture to success in the 21st century has been highlighted recently. In fact, several business writers believe that the challenges to firms in the 21st century will not be so much technical or rational as cultural: "how to lead the organizations that create and nurture knowledge; how to know when to set our machines aside and rely on instinct and judgment; how to live in a world in which companies have ever increasing visibility; and how to maintain, as individuals and organizations, our ability to learn."[69]

In combination, the attributes of a culture describe how the firm conducts its business; moreover, culture provides the context within which strategies are formulated and implemented. Thus, organizational culture is concerned with decisions, actions, communications patterns, and communication networks. Formed over the life of a company, culture reflects what the firm has learned across time through its responses to the continuous challenges of survival and growth. As an evolved context, culture is rooted in history, held collectively, and of sufficient complexity to resist many attempts at direct manipulation. Because it influences how the firm conducts its business as well as the methods used to regulate and control the behavior of organizational citizens, culture can be a competitive advantage.

In the global economy, strategic leaders capable of learning how to shape a firm's culture in competitively relevant ways will become a valued source of competitive advantage. Chrysler Corp.'s CEO Robert Eaton and President Robert Lutz are examples of strategic leaders thought to be sources of competitive advantage for their firm. To explain his company's recent recognition as "Detroit's profitability champion," Eaton suggested that the secret to Chrysler's late 1990's success is the "Chrysler difference; a corporate culture that rejects Motown's hidebound bureaucratic traditions." Some analysts support this suggestion, noting that "no group of managers has stirred up Detroit more since Ford's fabled Whiz Kids of the 1950s." Through their work with the firm's managers, Eaton and Lutz set a tone and pattern of interactions that have dramatically shaped Chrysler's culture. In one writer's view, the firm's tone ". . . is set by Eaton, whose low-key demeanor belies a fierce competitive streak, and Lutz, the swashbuckling ex-Marine with a flair for product creation. But behind Eaton and Lutz, Chrysler boasts a little-known cast of managers who've become the envy of the industry."[70]

The social energy that drives Southwest Airlines is thought by many to be both truly unique and a source of sustainable competitive advantage. Hosted by the company's University for People and detailed in a program delivered to employees on "Culture Day," the firm's culture is largely a product of CEO Herb Kelleher and the managers who surround him. Among other positive outcomes attributed to the social energy of the firm's culture are the company's steady growth, above-average profitability, and the avoidance of employee layoffs for 25 years. Actions that exemplify Southwest's effective culture include: "Pilots hold barbecues to thank mechanics; flight attendants sing safety instructions on board; agents hang mirrors on their computers to make sure they're smiling when taking reservations; Kelleher is generous with hugs and kisses." In the final analysis, the values shared throughout this firm are reflected by employees' commitments to treat co-workers and customers with respect and dignity, have fun, and work hard. An indicator of this culture's desirability is the fact that in 1996 alone, 137,000 people applied for only 5,000 Southwest Airlines' job openings.[71]

As these company-specific examples suggest, effective cultures are ones in which organizational citizens understand that competitive advantages do not last forever; as such, the firm must move forward continuously. When the firm's culture is one in which citizens are comfortable with the reality of constant change and the need for a never-ending stream of innovations, patterns and practices are in place that can enhance global competitiveness.

Emphasizing Ethical Practices

One characteristic of organizational cultures that may be critical to achieve a competitive advantage is an emphasis on the development and use of ethical practices. Among other positive contributions, ethical practices serve as a moral filter through which potential courses of action are evaluated.[72]

Top managers' influence on the firm's ethical practices and outcomes is accepted within the broader society and by business practitioners and academics. In the 21st century, effective strategic leaders will use honesty, trust, and integrity as the foundations for their decision-making processes. Strategic leaders displaying these qualities across time and different situations are capable of inspiring their employees as they pursue jointly the development of an organizational culture in which ethical practices are the behavioral norm. Acer CEO Stan Shih, for example, has noted that for his employees, there is simply no alternative to dealing honestly with all of the firm's stakeholders. Shih's belief that human nature is basically positive and good could be the force driving his forthright and ethical business practices.[73]

The challenge facing all strategic leaders desiring to establish and support the use of ethical practices throughout all parts of their firm is to determine how to instill normative values into the corporate decision-making processes. These values should guide corporate action and individuals' behaviors.[74] In the final analysis, ethical decision-making processes result in the use of organizational resources to obtain benefits desired by legitimate stakeholders. A strategic leader's commitment to pursuits in which legal, ethical; and social concerns have been taken into account is thought to be both morally right and economically efficient.

It will be difficult for strategic leaders to establish ethical practices—ones through which decision-making processes are used consistently that successfully serve the interests of all legitimate stakeholders—in the 21st century's global economy. Accounting for this difficulty is the significant diversity of the different cultures and economic structures within which the global firm will compete. Acquiring an understanding of the interests of all legitimate stakeholders will occur only through completion of in-depth analyses that are conducted through practices that are cognizant of and sensitive to cultural diversity. However, strategic leaders' commitments to serve stakeholders' legitimate claims will contribute to the establishment and continuation of an ethical organizational culture. Importantly, employees' practices that take place in an ethical culture become institutionalized throughout the firm. In other words, they become the set of accepted and expected commitments, decisions, and actions taken when dealing with the firm's stakeholders.

As discussed next, an organizations' control systems can support the use of ethical practices. In addition, control systems are vital links to the strategic leader's attempts to complete the other five components of effective strategic leadership we have examined.

Establishing Balanced Organizational Controls

Organizational controls exist to increase the probability the firm will achieve its desired outcomes. Effective controls build credibility for top managers and great groups alike, demonstrate the value of the firm's strategies to stakeholders, and promote the development of skills required for citizens to implement appropriate strategic changes.

Controls are the formal, information-based procedures strategic leaders and managers use to frame, maintain, and alter patterns of organizational activities.[75] The realities of the new competitive landscape increase the difficulty of establishing effective organizational controls; a key reason is that by their nature, controls limit employees' behaviors. Through interaction patterns demanded by controls, individuals' work is influenced and guided by strategic leaders in ways necessary to achieve performance objectives. However, the new competitive landscape is replete with opportunities that are addressed most effectively through innovation and creativity. Thus, in the 21st century, a competitive premium will be earned by strategic leaders able to establish controls that facilitate the display of flexible, innovation-oriented employee behaviors focused on the pursuit of agreed-upon performance objectives. Effective strategic leaders use organizational controls that strike an appropriate balance between employee empowerment, primarily to great groups, and behavioral parameters to ensure that the firm deals proactively and effectively with the new competitive landscape's uncertainties and discontinuities.

Top managers are responsible for the development and effective use of two types of internal controls—strategic controls and financial controls.[76] Strategic controls entail the use of long-term and strategically relevant criteria to evaluate performance; and, they focus on the content of strategic actions. In contrast, financial controls are concerned with *outcomes* resulting from actions taken. Strategic controls emphasize largely subjective and sometimes intuitive criteria for evaluation purposes.

Strategic controls require information-based exchanges among the CEO, top management team members, and organizational citizens. To exercise effective strategic control, top managers must acquire deep understandings of the competitive conditions and dynamics of each of the units or divisions for which they are responsible. Exchanges of information occur through both informal, unplanned meetings and interactions scheduled on a routine, formal basis. The effectiveness of strategic controls is increased substantially when strategic leaders are able to integrate disparate sets of information in ways that yield competitively relevant insights. Because their emphasis is on actions rather than outcomes, strategic controls encourage lower-level managers to make decisions that incorporate moderate and acceptable levels of risk. Moreover, a focus on the content of strategic actions provides the flexibility managers and other great group members require to take advantage of competitive opportunities that develop rapidly in the new competitive landscape.

Financial controls entail objective criteria (e.g., various accounting-based measures) that strategic leaders use to evaluate returns earned by company units and those responsible for their performance. By focusing on performance-induced outcomes, financial controls encourage the accomplishment of short-term performance goals. Additionally, an emphasis on financial rather than strategic controls results in managerial rewards being contingent on achievement of financial outcomes. Therefore, an emphasis on short-term financial performance goals encourages risk-adverse managerial decisions and behaviors.

Effective top managers seek to develop and use a balanced set of strategic and financial controls. Typically, this outcome is achieved by using strategic controls to focus on positive long-term results while pursuing simultaneously the requirement to execute corporate actions in a financially prudent and appropriate manner. In this fashion, strategic leaders are able to use strategic controls to increase the probability that their firm will gain the benefits of carefully formulated strategies, but not at the expense of financial performance critical to successful strategy implementation processes and to the firm's ability to satisfy selected stakeholders. Nonetheless, the diversity of the global economy, coupled with the dynamic challenges embedded within the new competitive landscape, highlight the increasing importance of strategic controls. Providing the leadership required for the firm to compete successfully in multiple countries and cultures demands strategic leadership practices oriented largely to the integration of disparate competitive information and the use of broad-based strategic controls.

In the next section, we present recommendations that will contribute to the use of effective strategic leadership practices in 21st century firms. These recommendations flow from the analyses and discussions presented above.

Recommendations for Effective Strategic Leadership Practices

In part, the arguments presented herein are framed around the belief that competition in the 21st century global economy will occur in the postindustrial era. Developed in industrialized Western societies over roughly the last quarter of the 20st century, postindustrial societies are characterized by conditions that differ somewhat dramatically from those associated with the industrial societies they are replacing.

In the industrial era (represented in the United States, for example, by the years between the industrial revolution and the later stages of the 20th century), industrial societies and the commercial enterprises operating within them were focused primarily on activities intended to create wealth. Technological and scientific advances were the principal means through which wealth was created during this time period. Among the many sectors in which technological and scientific advances led to the creation of wealth are medicine, agriculture, communications, energy, transportation, and electronics. In the postindustrial era, information-based technology and internationalization are the primary drivers of companies' wealth creation activities. Moreover, as shown by the following comments, the economic, social, and political attributes that are the foundation of the postindustrial era differ from those associated with its predecessor in some fundamental and important ways: "(1) much of the economic production occurs in service and high-technology sectors; (2) there is increasing globalization of finance, production, labor, and product markets, (3) economic growth is confronted with ecological limits, and (4) there is a movement toward democratization of markets and politics" in many of the world's countries.[77] This suggests that the postindustrial era will expand throughout the world during the 21st century, stimulating the development of additional competitors in many nations.

Collectively, the attributes of the postindustrial era interact to create more risk for firms, in terms of economic gains and losses, as they attempt to create wealth through decisions regarding how to compete in multiple marketplaces.

Thus, the nature of strategic leadership has changed from the industrial era, a time period in which the U.S. and other Western societies were viewed primarily as manufacturing societies. To successfully manage firms competing in the risk-laden postindustrial era, an era in which competition is more complex and hostile, strategic leaders face many challenges. Challenges of these types may become pervasive in the 21st century across multiple countries in light of increases in the number of market democratization processes occurring throughout the world.

Important orientations and actions associated with effective strategic leadership practices in the postindustrial era of the 21st century are presented in the following recommendations. In combined form, adherence to these recommendations will facilitate strategic leaders' efforts to successfully complete the activities comprising the six components of effective strategic leadership examined herein.

A Growth Orientation

The realities of competition in the global economy demand a corporate focus on growth rather than downsizing and cost reductions. A variety of strategic approaches can be used in the pursuit of growth, including those of acquisition, an emphasis on innovation and product development, a shift to extreme decentralization in the firm to stimulate entrepreneurial behaviors among organizational citizens, and a concentration on product line extensions intended to provide customers with additional value. The means chosen for growth are less critical than the desired outcome. In other words, to achieve strategic competitiveness consistently in the global economy, growth must be emphasized; but, an array of options can be considered as the means to achieve it. The most effective strategic leaders will be capable of working with all organizational citizens to find ways to match the firm's resources, capabilities, and core competencies with relevant growth-oriented opportunities in the external environment.

Knowledge Management

Increasingly, firms can be viewed as bodies of unique, idiosyncratic knowledge. As the intellectual capital on which a firm's competitive advantages are based and sustained, knowledge will be a primary driver and determinant of competitive success in the 21st century. Thus, it is the 21st century that the shift from the age of mass production to the age of brainpower will be finalized.

Because of its centrality to strategic competitiveness and the firm's financial returns, strategic leaders must enable their organization to develop, exploit, and protect the intellectual capital contained in citizens' knowledge bases. Fluid, elusive, and intangible, knowledge creation is often a product of interactions between the firm's citizens and other stakeholders. Strategic leaders are challenged to develop pathways through which knowledge can be transferred to people and units in which it can be further developed and used to pursue strategic competitiveness. Managing knowledge in this manner challenges conventional thinking and increases the likelihood that the firm will be able to create new competitive space in its markets. The importance of intellectual capital, both today and in the 21st century has been emphasized by Warren Bennis, as indicated in the following statements; "I am convinced that the key to competitive advantage in the 1990s and beyond will be the capacity of leadership to create the social architecture that generates intellectual capital. Success will belong to those who unfetter greatness within their organizations and find ways to keep it there."[78]

Cooperative strategies, voluntary interfirm collaborations involving the exchange, sharing, and co-development of new products and technologies, will be vital to the management of knowledge in the 21st century. Through these voluntary arrangements (e.g., strategic alliances, joint ventures, technology exchanges, licensing agreements, and so forth), firms pool their resources to create goods and services with economic value. Thus, interfirm collaborations have a strategic focus—the creation of knowledge that, in turn, facilitates the development of competitively valuable goods or services.[79] Strategic leaders who learn how to manage effectively the reciprocal interdependencies between their company and the other economic units with which interfirm collaborations have been formed will become a source of competitive advantage for their organization. Beyond this, the most effective strategic leaders will develop the skills required for their firms to engage simultaneously in competitive and cooperative behaviors.[80] Increasingly, the 21st century will be a time period in which companies that both effectively cooperate and compete with other enterprises will earn above-average financial returns more consistently. Throughout the firm, the creativity of great groups will be instrumental in isolating cooperative projects from those for which competitive behaviors are more appropriate.

Mobilization of Human Capital

Implied throughout herein is the need for companies to adapt to the significant changes that are a part of the global economy. Changes occurring in the world's societies, technologies, and markets are creating complex adaptive challenges for organizations. To cope with these challenges, 21st century strategic leaders will be challenged to mobilize citizens in ways that increase their adaptive abilities. to increase citizens' adaptive skills, leaders should refrain from providing answers; instead, their focus should become that of asking challenging questions. Framed around either cooperative or competitive issues, requesting that citizens working as members of great groups consider relevant information to determine how the firm can use its knowledge base to achieve strategic competitiveness will be an important task for the 21st century CEO and the top management team. Requesting that citizens proactively accept their roles as leader and colleague while working in great groups can be expected to mobilize efforts around key strategic issues. Facilitating citizens' efforts to challenge the historical conduct of business in the firm also can galvanize them as they seek to accomplish relevant goals. Importantly, the development and mobilization of human capital is vital if the firm is to achieve the strategic flexibility that is linked with success in the new competitive landscape.[81]

Developing an Effective Organizational Culture

As the social energy that drives the firm, culture exerts a vital influence on performance. To facilitate the development of values oriented to growth and success, 21st century strategic leaders should commit to being open, honest, and forthright in their interactions with all stakeholders, including organizational citizens.

These types of orientations and actions supported James Bonini's work as the manager of Chrysler Corp.'s big-van plant in Windsor, Ontario. At the young age of 33 and with limited manufacturing experience, some plant employees' initial response to Bonini was not favorable. Aware of this, Bonini knew his success would be influenced by his ability to gain the support of the plant's 84 managers, 1,800 workers, and officials of the local Canadian autoworker's union. In a display of candor and honesty, Bonini acknowledged immediately his youth and inexperience to those he was to lead. Moreover, he solicited help from all involved with the plant. Bonini also scheduled "town-hall" meetings to collect workers' ideas and listen to their complaints. He met with officials from the local union; based on their input that some workers had never met a plant manager, Bonini made certain that he was known by each employee. Meeting workers was facilitated by Bonini's frequent visits to the plant floor to verify that work was preceding as intended and to request workers' insights regarding how manufacturing processes could be improved. Contributing to Bonini's success in this plant assignment was employees' positive response to the candor, honesty, and integrity on which his decisions and actions were based.[82]

Because of extensive cultural diversity, developing an effective organizational culture (as James Bonini was able to do) in firms competing in the global economy will be quite difficult and challenging. Nonetheless, the competitive benefits of achieving success in these attempts are significant. Being candid about one's strengths and weaknesses, seeking and placing value on others' insights, and demanding that people reach their full potential while supporting their efforts to do so are actions that can help develop an appropriate organizational culture.

Remaining Focused on the Future

As noted above, the economic, social, and political attributes of the postindustrial era are expected to influence a growing number of nations as the 21st century commences. Because of this postindustrial era's anticipated pervasive effects, strategic leaders must use some of their time and energies to predict future competitive conditions and challenges.

In the latter part of the 1990s, companies based in several countries, including the United States, Europe, and Japan, have intensified their competitive actions in the world's emerging markets. This emphasis is understandable, given that emerging markets constitute a new and important competitive frontier. However, high levels of risk are associated with these significant opportunities. Some analysts argue, for example, that the "tides of capitalism" prominent in developing countries' economies following the former Soviet Union's collapse are beginning to recede. Major reversals in the trend toward democratization of countries' markets and their accompanying political structures would have significant implications for strategic leaders and their firms.[83] Given these possibilities, effective strategic leaders seek information that will allow them to predict accurately changes in various global markets. Strategic collaborations, with host governments and other companies, is a valuable means of dealing with changing conditions in emerging economic structures. By aligning their strategies with an emerging country's best interests, firms, operating either individually or in collaboration with others, increase their chance of competitive success in volatile situations. Failure to develop these understandings will inhibit strategic leaders' efforts to lead their firms effectively in the 21st century.

A Final Thought

Our interest has been to advance and consider an array of issues related to the practice of strategic leadership in organizations. As we have discussed, effective strategic leadership in the 21st century will differ somewhat dramatically from what is was in the 20th century. In particular, these variances call for different orientations and actions from the firm's chief strategic leader—the CEO.

Derived from analyses included in this article, the significant differences between effective strategic leadership practices in the 20th and the 21st centuries, as demonstrated by CEOs, are presented in Table 1. CEOs who approach strategic leadership in the 21st century as called for by the appropriate one-half of Table 1 will be a source of competitive advantage for their organization. In turn, the competitive advantage resulting from the work of the CEO as the chief leader and the contributions of great groups as members of an organizational community will allow the firm to improve its global competitiveness as it competes in the 21st century.

TABLE 1

Strategic Leadership Practices

The CEO and 20th Century Strategic Leadership	The CEO and 21th Century Strategic Leadership
Outcome focused	Outcome and process focused
Stoic and confident	Confident, but without hubris
Sought to acquire knowledge	Seeks to acquire and leverage knowledge
Guided people's creativity	Seeks to release and nurture people's creativity
Work flows determined by hierarchy	Work flows influenced by relationships
Articulated the importance of integrity	Demonstrates the importance of integrity by actions
Demanded respect	Willing to earn respect
Tolerated diversity	Seeks diversity
Reacted to environmental change	Proacts to anticipate environmental change
Served as the great leader	Serves as the leader and as a great group member
Views employees as a resource	Views organizational citizens as a critical resource
Operated primarily through a domestic mindset	Operates primarily through a global mindset
Invested in employees' development	Invests significantly in citizens continuous development

References

1. Five business thinkers, Peter F. Drucker, Esther Dyson, Charles Handy, Paul Saffo, and Peter M. Senge were asked recently by *Harvard Business Review* to describe the challenges they see already taking shape for executives as they move into the next century. The challenges discussed by these people are presented in: P.F. Drucker, E. Dyson, C. Handy, P. Saffo and P.M. Senge, "Looking Ahead: Implications of the Present," *Harvard Business Review,* 75(5), 1997, 18–32.

2. The importance of strategic leadership for 21ˢᵗ century firms is described in: M. Davids, "Where Style Meets Substance," *Journal of Business Strategy,* 16(1), 1995, 48–60; R.P. White, P. Hodgson, and S. Crainer. *The Future of Leadership* (London: Pitman Publishing, 1997).

3. Additional definitional information about strategic leadership can be found in: C.M. Christensen, "Making Strategy: Learning by Doing," *Harvard Business Review,* 75(6), 1997, 141–156; M.A. Hitt, R.D. Ireland, and R.E. Hoskisson, *Strategic Management: Competitiveness and Globalization,* Second Edition (Minneapolis: West Publishing, an International Thomson Publishing (ITP) Company, 1997).

4. John Browne, CEO of British Petroleum, describes a wide range of competitive approaches being used at BP. Among the multiple topics Browne addresses is how he defines competitive advantage. For more information about his views, see: S.E. Prokesch, "Unleashing the Power of Learning: An Interview with British Petroleum's John Browne," *Harvard Business Review,* 75(5), 1997, 147–168.

5. The universal need for each firm to develop a competitive advantage serves as a foundation for two authors analysis of how strategic management can be improved. For additional information on this subject, see: A. Campbell and M. Alexander, "What's Wrong with Strategy?" *Harvard Business Review,* 75(6), 1997, 42–51.

6. Mr. Gorman's viewpoint is included in an article in which potential reasons for the recent success of U.S. firms in the global economy are examined. For further information see: G.P. Zachary, "Behind Stocks' Surge is an Economy in Which Big U.S. Firms Thrive," *Wall Street Journal,* November 22, 1995, A-1, A-3.

7. Based on an argument that globalization is a reality of our time, one business writer offers intriguing perspectives regarding the level and degree of economic interdependence of the world's nations. To explore his views further, see: R. Ruggiero, "The High Stakes of World Trade," *Wall Street Journal,* April 28, 1997, A18.

8. In light of the global economy, an interesting set of predictions about the nature of business firms and their leaders in the 21st century can be found in: S. Makridakis, "Management in the 21ˢᵗ Century," *Long Range Planning,* 22, April, 1989, 37–53.

9. The director of the Institute for International Economics offers his optimistic perspective about the characteristics of a global economy in: C.F. Bergsten, "The Rationale For a Rosy View," *The Economist,* September 11, 1993, 57–58.

10. Peter Drucker made these observations in an address to the Knowledge Advantage Conference sponsored by the Ernst & Young Center for Business Innovation. Further details can be found in: "Peter Drucker on The Newt 20 Years," *Executive Upside,* March, 1997, 3.

11. To better understand the possible nature of the global marketplace in the future, a senior writer reviewed several books. His reviews can be found in: F.R. Bleakley, "The Future of the Global Marketplace," *Wall Street Journal,* March 15, 1996, A13.

12. Unpredictable events affect firms of all sizes. An analysis of the effects of the new competitive landscape on high-growth entrepreneurial firms, companies that may be able to take competitive advantage of the conditions resulting from these events, is presented in: R.D. Ireland and M.A. Hitt, "Performance Strategies for High-Growth Entrepreneurial Firms," Paper presented at the 1997 Babson Entrepreneurship Conference, April, 1997.

13. In a recent article, two prominent researchers argue convincingly that "the complexity of political, regulatory, and technological changes confronting most organizations has made radical organizational change and adaptation a central research issue." To further explore this central issue see: R. Greenwood and

C.R. Hinings, "Understanding Radical Organizational Change: Bringing Together the Old and the New Institutionalism," *Academy of Management Review,* 21, 1996, 1022–1054.

14. Rapidly changing business conditions result in a premium being placed on the firm's ability to "speed up" its operations. Recent research suggests that this ability is especially important to develop a competitive advantage in firms in industries with shortened product life cycles. Arguments supporting this position are presented in: E.H. Kessler and A.K. Chakrabarti, "Innovation Speed: A Conceptual Model of Context, Antecedents, and Outcomes," *Academy of Management Review,* 21, 1996, 1143–1191.

15. Both Drucker and Senge emphasize this point in their descriptions of events that have already happened that are shaping the future for 21st century firms. For more information, see: Drucker, Dyson, Handy, Saffo, and Senge, "Looking Ahead: Implications of the Present," 18–32.

16. This positive projection of growth for at least the beginning part of the 21st century is presented in: *Dallas Morning News,* "Futurists See Bright 21st Century," June 11, 1997, D2.

17. An insightful treatment of the link between corporate entrepreneurship and the pursuit of organizational growth in firms facing challenging competitive environments is presented in: S.A. Zahra, "Environment, Corporate Entrepreneurship, and Financial Performance: A Taxonomic Approach," *Journal of Business Venturing,* 8, 1993, 319–340.

18. For additional information about how firms can mobilize to adapt their behaviors for competitive reasons, see: R.A. Heifetz and D.L. Laurie, "The Work of Leadership," *Harvard Business Review,* 75(1), 1997, 124–134.

19. Further arguments regarding the choices firms can make through the work of their strategic leaders and other key decision makers can be found in the following classic: J. Child, "Organizational Structure, Environment and Performance: The Role of Strategic Choice," *Sociology* 6, 1972, 1–22.

20. In a recent article, two researchers present a detailed analysis of different perspectives of strategic leadership that appear in the academic literature. This work is intended to present what the authors consider to be a "more realistic view of top managers' work." To examine the researchers' perspectives, see: A.A. Cannella, Jr. and M.J. Monroe, "Contrasting Perspectives on Strategic Leaders: Toward a More Realistic View of Top Managers," *Journal of Management,* 23, 1997, 213–237 (the quote in our article appears on page 213 of the Cannella and Monroe publication).

21. The historical isolation between strategic leaders and those they led is described in: P.M. Senge, "Communities of Leaders and Learners," *Harvard Business Review,* 75(5), 1997, 30–32.

22. W. Bennis, "Cultivating Creative Genius," *Industry Week,* August 18, 1997, 84–88.

23. This point is described in greater detail in Bennis, "Cultivating Creative Genius."

24. Some believe that understanding how to gather and interpret data is the organizational challenge of the next century. To evaluate this possibility, see: J. Teresko, "Too Much Data, Too Little Information," *Industry Week,* August 19, 1996, 66–70.

25. For a discussion of how uncertainty affects people at both upper and lower organizational levels, see: R.P. White, "Seekers and Scalers: The Future Leaders," *Training & Development,* January, 1997, 21–24.

26. Known widely as a preeminent business "thinker," Charles Handy explains his thoughts about organizational communities in: C. Handy, *The Age of Unreason* (Boston: Harvard Business School Press, 1989).

27. This quotation appears in: Bennis, "Cultivating Creative Genius," 88.

28. To explore the concept of great groups further, see: Bennis, "Cultivating Creative Genius."

29. The global economy demands that firms be able to adapt quickly to what often are rapid changes in the environments facing them. To study the view that effective leaders allow all organizational employees to play an active role in helping a firm become adaptive, see: Heifetz and Laurie, "The Work of Leadership."

30. To consider the view of British Petroleum's CEO about the value and nature of teams (or great groups) in the global economy, see: Prokesch, "Unleashing the Power of Learning: An Interview With British Petroleum's John Browne."

31. The importance of group members accepting the responsibility to support one another in their work is discussed in another one of Charles Handy's books: C. Handy, *The Age of Paradox* (Boston: Harvard Business School Press, 1994).

32. Among many points discussed by John Browne, the importance of learning how to leverage knowledge is perhaps given the most attention. To consider Browne's perspectives further, see: Prokesch, "Unleashing the Power of Learning: An Interview With British Petroleum's John Browne."

33. The criticality of external information for firms seeking high performance in the global economy is described in: P.F. Drucker, "The Future That Has Already Happened," *Harvard Business Review,* 75(5), 1997, 20–24.

34. The importance of collective work, and how such work can be stimulated, is discussed in: P.B. Vaill, *Managing As a Performing Art: New Ideas for a World of Chaotic Change* (San Francisco: Jossey-Bass, 1989).

35. The inclusive roles of organizational leaders is noted in: G. Dutton, "Leadership In a Post-Heroic Age," *Management Review,* October, 1996, 7.

36. An excellent, comprehensive analysis of strategic leadership and the role of the top management team as part of strategic leadership, appears in: S. Finkelstein and D.C. Hambrick, *Strategic Leadership: Top Executives and Their Effects on Organizations* (St. Paul: West Publishing, 1996).

37. This quote is taken from: Bennis, "Cultivating Creative Organizations."

38. Research results regarding the value of heterogeneous top management teams is explored carefully and in a detailed manner in: Finkelstein and Hambrick, *Strategic Leadership.*

39. D.F. Abell, "Mastering Management—Part 16," *Financial Times,* February 23, 1996, 13.

40. The important link between self-confidence and the successful completion of significant types of organizational work is discussed in: R.D. Ireland, M.A. Hitt, and J.C. Williams, "Self-Confidence and Decisiveness: Prerequisites for Effective Management in the 1990s," *Business Horizons,* 35(1), 1992, 36–43.

41. B.A. Nagle, "Wanted: A Leader for the 21st Century," *Industry Week,* November 20, 1995, 29.

42. This quote, and the importance of letting organizational citizens know that their strategic leaders want them to try different methods to satisfy the demands of new challenges, appears on page 158 of: Prokesch, "Unleashing the Power of Learning: An Interview With British Petroleum's John Browne."

43. Viewpoints of other leaders, in addition to von Pierer, can be found in: W.H. Miller, "Leadership at a Crossroads," *Industry Week,* August 19, 1996, 43–57.

44. Other aspects of Mr. Gorman's perspectives about the value of a corporate purpose are included in: Miller, "Leadership at a Crossroads."

45. Mr. O'Rourke offered this viewpoint as part of his description of what a leader must do to lead effectively. His perspectives can be studied fully by reading: W.H. Miller, "Leadership's Common Denominator," *Industry Week,* August 19, 1997, 97–100.

46. A full list of the 21 competencies identified by the survey's 1,450 participants can be viewed by reading: Davids, "Where Style Meets Substance."

47. This view is explained more fully in: Prokesch, "Unleashing the Power of Learning: An Interview With British Petroleum's John Browne."

48. Charles Handy considers these points in two books: *The Age of Paradox* and *The Age of Unreason.*

49. This point is articulated in: *The Economist,* "The Changing Nature of Leadership," June 10, 1995, 57.

50. Full details regarding actions framed by Rockwell's strategic leaders to achieve the firm's vision can be found in: "Its Time to Change Your Perception of Rockwell," Rockwell International Corporation Annual Report, 1995.

51. An intriguing analysis of decisions made by Samsung Group's strategic leaders regarding the firm's entry into the world's automobile manufacturing industry is featured in: L. Kraar, "Behind Samsung's High-Stakes Push Into Cars," *Fortune.* May 12, 1997, 119–120.

52. Large conglomerates, called chaebols, have played important roles in the growth of South Korea's economy. However, some evidence suggests that these huge firms may encounter additional competitive challenges in the future. Details of these challenges, and some of the chaebols' responses to them, are presented in: M. Schuman and N. Cho, "Troubles of Korean Conglomerates Intensity, Signaling End of an Era," *Wall Street Journal,*: April 25, 1997, A11.

53. Kraar, Behind Samsung's High-Stakes Push Into Cars, 119.

54. Some research proposes that knowledge is the most strategically significant source of core competence and thus, of competitive advantage for firms competing in the complex global economy. In a recent publication, this issue is explored through the development of a knowledge-based theory of organizational capability. To examine this theory see: R.M. Grant, "Prospering in Dynamically-Competitive Environments: Organizational Capability as Knowledge Integration," *Organization Science,* 7, 1996, 375–387.

55. Jay Barney's work informs our understanding of the criteria of sustainability. Two publications in which Barney's arguments are detailed are: J.B. Barney, "Looking Inside for Competitive Advantage," *Academy of Management Executive.* IX(4), 1995, 49–61; J.B. Barney, "Firm Resources and Sustained Competitive Advantage," *Journal of Management,* 17, 1991, 99–120.

56. The value of understanding the nature of a firm's core competencies is accepted widely. However, one researcher suggests that little guidance is available to help strategic leaders and their co-workers to define carefully their firm's capabilities and core competencies. The experiences of three top-level management teams to reach consensus about their respective firms' core competencies are described in: K.E. Marino, "Developing Consensus on Firm Competencies and Capabilities," *Academy of Management Executive,* X(3), 1996, 40–51.

57. Authored by a *Fortune* magazine writer, the following book examines the strategic nature and increasing value of knowledge for firms competing in the global economy: T.A. Stewart, *Intellectual Capital* (New York: Doubleday/Currency, 1997).

58. T.A. Stewart, "Owens Back From the Dead," *Fortune,* May 26, 1997, 118–126.

59. Based on the competitive value of the firm's collective intellect, three researchers have identified actions effective strategic leaders and their firms take to maximize the value of this critical organizational resource. These guidelines are offered in: J.B. Quinn, P. Anderson, and S. Finkelstein, "Leveraging Intellect," *Academy of Management Executive,* X(3), 1996, 7–27.

60. Based on organizational meta-learning processes, firms are able to continue gaining competitive advantages by exploiting dynamic core competencies. How this is accomplished is described in: D. Lei, M.A. Hitt, and R. Bettis, "Dynamic Core Competences Through Meta-Learning and Strategic Context," *Journal of Management,* 22, 1996, 549–569.

61. Economist Paul M. Romer's work is thought by some to be controversial. Romer's analyses suggest that ideas and technological discovery are the main drivers of a nation's economic growth. An introduction to these arguments is offered in: B. Wysocki, Jr., "For This Economist, Long-Term Prosperity Hangs on Good Ideas," *Wall Street Journal,* January 21, 1997, A1, A8.

62. H. Rudnitsky, "One Hundred Sixty Companies For the Price of One," *Forbes,* February 26, 1996, 56–62.

63. The potential value of additional national expenditures being allocated to education and training initiatives is explored by a prominent economist in: G.S. Becker, "Why the Dole Plan Will Work," *Business Week,* August 26, 1996, 16.

64. These points are discussed in Bennis, "Cultivating Organizational Genius."

65. J. Katkin, "Close the Talent Gap," *Houston Chronicle,* November 9, 1997, C1, C5.

66. These statistics are drawn from the following two sources: S. Baker, A. Barrett, and L. Himelstein, "Calling All Nerds," *Business Week.* March 10, 1997, 36–37; D. Kunke, "In Search of Expertise," *Dallas Morning News.* April 16, 1997, D1, D10.

67. A business practitioner who participated in a "debate" expressed this view. The focus of the debate was the extent to which the traditional model of the MBA degree is outdated. The full text of this debate appears in: "MBA: Is the Traditional Model Doomed?" *Harvard Business Review,* 70(6), 1992, 128–140.

68. For more information about Mr. Brabeck-Letmathe's views, see: Miller, "Leadership's Common Denominator."

69. These questions appear at the beginning of the interviews with Drucker, Dyson, Handy, Saffo, and Senge. For more information, see: "Looking Ahead: Implications of the Present."

70. B. Vlasic, "Can Chrysler Keep it Up?" *Business Week.* November 25, 1996, 108–120.

71. Southwest Airlines' culture has been cited frequently as a competitive advantage for the firm. Interestingly, everyone (except consultants and U.S. competitors) is welcome to attend the sessions in which the company's culture is discussed. Additional details about the firm's culture sessions are offered in: W. Zellner, "Southwest's Love Fest at Love Field," *Business Week,* April 28, 1997, 124.

72. To explore in greater detail how ethical practices can be used as decision filters, see: J.M. Lozano, "Ethics and Management: A Controversial Issue," *Journal of Business Ethics,* 15, 1996, 227–236; J. Milten-Smith, "Ethics as Excellence: A Strategic Management Perspective," *Journal of Business Ethics,* 14, 1995, 683–693.

73. L. Kraar, "Acer's Edge: PCs to Go," *Fortune,* October 30, 1995, 187–204.

74. The developing relationship between corporate social responsibility and society's expectations of corporations was considered through a special issue of *Academy of Management Review.* To examine the special issue's topics, consult the introductory comments included in: S.P. Sethi, "Introduction to *AMR's* Special Topic Forum on Shifting Paradigms: Societal Expectations and Corporate Performance," *Academy of Management Review,* 20, 1995, 18–21.

75. R. Simons, "How New Top Managers Use Control Systems As Levers of Strategic Renewal," *Strategic Management Journal,* 15, 1994, 169–189.

76. Extensive considerations of the differences between strategic controls and financial controls are presented in several publications including: M.A. Hitt, R.E. Hoskisson, R.A. Johnson, and D.D. Moesel, "The Market for Corporate Control and Firm Innovation," *Academy of Management Journal,* 39, 1996, 1084–1119; M.A. Hitt, R.E. Hoskisson, and R.D. Ireland, "Mergers and Acquisitions and Managerial Commitment to Innovation in M-form Firms," *Strategic Management Journal,* 11 (Special Issue), 1990, 29–47.

77. P. Shrivastava, "Ecocentric Management for a Risk Society," *Academy of Management Review,* 20, 1995, 119.

78. Bennis, "Cultivating Creative Genius," 87.

79. In the following publication, three researchers explain theoretically the value firms can derive through implementation of cooperative strategies formed through interfirm collaborations: A.A. Lado, N.G. Boyd, and S.C. Hanlon, "Competition, Cooperation, and the Search for Economic Rents: A Syncretic Model," *Academy of Management Review.* 22, 1997, 110–141. An extension of this argument is provided by two other researchers, who suggest that at least in a sample of entrepreneurial semiconductor firms, interfirm collaborations were found to form because of strategic needs and social opportunities. Based on their results, these researchers reported that alliances sometimes form when ". . . firms are in strong social positions such that they are led by large, experienced, and well-connected top management teams." This reasoning is examined in: K.M. Eisenhardt and C.B. Schoonhoven, "Resource-based View of Strategic Alliance Formation: Strategic and Social Effects in Entrepreneurial Firms," *Organization Science,* 7, 1996, 136–150.

80. In addition to explaining theoretically how firms earn economic rents individually from competitive strategies and from cooperative strategies, Lado, Boyd, and Hanlon also argue that "Success in today's business world often requires that firms pursue both competitive and cooperative strategies *simultaneously.*" Called syncretic rent-seeking behavior, these researchers explain in their *AMR* article (cited in footnote #79) what firms can do to earn economic rents while engaging jointly in competitive and cooperative behaviors.

81. This point is discussed in some detail in: M.A. Hitt, B.W. Keats and S. DeMarie, "Navigating in the New Competitive Landscape: Building Strategic Flexibility and Competitive Advantage in the 21st Century." *Academy of Management Executive,* 1998, in press.

82. A comprehensive description of James Bonini's experiences as a young, inexperienced manager at a Chrysler Corp. plant is offered in: G. Stern, "How a Young Manager Shook Up the Culture At Old Chrysler Plant," *Wall Street Journal,* April 21, 1997, A1, A6.

83. These possibilities, and their accompanying competitive implications for firms committed to achieving success in the global marketplace are examined in: J.E. Garten, "Troubles Ahead in Emerging Markets," *Harvard Business Review,* 1997, 75(3), 38–49.

Gray Flannel Suit?

Yes, *vous*. Ties between employees and companies are looser. But powerful new forces link them together. Smart people—and smart companies—should exploit both continuity and change.

by Thomas A. Stewart

He's gone, right? The man in the gray flannel suit, briefcase in hand, fedora on head, waiting on the platform for the 7:37 to go downtown. Stable, conservative, educated but not too clever, slightly behind his time rather than slightly ahead of it, the Organization Man seems more passé than a Rob Roy before lunch.

FORTUNE's William H. Whyte, who named Organization Man, described his kind in 1956: "They are all, as they so often put it, in the same boat. Listen to them talk to each other over the front lawns of their suburbia and you cannot help but be struck by how well they grasp the common denominators which bind them. . . . They are keenly aware of how much more deeply beholden they are to organization than were their elders. They are wry about it, to be sure; they talk of the 'treadmill,' the 'rat race,' of the inability to control one's direction. But they have no great sense of plight; between themselves and organization they believe they see an ultimate harmony. . . ."

The new orthodoxy is that there is no such orthodoxy. There are no implicit contracts and not many explicit ones. No loyalty. No common lot. No harmony of interests, no trust that what's good for General Motors is good for us, personally. No one who can promise anyone a job, except a customer—and customers force us to apply for our jobs again and again; not faithful wives but fickle mistresses, customers daily remind us that they will leave for a younger guy with thicker hair if we don't bring bigger roses at a lower price. And since no one promises us a job, the only promise we make to an employer is to take him for all he's got (see "The *New* Organization Man").

Yet, two full generations after Whyte christened Organization Man, his hold on our collective imagination remains powerful. In the flesh he was anything but memorable; bland was the whole point. But he is vivid in our minds.

We respond to him because he is still us. Organization Man did not die; he morphed. The hat's gone. The briefcase contains a laptop. The 737 is probably a plane at O'Hare, not a train at Winnetka. He underwent a sex change too: In 1956, 85% of civilian men were in the labor force, vs. only 37% of women; by 1997, men's participation rate had fallen to 75%, women's risen to 60%. (No, Desmond isn't living off Molly: Men's lower participation chiefly reflects a larger retiree population.) The attachment between the Organization and the Organization (Wo)Man has changed as well, in both profound and superficial ways.

In cataloging the alternations, however, we risk ignoring deep continuities. This is a mistake. People and companies that figure out how to use both—how to catch the waves of change and also ride the tides of continuity— can prosper from the knowledge.

There is still, to start with a small example, that shared sense of running a rat race; we're proud of it, though we worry that the exercise shrivels the soul to the dimensions of a rodent's. In a remarkable diary, Thomas Asacker, founder of Humanfactor, a New Hampshire medical devices company, writes: "I'm amazed at how few interesting people I meet in my business life—for me a redundant expression. It seems that most of the people I run into simply want enough money and free time for things like annual vacations, watching television, surfing the Net, or kibitzing about this or that. Questioning the way things are and trying to improve them appears to be nothing but a waste of their 'downtime.' Business people seem particularly prone to this status quo way of living. We're running so fast that we often forget to stop, take a breath, look at the map, and question the route."

Also like our 1950s forebears, we show an easy grasp of the "common denominators" that connect us regardless of industry or geography; perhaps we're less likely to chat across suburban front lawns—who's home anymore?—but in airport lounges, at offsite after offsite, conference after conference, whether we work for Russell Reynolds, Reynolds & Reynolds, or Reynolds Metals, we talk about the boat we're all in. We chat about golf and upgrades rather than lawn seed and Chevrolets, but that's a difference of degree rather than of kind, what you'd expect given a 240% rise in real GDP since 1956. The backbiting between Generation X and middle-aged baby-boomers is almost word-for-word the same as it was when parents complained: "I don't know what's wrong with these kids today. . . . Noisy, crazy, sloppy, lazy loafers" (*Bye Bye Birdie,* 1960); and their offspring returned the disfavor: "Your sons and your daughters are beyond your command; your old road is rapidly agin' " (Boy Dylan, 1964).

Significantly, we share a jargon—phrases like "actionable plans" and "jump to a new S-curve"—that is a sure mark of a common culture. The words themselves change, but business jargon is as universal today as when E. B. White derided it in *the Elements of Style* (© 1959).

Yet clearly today's Organization Man is not just yesterday's without the skinny necktie. Business types, for all their bluster and (more jargon) "bias toward action," tend to be more acted upon than acting. They still "do it the company way," like J. Pierpont Finch, hero of *How to Succeed in Business Without Really Trying.* Dilbert resents the obedience demanded of him—but he relents.

If we're to understand the new shape of Organization Man, therefore, we must learn what bent him. There are two big causes of the change—drivers, in our lingo. First: the acceleration of the rate of change itself. "I've been in business for 35 years, and I've never seen change of such complexity, pace, scale, and speed," says Vincent DiBianca, who spent two decades at Touche Ross, then founded DiBianca Berkman, a consulting firm he sold to CSC Index in 1993. "How quickly our competitors can copy us," confides Asacker in his diary—not that this is a secret from anyone in business today. In information technology, the already punishing rate of change expressed by Moore's law—which says that computing power per dollar doubles every 18 months—is now being pushed even faster by advances in chip design. In the swiftest of all industries, financial services, products have the life span of weird subatomic particles; they might be designed and introduced in a matter of minutes, and might disappear in a matter of hours. Says Sir Brian Pittman, chief executive of Lloyds TSB in Britain: "If we introduce a new consumer banking product in the morning, we know if it is a success before we go to lunch."

Supersonic change warps managerial roles and structures. When advantage is fleeting, one must exploit it stat. This demands that one rapidly move people and resources both inside corporations and among them, creating teams where there's not time to set up departments, alliances where there's not time to build capabilities. DiBianca tests agility by asking executives how long their companies would need to get a smallish group of people (a dozen or two) up and running on a new project in a new location—the whole setup, including getting the funds, picking the people, getting their bosses to sign off, backfilling their old jobs, preparing facilities, running in phones and local-area networks, etc. Answers run the gamut from six months to six weeks. But some companies—Warner Lambert is one—say they've got it down to just six days.

Change loosens the tie between Organization Man and the Organization; there is less routine to hitch to. What knots there are might be re-tied overnight, as happened in 1997 for 2,600 information-system employees of Du Pont who, after an outsourcing deal, are doing the same work, in the same offices, for paychecks that now say Computer Sciences Corp.

There is a second big reason Organization Man has taken on a new form: a change in the character of the capital of which managers are custodians. Says Elizabeth Lanier, a self-described "recovering lawyer" who is chief of staff of Cinergy, the $3.2-billion-in-sales gas, electric, and energy services company based in Cincinnati: "Organization Man was on a short leash because there was a relative shortage of capital. When you are capital constrained, you want people who think like you and use capital just like you. Capital markets themselves were much narrower—just banks and bonds and insurance companies—and more narrow-minded."

Lots of that capital was tied up in facilities—factories, stores, refineries, warehouses, offices—and Organization Man, in turn, was tied to them. Says Richard M. Zavergiu, a transportation consultant in Canada: "Manual workers as well as highly skilled managers were rooted in physical place." Sometimes this was because a place was specially designed for one kind of work—a factory, a refinery. But even a drone in a generic office beehive had to be there. It was impossible—or impossibly expensive—to work together without being together physically.

Long-distance phone calls were exotic enough that you'd leave a meeting to accept one; in a world where memos circulated because they could not be photocopied, where phone calls came through a switchboard and international communications through a bulky telex in the mailroom, you had to be downtown. Today, with Albuquerque a mouse-click away from Zimbabwe, it's easy to forget that voice mail and fax machines were novelties a dozen years ago.

Now capital is not scarce and not rooted in a place. It is, says Lanier, "democratically abundant" from all kinds of sources. Moreover, the financial and physical capital that companies need is less valuable than their intellectual capital. When it seemed as if physical capital was most valuable—and when human beings couldn't communicate at a distance greater than a few hundred feet—Organization Man went to a central place, like Mohammed to the mountain. Now, says Zavergiu, "the capital value of knowledge exceeds the capital value of fixed assets for many corporations." The worker is worth more than his tools. The mountain must come to Mohammed. In New England, in Portland, Me., two semiconductor fabs—one owned by national Semiconductor, the other by Fairchild Semiconductor—stand next to each other. Why Maine? Quality of life: Many skilled workers like Maine's lifestyle. In Old England, the trains between London and Amsterdam are full of software programmers. Why? Says Keith Bradley, professor at Britain's Open University Business School: "In London we have a great need for smart programmers, but Holland has become the hot place for them to live because Dutch dope laws are so liberal. A lot of software companies are starting up in Holland."

In a knowledge economy, then, technology untethers the man. At the same time, he is less beholden to the organization for capital. As the value of human capital rises compared with the value of fixed assets, the organization becomes more beholden to the man. Says Lanier: "I could quit my job today and go back to law. I don't need Cinergy. Cinergy needs me."

That's also what twentysomethings say who have never known anything other than the new economy in boomtime. Mind you, legions of U.S. managers who were kicked in the teeth by their employers in the 1980s and 1990s—and legions in Europe who face the same boot in the next decade—will dispute the notion that the company needs them. But it does, and that is a major change. The Organization never did need Organization Man, though it employed him in vast numbers. It needed a certain amount of output, pushed paper mostly. Dilbert's creator, Scott Adams, has talent worth tens or hundreds of millions of dollars. His former employer, Pacific Bell, needed someone in the job he held, but it had no need for Adams, no way to use his talent. So Adams left as others did—some who jumped, some who were pushed.

The transition has been ugly; transitions usually are. Consider how the reputation of General Electric's John F. Welch changed. A dozen years ago he was "Neutron Jack"—the man who kept the buildings and fired the people; now he is the CEO of America's most admired corporation, a man who is believed when he says, "None of this is about squeezing anything at all—it is about tapping an ocean of creativity, passion, and energy." The Organization needs you. Maybe not for long, but for now.

Out of these changes—an economy that rewards agility and a company that needs our minds and souls—has emerged the notion of a "new contract" between employer and employee. The old contract supposedly promised employment: If you do it the company way, if executive policy is okay by you, you will still be here. The new contract supposedly goes like this: Rather than promising employment, we will strive to make you employable by offering a challenge and the chance to learn valuable skills.

That's not hogwash, but it's not a pure, cool, mountain stream of truth either. For one thing, there never was an old contract legally or in any other sense. U.S. labor markets are—and always have been—the freest in the developed world. "Employment at will" (the employer's will) is a matter of law in many states; if anything it's harder to fire someone in the U.S. today than it was in the 1950s, the supposed heyday of employment for life.

Furthermore, the employability stuff, which does a fine job of rationalizing quitting and firing, doesn't explain why people yearn to stay. And yearn they do; even the most gung-ho players in the wild, wired new economy, if they had their druthers, would prefer to have one employer than hop-skip-and-jump from one knowledge-worker gig to another. By a two-to-one ratio, according to a survey taken for *Wired* magazine and Merrill Lynch, "superconnected" people—who regularly exchange E-mail and use a laptop, cell phone, beeper, and home computer—would rather stick with one employer for 20 years than have five jobs for four years each, even if the money and responsibilities were the same.

ESCAPE FROM THE CULT OF PERSONALITY TESTS

Several years ago I visited an AlliedSignal factory in Virginia where managers wore name badges color-coded to reveal how they had scored on a test of personality type. The idea was that people could communicate better if they understood their interlocutors' characters. To be labeled by personality type is perhaps the inevitable result of the primacy of relationship over task in employee-employer dealings. No wonder sales are at an all-time high for the granddaddy of these instruments, the Myers-Briggs Type Indicator; that's the one people have taken who tell you "I'm an ENTJ"—an extroverted intuitive thinking judger, a born leader—or "I'm an ISFP"—an introverted sensing feeling perceiver, a loyal follower. About a third of the time, the Myers-Briggs is administered by colleges or career counselors; most often it's given by companies to employees or job candidates.

Test publishers caution against using their instruments to judge applicants or candidates for promotion—these are tools for counseling, team building, and development, they say—but it's an open secret that they're used to screen candidates. One FORTUNE 100 company routinely gives a battery of standardized tests to would-be executives; others mix tests among other assessments, ranging from good old-fashioned interviews to unstructured group situations where a trained observer watches to see if you assume the role of leader, consensus-builder, nuisance, or what. Applicants might spend a fictional day on the job, going through an in box full of "problems," interrupted by "subordinates." The best approach, says Dee Soder, president of CEO Perspective Group, who coaches executives and evaluates job candidates for companies, is to consider what character traits matter most—stability, adaptability, quickness of learning, whatever—then design an assessment process that includes at least two different ways to get at each trait.

It's possible to cheat on standardized tests. "Just ask my client, who is now an executive vice president at [the FORTUNE 100 company]," one psychologist says, anonymous because psychology, like most professions, considers it wrong—or bad business practice—to share

What, then, does tie us to the company? Ask people with a choice why they choose to stay. A good answer in the 1950s, says Brent Snow, an organizational development consultant, would have emphasized the safety and resources big groups offer small individuals: "It's a good company; I have an opportunity to move up; I have a future here." Recently, Snow has been asking employees at Oracle why they work there. The response? "Every one of them, I suspect, could be making more money. But they all start talking about the challenges, the chance to do interesting work on the cutting edge."

Learning is a piece of the "new contract" that people truly buy. Listen, for example, to a trio of thirtysome-things at Price Waterhouse consulting:

John Waterman, 30: "I'm here because I keep learning. Whenever I start to get a little bored, a new project comes along with opportunities for learning."

Tracy Amabile, 33: "The people and the learning are what's primary. I've been provided a lot of opportunities, lots of challenging work in different industries."

Ed Germain, 35: "I've had a lot of training, a lot of project opportunities. For me stagnation would lead to restlessness."

Leaders at another Big Six (or Five, or Four) consulting firm talk about "knowledge handcuffs." At a time when these fast-growing firms are offering big bonuses to poach the others' talent, they have found people often

trade secrets with the laity. On the Gordon Personal Profile, never forget that you "take the lead in group activities," are "able to make important decisions without help," or find it "easy to influence other people." You will get credit for a trait called "ascendancy," which, test developer Leonard Gordon says, "has been a consistent predictor of managerial success."

Tests have questions that trip up phonies, but there's a difference between fakery and shifts of emphasis. The best advice for beating the tests comes from William H. Whyte in *The Organization Man:* Stay in character. Gild the lily, but don't pretend to be a magnolia. On the 16PF test, for example, you'll look more like a leader if you answer questions as if you were just a tad more outgoing, a bit bolder, and little livelier than you ordinarily are, and just a smidgen less anxious and self-reliant. (Leaders, say the authors of this test, are independent but not self-reliant. If you get the difference, you can game these tests.).

But why fool the tests? You'll only get yourself a job at which you'll fail, right? That assumption is, at least to a contrarian INTP (with a strong streak of J) like me, more troubling than the mystique surrounding testing. It's a tenet of American's faith that anyone can become anything. Whether we start in a log cabin or a mansion, graduate from Harvard or the William Morris mailroom, Americans are not what we are: We are what we can become. Self-help books—starting with Dale Carnegie's 1938 *How to Win Friends and Influence People*—find a bigger audience in America than anywhere else. In F. Scott Fitzgerald's novel *This Side of Paradise,* the young hero, Amory Blaine, says, "We're not personalities, but personages." A personality, he explains, "is what you thought you were. . . . A personage, on the other hand . . . is never thought of apart from what he's done. He's a bar on which a thousand things have been hung—glittering things, sometimes." Whether it's scientifically right or wrong, the determinism that lurks behind tests of personality type is, in other words, downright unAmerican. I can be whatever I want: Just give me the chance.

—T.A.S.

stay because they feel bound to the knowledge of their firm—the networks, electronic and (chiefly) human, of experts and expertise upon which they rely.

Learning has taken on such psychic importance that schooling—or at least credentials—has begun to take the place of promotions. Quasi-professional certification exams are showing up in all kinds of general management areas, such as project management, management consulting, and human resources management. The newly flat and lean HR department may no longer have "benefits managers" and "senior benefits managers," but you can take a test (offered by the Human Resources Certification Institute) and become a "professional of human resources," then take a harder test and become a "senior professional of human resources." In 1997 about 9,000 people say down for the HR exams, ten times the number in 1990. When asked why they came, the No. 1 reason they offered was "I did it for personal growth."

And for a fringe benefit of potential gain too: The sheepskin helps you get work. John Bishop, chairman of the human resources studies department at Cornell University, has discerned a fascinating nascent trend in U.S. labor markets. People are beginning to have more different employers (no surprise) but fewer different occupations. In the old dispensation, IBM might have hired you as a salesperson, then over the years moved you into marketing, manufacturing, finance: One company, four occupations. That still dominant pattern is starting to evolve toward one in which you stay in marketing but move from IBM to Procter & Gamble to Ameritech to Wells Fargo. Credentials can help you make such leaps: By gum, the next applicant in the waiting room is a *senior* human resources professional. Says Peter Capelli of the Wharton School: "Increased mobility across companies means that investments in skills pay off relatively more for individuals and relatively less for companies."

Cinergy has changed how it trains and develops people to recognize that individuals must be the prime investors and beneficiaries in learning. Gone are executive and leadership development; in their place is "talent development," and it's available to everyone. Says Lanier: "The premise is that we want to have the smartest people in every layer in every job. If it's a janitor in a power plant, I want him smarter than any other janitor." If you recruit and train only high-potential leaders for the organization, says Lanier, you not only run the very high risk that your best talent will take your investment to the competition but "you get a high piss-off factor. You tick off all existing employees. Our business is changing fast. Our ability to respond to opportunities is not a function of how well we recruit MBAs but of how many smart people we have that we can lateral to and say run with it." You stay, then, because the Organization, so long as it needs you, gives you a way to invest in skills you truly want.

A second powerful force that ties Man to Organization: The company gives you a field on which to strut your stuff. Paradoxically, that is, you are dependent on the organization to provide the arena in which to be independent. Explains David Witte, CEO of the Ward Howell International executive search firm: "Freedom and responsibility are the very best golden handcuffs there are." For example, in the oil business, says Witte, "I can easily take people from bureaucratic companies like Amoco or Exxon, but there's no way in hell I can steal from Joe Foster." Foster, when he was at Tenneco Oil, was one of the first in the energy business to offer employees the freedom and authority of self-managing teams; in 1989 he and 22 others left Tenneco to start up Newfield Exploration Co. in Houston (1996 sales: $149 million), built on the philosophy that independence and equity ownership are the keys to retaining expert employees, who are, in turn, the key to success.

This independence is not the same as—is dramatically at odds with—the "You Inc." view of the new contract, which holds that we are each of us on our own, and which would substitute fluid, internal labor markets for the old organization's hierarchies. To rely chiefly on market mechanisms to allocate talent is to admit being unable to do it yourself, says Howard Stevenson, a professor at Harvard Business School. "The myth of atomistic man is wrong, and companies that are acting on it are wrong. Markets result when organizations fail, not the other way around."

In chaotic times, Stevenson argues, some people become lone wolves (the You Inc. approach); others join cults, following a leader who offers simplistic solutions (the guru du jour approach); and some form tribes. Tribal loyalty—along with learning and independence—is the third great rope tying the New Man to the Organization. The tribe is not the organization as a whole (unless it is relatively small) but rather teams, communities of practice, and other groups within the company or one's occupation.

Tribalism explains an otherwise baffling phenomenon: If the employment "contract" has shifted from paternal and permanent to individualistic and transactional, why have we become so obsessively concerned with interpersonal relationships at the office? Why do we care about "fit" and culture? Why not just snarl at one another eight hours a day and be done with it?

Brian Hall, CEO of Values Technology in Santa Cruz, Calif., has documented a shift in people's emotional expectations from work. Hall has taken speeches, letters, interview transcripts, and brochures from the entire history of two long-lived companies (a midsized financial services company and a global electronics giant), scanned them into a computer, and searched for words and phrases that refer to values such as independence, entrepreneurship, loyalty, etc. In both companies Hall finds a "massive transition" in progress. From the 1950s on, a "task first" relationship to the company—"tell me what the job is, and let's get on with it"—dominated employee attitudes. Emotions and personal life were checked at the door; you might have worked 30 years with strangers, or be like the Boston banker Hall met who never told his colleagues he had developed Parkinson's disease.

In the past few years, a "relationship-first" set of values has risen to challenge the task orientation, and Hall believes it will become dominant: Employees want to share attitudes and beliefs as well as workspace, want to establish the relationship (with one another and with the company) before buckling down to the task.

That's not touchy-feely. When the task changes abruptly and often, people need to cling to something that has continuity. As Stevenson points out, "We have to know each other, know how we work together, so that when a crisis comes we don't have to spend a long time coordinating." At Hewlett-Packard, for example, tasks change constantly; more than 50% of the company's orders derive from products that did not exist two years ago. The performers, however, don't change. HP's employee attrition rate is usually half the average in the labor markets where it operates; in the 1990s attrition has actually fallen by a third. "I get bench-marked on this frequently," says Sally Dudley, a manager of human resources and a 24-year HP veteran. "We don't do anything special. We're 'among the leaders' on pay. Our total compensation package is fairly traditional for a large company." HP's magic lies in the primacy of relationships over tasks. Says Dudley: "I've done 14 different jobs here. Those who have spent most of their careers at HP—and most of us have—don't identify with doing the same thing."

So learning supplants security; freedom to maneuver supplants power; and relationship supplants task. But there is one price the Organization exacts as implacably as ever: conformity, though with a characteristic *fin-de-siècle* twist. The Organization these days demands a stereotype of original thinking, an orthodoxy of the unorthodox. Change management is a discipline, its practitioners experts in something called the "change piece": "Tell me how you did the change piece," they ask one another. The definition of the ideal manager may be different from what it was in 1958, but it is just as rigid. See how far you'd get in a job interview if you proclaimed yourself an "inside-the-box thinker."

Says headhunter Witte: "For a huge percentage of searches, the client asks for the same thing: 'I want someone who has been in consumer goods for ten years and telecom for five years. I want that guy—find me him. I want him to come into my steel mill, into my chemical plant, into my whatever.' " It's not that they want someone from Procter & Gamble or Pacific Telesis in particular, Witte says. Instead, they want a "change agent"—another piece of jargon—which Witte defines as follows: "Someone who has had a lot of change, been promoted quickly, has shown he can change industries, identify new opportunities, throw them into a business plan, and deliver on it."

It seems sensible until you wonder, Why do we all want to be different in the same way? Orthodoxies come, it seems, and orthodoxies go, but the fact of orthodoxy—that remains.

Genentech Changes Research Approach and Seems to Reap a Number of Benefits

by Ralph T. King Jr.
Staff Reporter of THE WALL STREET JOURNAL

For years, Arthur Levinson, the chief executive officer of *Genentech* Inc., kept a framed comment by Merck & Co.'s research chief on his office wall: "Genentech can only develop one product at a time."

And for years, those words were apt. No more, though. At a meeting of securities analysts in New York Friday, Dr. Levinson is expected to unveil the results of a long-range project—the Secreted Protein Discovery Initiative—that has generated five hot product leads, including a surprising antiviral molecule, and could spawn as many as 20 more within two years.

The project—called "Speedy" by company insiders—reflects an overhaul of the biotechnology company's traditional approach to research, in which scientists worked alone or in tiny teams. Under a new approach approximating an assembly line, some 80 scientists—a quarter of the company's research staff—comb through massive gene-data warehouses.

Another departure: Genentech, long known for its go-it-alone style, has bought rights to a group of experimental drugs created outside the company, which is based in South San Francisco, Calif.

Responding to Threat

For Dr. Levinson, a 47-year-old molecular biologist who has spent his career at Genentech, the changes are an attempt to revive a sluggish drug pipeline and respond to an ominous threat: Swiss drug giant Roche Holding Ltd., the company's majority owner, has the right to take over Genentech under an option agreement, which it is likely to do if Genentech's stock price doesn't gain momentum.

So far, Dr. Levinson's strategy seems to be working. Today, Genentech has eight products in the final stage of clinical testing, three of them from outsiders. Last December, it launched Rituxan, a lymphoma drug developed jointly with *Idec Pharmaceuticals* Corp. of La Jolla, Calif. The company's stock has been trading recently in the range of $66 to $68 a share, its highest level in a decade.

Genentech isn't completely out of Roche's shadow. The company's stock runup makes it unlikely that shareholders will exercise their right to sell out to Genentech for $60 a share under the complex option expiring in July 1999. Yet Roche could still elect to buy the 33% of Genentech it doesn't already own for as much as $82.50 a share. That leaves Dr. Levinson 15 months to convince Roche not to do so.

Dr. Levinson seems to thrive on such pressure. A workaholic who talks in rapid-fire bursts, he admits he finds deadlines "motivating, focusing." He recalls feeling depressed on his seventh birthday by his lack of accomplishment.

Dr. Levinson's fondness for deadlines can lead to prodigious effort. Two dozen employees are putting in 80-hour weeks to submit a marketing application for Hereceptin, a breast-cancer drug, to the Food and Drug Administration three months ahead of schedule.

167

Hefty Checks

Dr. Levinson has promised employees "Genenchex" of $3,000 or more if they make the deadline. "There will be patients alive if we save those several months," he says. The drug is expected to win approval by the end of this year.

Even Genentech's partners have risen to Dr. Levinson's challenge. His voluntary decision to give Idec extra funds in the home stretch of Rituxan's development helped shave six months off its launch. The drug could generate sales of as much as $170 million this year and "has changed the face of lymphoma treatment," says David Golde, chief physician at New York's Memorial Sloan-Kettering Cancer Center. Many patients start to feel better fast without the drastic side effects of chemotherapy, the standard treatment for low-grade, non-Hodgkins lymphoma.

Genentech will pocket a majority of the Rituxan profit but declines to give a precise figure.

Dr. Levinson's broad-based R&D strategy isn't without risks for Genentech. Some veterans see it acting more and more like a big pharmaceutical company, potentially stifling creativity and hurting morale among researchers. In January, for example, Genentech scrapped five years of research and ended a competition with *Amgen* Inc. to market a blood-clotting agent and cited other priorities in licensing the drug to *Pharmacia & Upjohn* Inc. "You can't do it all," says Dr. Levinson, who has killed dozens of projects over the years. "As a manager, it often comes down to intuition. Is it going to work or not?"

The Speedy project, based on the premise that classical biotechnology is outmoded, has also been controversial. Traditionally, scientists chased the obvious drug leads, known proteins like insulin and growth hormone, by laboriously cloning, or synthesizing, them into marketable products.

Protein Focus

Today, drug prospects are more likely to lie buried in human genetic code piling up in databases around the country and are uncovered only by a massive computer-assisted effort. With Speedy, Genentech simplified the task by focusing on the 10% of all proteins that travel outside the cell, blocking or spreading disease. Those 10,000 or so proteins are identified by using high-tech screens called signal sequence traps, or SSTs, and then run through scores of tests to determine their therapeutic benefit.

So far, the five promising leads spotted by Speedy include a protein that could treat diabetes, a molecule that seems to spur blood-vessel growth, several antitumor agents and the antiviral compound, which Dr. Levinson declines to discuss for competitive reasons.

Other, far larger companies have long had protein factories that resemble Genentech's in some respects. *SmithKline Beecham* PLC is collaborating with the pioneer warehouser of gene data, *Human Genome Sciences* Inc. *American Home Products* Corp. is using SST technology to generate leads at Genetics Institute Inc., its Cambridge, Mass., unit. Moreover, analysts say it is too soon to tell whether any of these highly touted approaches, including Genentech's, will actually accelerate the discovery of important drugs.

Meantime, some Genentech staffers are outspoken in the criticism of Speedy. At a Genentech party last Halloween, one employee came dressed as a homeless person with a sign that read "Will analyze SSTs for food."

Timothy Stewart, a Genentech staff scientists, says he worried at first that Speedy wouldn't work. "It made me very uncomfortable," he says. But Dr. Stewart and other doubters have come around as the computer search has begun bearing fruit, potentially catapulting Genentech ahead of competitors.

"You can't do this kind of science alone anymore," says David Botstein, the renowned Stanford University geneticist who is spending a yearlong sabbatical at Genentech. "Nobody wants to be a dinosaur," says Dr. Botstein, who played a big role in advancing Speedy.

Says Dr. Levinson: "There is no guarantee we'll find the Next Great Molecule and it's not a style of science that appeals to everyone. But if we had waited two more years, someone would have eaten our lunch."

Success Stories

Genentech's Big Sellers, the Year of Commercial Launch, Sales in Millions

Year	Brand Name	Drug Type and Use	1997 Sales
1985	Protropin/Nutropin	growth hormone for short stature	$224.0
1987	Activase	blood-clot buster for heart attacks and strokes	261.0
1994	Pulmozyme	enzyme relieves lung congestion in cystic fibrosis	92.0
1997 (Dec.)	Rituxan	antibody for low-grade, Non-Hodgkins lymphoma	29.4*

*Sales through Feb. 1998

Source: Genentech

Sony Changes the Game

PlayStation zapped Nintendo and Sega to become a $5 billion video game juggernaut. The lesson: to win big, make your own rules.

by Paul Roberts

In a small office inside Sony interactive studios America, a tightly packed collection of programmers, artists, and marketing specialists in San Diego, Holliday Horton is putting all-pro wide receiver Tim Brown through his paces. At Horton's command, the 6 foot, 190 pound Oakland Raider breaks into a sprint, stops cold, and leaps for a pass. Then he does it again. And again. "Now watch this," Horton says, clicking her mouse and magically removing all lateral motion from the athlete's powerful stride. On Horton's screen, the digital line drawing of Brown seems suspended in mid-air. The receiver's legs are churning uselessly. "That's how *some* people do it," she scoffs. "But without that side-to-side motion, it's like he's a bug pinned to the wall. It's totally unrealistic."

These are not idle criticisms. As a top artist in Sony Corp.'s North American video game group, formally known as Sony Computer Entertainment America (SCEA), Horton, 31, has a big stake in the degree to which little simulated men can be made to run and jump and smash into one another, realistically, on a television screen. Two years ago, she was a lead artist on NFL *GameDay*—one of the most important titles behind the rise of PlayStation, Sony's blockbuster entry in the $15 billion video game market. With sophisticated on-field simulations and astonishing 3-D action, Horton's game was an instant smash. More important, it made other sports games look like *Pong*. Virtually overnight, *GameDay* was heralded as the first true "second generation" console title.

Expectations are already just as high for *GameDay '98,* the second sequel to the original hit. And until it ships, Horton and her colleagues will put in 12 to 14 hour days, every day, as will the PlayStation programmers creating other sports games (NHL *Face Off, NBA ShootOut*) plus a collection of action, adventure, and fantasy titles with names like *Blasto* and *Spawn: The Eternal.*

Somehow, though, the San Diego studio remains calm—and visibly free of "management." Horton sets her own hours (she usually rolls in about 11 a.m. and stays until midnight) and is basically left alone to get things done. Her explanation: "They trust me." In fact, during crunch times, Horton's manager, Chris Whaley, has actually barred Sony brass from so much as visiting the studio. "As long as we keep bureaucracy at bay," says Whaley, 38, a jock and computer whiz with a taste for loud shirts, "we can get the job done."

Someone is obviously doing something right. PlayStation is the most successful new product from Sony since the Walkman and one of the most successful consumer products from *any* company in a long time. Until recently, the global video game market was dominated by two seemingly invincible giants: Nintendo and Sega. Then came PlayStation—and everything changed. Sony launched PlayStation in Japan in December 1994; SCEA launched it in North America in September 1995. By Christmas 1996, Sony had shipped nearly 3 million units in North America and 9 million worldwide. Through May 1997, it had shipped nearly 5 million units in North America and 16 million worldwide.

That's just hardware. PlayStation owners have also purchased 30 million pieces of game software in North America and 114 million worldwide. And many of its titles have made the transition from video game hits to pop-culture touchstones. Crash Bandicoot the star of one of PlayStation's most beloved games, comfortably holds his own against Nintendo's Super Mario and Sega's Sonic the Hedgehog as a digital celebrity.

Talk about *growth:* a business unit with literally no sales three years ago will generate worldwide revenues of more that $5 billion this year (on gross retail sales of $9 billion). Talk about *productivity*: PlayStation has achieved these staggering results with roughly 1,500 employees worldwide and just 500 people in North America. That means the unit generates $3.3 million of revenue *per person*. Microsoft, a company legendary for its productivity, generates only $420,000 of revenue per person.

But what's most compelling about PlayStation isn't the breathtaking scale of its growth but the subversive logic behind it. How did Sony become a force in the video game industry? *By changing the rules of the game.* It redefined the market to include customers that Nintendo and Sega had ignored. It made technology choices that both enhanced the performance of its hardware and recast the economics of selling software. It designed a tough-minded approach to innovation that helps its in-house studios (and outside developers) churn out a string of popular games. And this year, in a unique effort to "close the loop" between producers and consumers, it released a product that lets players develop their own games.

"We are in uncharted waters," says Kazuo (Kaz) Hirai, SCEA's executive vice president and the highest ranking PlayStation executive in North America. Hirai runs the unit's day-to-day operations out of SCEA headquarters in Foster City, California, a Silicon Valley town about 20 miles south of San Francisco. "That means we're setting our own course. From the beginning we said we didn't simply want to take the gaming business away from Nintendo and Sega. We wanted to present our customers with a new form of entertainment. PlayStation is more than a toy. It's our dream to see a PlayStation console in every house, just like VCRs and CD players."

Fresh Eyes, New Vision

The first thing a visitor to PlayStation headquarters notices is how fresh everything looks. Cubicles and offices are spangled like dorm rooms with posters, plants, and sci-fi monsters. The Foster City staff looks like it should be running a college newspaper, maybe an independent record label, but not a multibillion-dollar division of one of Japan's most powerful companies. Top management sports remarkably few gray hairs.

The look is appropriate; almost everything about PlayStation represents a fresh take on the industry. Kaz Hirai is just 36 years old. Almost everyone in his management team is in their 30s—too young, they say, to have much regard for the status quo. "Young people don't have preconceived notions about how things should be done," says Phil Harrison, SCEA's vice president for third-party relations and R&D. "They just come up with solutions—without even realizing that they've arrived at success in a 'strange' way."

Harrison personifies the point. AT 27, the tall, amiable Englishman works with outside game developers (Electronic Arts, Lucas Arts, Crystal Dynamics) to create a relentless stream of killer PlayStation titles. It's a role for which he seems born: ambitious, bright, and deeply interested in computers and video, he programmed his first game at 13 and at 16 quit school to become a consultant. Six years later he joined Sony and was assigned to a top-secret project known only as PSX. After two years of work, PSX became PlayStation. Harrison, still a kid, became an executive.

But the leaders of PlayStation aren't just young. Most of them are also *outsiders*—a status for which they make no apologies. Back in the late 1980s, when Sony was creating its enormously successful music division, it staffed the venture almost entirely with people from outside the music industry. "We didn't want people from the record business," explains Hirai. "They would just bring their old ways with them. We wanted people who would have to figure things out all over again, who would question everything, people who 'didn't know any better.' " Sony took the same approach to PlayStation. Half the unit's top personnel, including Hirai, came from Sony Music rather than the video game business. "The last thing I want to hear is, 'We tried that last year and it didn't work,' " Hirai says. "Our business changes constantly. What didn't work a year ago might work today."

Those fresh eyes saw a number of strategic vulnerabilities at Sega and Nintendo—and created a business model to take advantage of them. The most serious vulnerability was vanishing variety. Although Sega and Nintendo made some undeniably exquisite games, the two giants were increasingly unwilling, or unable, to develop successful titles outside a few proven genres. "In 1994, there were something like 16 baseball video games," says Kelly Flock, 43, president of Sony Interactive Studios America. "It was a perfect example of the dying creativity of a stagnant industry."

This timidity was understandable. The early 1990s were littered with failed attempts to develop "second generation" consoles, and gaming companies had grown wary of big risks. The industry's economics also worked against innovation. Nintendo, for example, has always sold games on proprietary cartridges that are expensive for developers to buy (a blank cartridge sells for up to $35) and take months to manufacture. It expects its partners to bear these costs. Nintendo insists that third-party developers place huge orders for cartridges and pay their manufacturing fees upfront. Forget just-in-time inventory; long manufacturing lead times mean retailers have to bet months in advance on which games will be hits.

The result? Developers worked only on games with huge market potential. Retailers featured a limited selection of titles. Video games, like Hollywood and book publishing, became a business of blockbusters, sequels, and knockoffs. "As a business model, a creative platform, and a consumer value, the industry had run out of steam," says Phil Harrison.

Hence PlayStation's first strategic innovation: maximize the number and variety of titles available to customers. "This industry is full of dreamers," says Kelly Flock. "But the technology and economics had been limiting creativity. We believed that we could inspire the creative side of the industry, that we could help the artists and engineers do the things they had been dreaming about."

PlayStation's second big innovation involved customers themselves. In PlayStation's view, Nintendo and Sega had focused too narrowly on traditional gamers—boys between the ages of 10 and 16. It was an undeniably huge audience; the worldwide installed base of video game consoles exceeds 30 million. But PlayStation concluded that its long-term growth prospects were with the tens of millions of people who had stopped playing games or were never interested. (See "Different Market, New Message," on p. 124) This audience was older and more sophisticated than young boys, with harder-to-predict tastes. No one knew what kinds of games would resonate. The only way to find out was to experiment.

Which was a problem. Every constituency in the business had become addicted to blockbusters. Reaching a different audience meant persuading lots of players to try something different, to get a little wild. That meant reinventing the economics of the industry—and *that* meant embracing a new technology platform.

Here too the establishment was vulnerable. Nintendo stuck with cartridge-based hardware because of its blazingly fast performance—and because it was the platform on which it rose to power. But PlayStation concluded that CD-ROM technology was superior on almost every other dimension. CDs are cheaper than cartridges—$5 to $10 versus $35. They're easier to turn into games. PlayStation manufacturers CD-ROMs in three U.S. factories and fills orders within two weeks. Nintendo manufactures cartridges in Japan and takes as long as *three months* to fill orders. And CDs can store vastly more data than cartridges (650 megabytes versus 16 megabytes), which allows for more complex graphics and games.

"It's amazing how much more value you get with a CD," says Flock. "Not to mention manufacturing turnaround. The cartridge model does not allow for any meaningful inventory management among retailers. It also means publishers will not take any creative risks. The only innovation in interactive gaming is with CDs."

It's hard to overstate the importance of CD economics to the PlayStation model. Its flexibility lets the company test offbeat games in small batches and, if a hit appears, bring large volumes to market quickly. It also helps developers try to defy cultural barriers. Games that do well in Japan often bomb in Europe and North America. CDs let PlayStation troll for crossover titles by doing test runs of, say, 5,000 copies and monitoring the market response.

Parappa the Rapper, perhaps the most unusual video game every published, epitomizes PlayStation's willingness to experiment with genres and demographics. Parappa is a little dog who lives in a pop-art world with his friends, a cat and a bear, and his girlfriend, a sunflower. It's the flower's birthday, but Parappa has dropped the cake and, lacking money, heads to a flea market. There, he meets a rapping frog. Each time the frog raps out a tune, the players must match its rhythm by hitting the correct sequence of buttons on their PlayStation consoles.

Developed by Sony Music, *Parappa the Rapper* was launched in Japan last fall. Little kids didn't get it and teens were turned off by the childlike graphics. But the game was a surprise hit among twenty-somethings. It's been among the country's top 10 titles for a year and has sold more that 700,000 copies. With high hopes for a geographic crossover, Sony plans to release the game in North America this November. The company still needs plenty of hits in traditional genres—sports, action, racing—but offbeat games like *Parappa* are what distinguish PlayStation from the competition.

DIFFERENT MARKET, NEW MESSAGE

Sophia is the kind of woman you don't take home to mother. She's big and tough, with a thing for leather and a history of kicking the stuffing out of guys twice her size. Yet if someone in your family plays video games—or watches television, for that matter—chances are Sophia has spent time in your living room. Not only is she the main character in *Toshinden,* a popular PlayStation game, but she is also one of the company's mass-market mascots. Last fall in a series of intense, rapid-fire TV spots, the lithe warrior made short, loud work of a progression of opponents, after which viewers were taunted with a sinister voice-over. "You are not ready."

The spot was unabashedly risqué—and targeted at a twenty-something audience rather than the pimply teenagers normally associated with video games. Which means it was perfectly consistent with Sony's aim to redefine its market and create new techniques for reaching it. Indeed, almost everything about the rise of the PlayStation—from the console itself to Sony's relationship with gaming "evangelists"—reflects a strategy to beat the competition by changing the rules of competition.

Early on, Sony concluded that it had to reach an older, more sophisticated crowd—which meant changing the image of games from a dubious juvenile pastime to a legitimate hobby that responsible adults could enjoy. That's why it designed the PlayStation console to look less like a toy and more like a sleek consumer product. It's also why Sony keeps slashing prices for hardware and software. (PlayStation launched at a list price of $299 and now sells for $149; games list for $49.99 but are often available for much less.) Sure, cheaper is always better. But PlayStation's ultimate goal is to make buying a video game a legitimate economic alternative to a night at the movies or a restaurant—which means slashing prices further.

Still, Sony's core challenge is to create excitement rather than cut prices—to craft a message for PlayStation that resonates with people who might never otherwise think about video games. That means more TV spots, the best of which remains a celebrated ad featuring Crash Bandicoot. But rather than use the game's animated character, the ad features an obviously human actor dressed in a clumsily fabricated Crash Bandicoot suit, who drives a pick-up truck to Redmond, Washington, home of Nintendo. Crash arrives at the company parking lot, megaphone in hand, and challenges "Mr. Super Mario" to come out and fight—only to be dragged off by security guards.

The goofball character is almost as memorable—and nearly as deep—as Bill Murray's Carl the Greenskeeper from *Caddyshack.* The spot itself is a shrewd take on popular culture, a mixture of MTV, "Saturday Night Live," and "Twin Peaks," designed to appeal to an older crowd unaccustomed to the peculiarities of gaming but happy to try something associated with wit and hipness.

In that sense, it captures the essence of PlayStation's market position. Andrew House , the 32-year-old vice president for marketing, puts it this way. "If Nintendo owns 'fun,' then we own 'cool.' "

To be sure, for all of PlayStation's triumphs, the game is far from over. Last September, Nintendo launched its own second-generation video console (dubbed N64) with speed and graphics that clearly outperform the PlayStation. During its first nine months on the market, North American consumers bought an impressive 2.6 million units. But Nintendo continues to struggle with its blockbuster complex. As of this summer, PlayStation customers have 250 game titles from which to choose. When Nintendo launched the N64, there were just 2 titles on the market. There are still fewer than 20. For PlayStation, variety remains the spice of business life.

Free Spirits, Hard Work

So what is this? A military simulation? Rambo in a tank? A dessert topping?" In a conference room in Foster City, Jeff Fox sits at the head of a long oval table, looking mildly cross. For the past half hour, the 33-year-old senior PR director has been meeting with a dozen sales and advertising types, watching as Susan Nourai, an assistant marketing manager in Foster City, rolls out a tank-battle game called *Steel Reign*. Nourai, 25, is understandably nervous: a warm reception today means a generous marketing budget, which means more sales and fatter royalty checks for her team.

The first part of the demo goes reasonably well. Nourai lays out the concept (tanks shooting at other tanks) and describes the weaponry (cannons, guided missiles, machine guns). She goes over the game's story line and setting, brushes off a friendly heckle ("It's the future, and all the bowling alleys are closed!"), and, after nervously driving her tank into a building ("oops!"), proceeds to set the 3-D landscape on fire. Tracer streaks fill the screen. The room echoes with explosions. Nourai dispatches a progression of enemy tanks, then blows a helicopter out of the sky. The table erupts in cheers. "Check out how good that smoke looks," someone says.

But as the talk turns to marketing, Fox, a small, dark-haired man with a probing wit, voices concern. As the guy who must pitch *Steel Reign* to a jaded trade press, he worries that the game's audience is not sufficiently defined. What's the message? How's the game being billed? As a serious battle "sim" (simulation) for armchair strategists? As an action game? As both? Neither? Gradually, under steady questioning by Fox and others, the *Steel Reign* team refines its marketing strategy. The game is scheduled for a September release.

High-stakes decisions like this are a regular part of life at PlayStation. Sure, the programmers in San Diego and Foster City make games. But they're really in the business of manufacturing creativity. Their work is a daily struggle to balance chaos and control, brilliance and budgets, experimentation and efficiency. In this sense, they face the same challenges as people in any business—Hollywood, Madison Avenue, Wall Street—that fuses open-minded innovation with tough-minded execution.

As video games become bigger, faster, and more lifelike, the stakes keep rising. Three years ago, Jonathon Beard, a 28-year-old producer and graphic artist, could sit down with a few programmer friends and create a game in six weeks. Beard's current project, a complex fighting game called *Blasto,* took 18 months of work and a small army of professionals: four programmers, four modelers, three animators.

That's typical. Between 1988 and 1993, the average cost of making a video game jumped from $80,000 to $500,00. Since then, it has leaped to $1.5 million—with a few projects burning as much as $8 million to $10 million. Yet by all indications, *Blasto* will not only make its deadline but also make a major splash in the Christmas market. Some insiders are predicting it will be one of PlayStation's biggest games ever.

That's typical too. PlayStation works hard to master the personal and organizational tensions inherent in designing cutting-edge software for a fast-moving industry. "Things change so quickly that we *do* want people to reinvent the wheel," argues Phil Harrison. "Our biggest competitor is complacency, and the only way to combat complacency is to challenge yourself with extraordinary goals."

How does PlayStation rise to the challenge? First, it makes work playful—even as it keeps it serious. Most designers got into the video game business because they loved games, not business. That simple reality has big management implications. Game designers are supremely motivated to complete their individual projects. But they lack traditional career ambitions or a corporate navigational sense. "These people tend not to be real aggressive self-promoters," explains Kelly Flock. "They want to be noticed without being a squeaky wheel, which means that part of being their manager is being their advocate." Translation: designers are gamers first and businesspeople second.

That said, everyone understands that PlayStation is serious business. Most titles sell for somewhere around $50; a hit can ship as many as 2 million units world wide. That means a single project team can generate as much as $100 million in retail revenue. Team members receive sizable bonuses (a fixed percentage of their salaries) when they meet their alpha, beta, and final-ship milestones. They also receive quarterly royalties for the games they design. PlayStation calculates each game's revenues, subtracts development costs and an allocation for marketing and overhead, and then divides a royalty pool among the team. These royalties can add up to real money—the best evidence of which is the number of expensive sports cars parked outside Sony's studios.

PlayStation also encourages autonomy—but demands accountability. Game designers like to be left alone. A sense of independence—defiance, really—oozes from every corner of the studios. In Foster City, gamers openly deride the executive offices as "Mary Kay Headquarters." Half the cubicles are off-limits to outsiders. One sign announces: "We don't mean to sound rude, but for development security reasons, visitor are not allowed past this point." For added emphasis, storm troopers from *Star Wars* stand guard. The message is unmistakable: Nobody tells us what to do.

The flip side of all this autonomy is accountability. And the essence of accountability is shared goals. Once a project has been "green-lighted"—that is, once a producer, a programmer, and an artist have developed an outline, and a development team has been assembled—members of the team strike a formal agreement about how work will proceed. The agreement includes lots of traditional metrics: project objectives, deadlines, milestones. It also includes metrics that reflect life on software teams: worst-case scenarios, required work hours, "all the things people need to be prepared for," Flock says.

Job assignments are especially contentious. In the old days, when game teams involved just two or three people, the ideal designer was a brilliant generalist with multiple skills. Today's games require much larger development teams—and much narrower specialties. This new reality can irk industry veterans. "They're playing a smaller role in a bigger process, and a lot of them don't like it," Flock says. That's why it's critical for everyone to know exactly what's expected of them, what they will and won't be doing.

Third, PlayStation encourages people to work in teams—and to compete. The studios revel in an organizational tension that would make most companies very uncomfortable: just because everyone is on the same side doesn't mean they always have to get along. At PlayStation, creativity and competition are two sides of the same coin.

Paul Forest, 25, an artist based in San Diego, shares a cubicle with four team members. Forest is working on *Spawn: The Eternal,* a game in which an unlucky traveler is doomed to wander hell's many levels—and battle whomever he meets. *Spawn* is not a sports title. In fact, although this cubicle is less than 200 feet away from where *NFL GameDay '98* is being produced, it might as well be 200 miles away. Forest barely tolerates his sports-minded neighbors. Chris Whaley, who runs the sports studio, laughs at the conflicts between teams that work on sports games and those that don't: "We call them the 'Ghouls and Goblins' and they call us the 'Dumb Jocks.' "

Recently, in fact, after sharing one giant studio, the sports and nonsports teams were given quarters in separate buildings and now operate almost totally independent of one another. "Teams are competing for internal resources," says Flock, "for marketing dollars, support for their products. And they know how much that matters."

Finally, PlayStation expects success—but prepares to manage failure. Even the best-designed systems can't guarantee creative perfections. PlayStation pulls the plug on about 15% of the projects it starts. The studios rarely assign those teams another project.

"When you terminate a project," Flock says, "you have to break up the team. Failure usually means that the team dynamics weren't working. Chances are that the dysfunction will continue into the next project."

Interestingly, "hot teams" face a similar fate. Teams that are clicking get subdivided into two or more new teams. "After a killer project," Flock says, "the number two person is ready to become number one on a new project. The second artist is ready to become a lead artist, and so on." The studio often creates new teams before it knows what projects they'll be working on. "The industry is moving so fast now that you almost have to start on a project before you really know exactly what it will be," says Flock. "You want your teams in constant motion."

Tough Customers, Great Developers

What do you do after you've conquered an industry with relentless innovation in hardware, software, and business strategy? Generate more innovation in all three areas. After all, Nintendo and Sega are pursuing aggressive comeback strategies—and making genuine headway. PlayStation's only option is to keep changing the game.

That's why the mass market isn't the only arena where PlayStation is rethinking how it develops products and relates to customers. It has devised new techniques for reaching hard-core gamers known as "evangelists"—people recognized by their peers as gurus. Most of us have a friend or neighbor whose advice we seek before buying a car or computer. Gamers are the same way. By targeting these evangelists, says Phil Harrison, the company's ambassador to outside developers, PlayStation is "reaching the top of our consumer pyramid: the experts, the know-it-alls, a group that understands the industry but isn't developing games."

PlayStation Underground, the company's customer magazine, is one vehicle to reach this constituency. It's available on CD-ROM and online, and it's an evangelist's dream. It features everything from samples of coming games to coded tips for how to win existing games. That's a big deal. Game tips (secret codes that give players access to better weapons or more "lives") are an important part of hard-core gaming culture. PlayStation doesn't just tap into that language; it uses that language to influence behavior. "Gamers are notorious for never reading instruction manuals," says Colin MacLean, 36, manager of online and direct marketing. "So we hide codes in the instructions, and they read every word!"

PlayStation's most recent—and most radical—initiative is Net Yaroze, a special edition of the video console that allows players to create their own games. SCEA unveiled Net Yaroze in March. The consoles are available only direct from Sony (list price: $750), which means the company knows exactly who is buying them. And PlayStation is not just selling Yaroze hardware and programming software. It's also creating a Yaroze community. Users will be able to design their own games, discuss them with other Yaroze owners, collaborate on games through a private Yaroze Web site, even get expert tips from PlayStation programmers in San Diego and Foster City.

Among hard-core gamers, Yaroze has been hailed as a breakthrough concept. Harrison thinks of it as a challenge: "OK, Mister Gameplayer. You've always sat at home and said, 'This game sucks, I could do better.' Well, here you are, go do it."

No one know how many PlayStation games Net Yaroze will create. But the mere fact that it exists creates a rare sense of openness in an industry notorious for proprietary technology and tight controls. And who knows? It just might produce a hit or two.

Harrison says he looks forward to the day when a magazine interviews the developer of a hot PlayStation game—and the developer says the game took shape when he was a Yaroze owner. Maybe he pitched the idea to an outside company, maybe to PlayStation itself. But somehow he got the chance to build a full-fledged consumer title based on what he did at home with Yaroze.

Far-fetched? Perhaps. "But that," says Harrison, "is the dream."

Crash Bandicoot *Developer* Naughty Dog. *Released* September 1996. *Copies Sold* More than 1.5 million. *Storyline* "Bandicoot" is Australian for a small, foxlike mammal. It's also the title character of one of PlayStation's best-known games. Invented by the crazed Dr. Neo Cortex for his army of animal warriors, Crash is found unworthy and dismissed. But he has fallen for the lovely Tawna, a member of Cortex's staff. The game, distinguished by its attractive sets and in-your-face graphics, chronicles his efforts to reclaim her.

Tekken 2 *Developer* Namco. *Released* March 1996. *Copies Sold* More than 2.5 million. *Storyline* Roam a futuristic 3-D world, meet interesting characters—and kill them. That's the gist of this classic fighting game. PlayStation emphasizes game genres beyond conventional shoot-'em-ups, but fighting games still account for roughly 25% of its sales. *Tekken 2* is the most popular PlayStation title in North America. It provides dozens of characters, from a medieval warrior to a kangaroo, that players can become or fight or both.

Formula 1 *Developer* Psygnosis. *Released* September 1996. *Copies Sold* 1.5 million. *Storyline* **Formula 1** gives you the power and feel of a monster race car and a virtual track to test it on. Driving games make up nearly a quarter of all video game sales, and **Formula 1** has lots of competition. Veteran players, however, give this title high marks for the realism of the environment and, most of all, the sensitivity of the car. **Formula 1** is the biggest selling foreign-produced game in Japan.

Tomb Raider *Developer* Eidos Interactive. *Released* October 1996. *Copies Sold* more than 2 million. *Storyline* This fast-paced treasure hunt lets PlayStation shine. Players explore a vast, exquisitely rendered multi-level maze. They evade obstacles and solve riddles on their way to the treasure. **Tomb Raider** has several things going for it. The environment grows larger and more convoluted as players advance through the levels. And the lead character is a young woman with great athletic ability and an astonishing physique.

Paul Roberts (PRoberts@aol.com) is a writer based in Seattle and a frequent contributor to Fast Company.